There is no greater misconcepti⟨ epistemology of Van Til than that dences for the truth of Christianity. There is no more important recognition about this epistemology, rooted in Scripture as the self-attesting revelation of the triune God essential for interpreting the whole of reality, than that it provides the only sound basis for a truly compelling presentation of the manifold evidence there is. The value of this seminally important work is greatly enhanced by Oliphint's foreword and his editorial comments throughout.

—RICHARD B. GAFFIN JR., Professor of Biblical and Systematic Theology, Emeritus, Westminster Theological Seminary

Christian Theistic Evidences may not be the catchiest title for an apologetics text, but readers who have digested Van Til's revolutionary insights will understand that it carries a profound double meaning. Not only are there abundant evidences for the truth of Christian theism, but the very idea of "evidences" presupposes the truth of Christian theism. Evidences are, by nature, Christian theistic. If the sovereign God of the Bible exists, they can be nothing less. No one has pressed this point with more conviction than Van Til. I'm immensely grateful to P&R for issuing these new editions of Van Til's major works with insightful editorial annotations by Scott Oliphint and William Edgar.

—JAMES ANDERSON, Associate Professor of Theology and Philosophy, Reformed Theological Seminary

Does the defense of the faith require evidences? Absolutely, as long as they are accounted for within the biblical worldview. *Christian Theistic Evidences* deserves to be better known than it is. Historically, it represents Cornelius Van Til's first, revolutionary statement of presuppositional (or covenantal) apologetics. It contains all his major statements against the pretended neutrality of fact, of reason, and of foundations. Dr. Oliphint's masterful annotations clarify and enhance the beauty of the text. His introduction is pure gold. This is *must* reading for anyone who wishes apologetic method to be consistent with sound theology.

—WILLIAM EDGAR, Professor of Apologetics and John Boyer Chair of Evangelism and Culture, Westminster Theological Seminary

Critics of Cornelius Van Til often complained that in Van Til's presuppositionalist apologetics there was no room for the use of evidences to verify the Christian faith. But Van Til often said that evidences were an important part of apologetics. In fact, he taught a required course on Christian evidences at Westminster Theological Seminary. Now the textbook for that course is available again in a new edition with an introduction and new footnotes by Scott Oliphint of Westminster, who has produced recent editions of other Van Til works. *Christian Theistic Evidences* is Van Til's philosophy of fact, his philosophy of science, and as such it should interest everyone who seeks to understand Van Til's work.

—JOHN M. FRAME, Author, *A History of Western Philosophy and Theology*

CHRISTIAN THEISTIC EVIDENCES

CHRISTIAN THEISTIC EVIDENCES

CORNELIUS
VAN TIL

SECOND EDITION,

INCLUDING THE COMPLETE TEXT OF
THE ORIGINAL 1978 EDITION

EDITED BY K. SCOTT OLIPHINT

P&R
PUBLISHING
P.O. BOX 817 • PHILLIPSBURG • NEW JERSEY 08865-0817

Text based on *The Works of Cornelius Van Til, 1895–1987*, CD-ROM, edited by Eric
Sigward (New York: Labels Army Co., 1997). Used by permission. Italics have been
harmonized with the print version and minor corrections have been made to the text.

Page design by Lakeside Design Plus

Printed in the United States of America

Library of Congress Cataloging-in-Publication Data

Names: Van Til, Cornelius, 1895-1987, author. | Oliphint, K. Scott, 1955-
 editor.
Title: Christian theistic evidences / Cornelius Van Til ; edited by K. Scott
 Oliphint.
Description: Second Edition, including the complete text of the original 1978
 edition. | Phillipsburg : P&R Publishing, 2016.
Identifiers: LCCN 2015043792| ISBN 9781596389236 (pbk.) | ISBN 9781596389243
 (epub) | ISBN 9781596389250 (mobi)
Subjects: LCSH: Apologetics. | Philosophical theology.
Classification: LCC BT1103 .V365 2016 | DDC 239–dc23
LC record available at http://lccn.loc.gov/2015043792

Contents

FOREWORD
BY K. SCOTT OLIPHINT

When Cornelius Van Til first prepared to teach his "Evidences" course in the summer of 1930, just one year after the founding of Westminster Theological Seminary, he was uneasy about it. His discomfort stemmed from his desire to please his mentor, the founder of Westminster, J. Gresham Machen. Specifically, Van Til was aware that he would have to distance his course from the teaching that he had received as a student in his apologetics courses at Princeton Theological Seminary.[1] He was concerned that Machen would not approve of his disagreement with the content of those courses, since Westminster was founded to be the continuation of Old Princeton, not its nemesis. So Van Til wrote to Machen that summer to ensure that he would prepare and teach the course in a way that Machen could approve.

The response from Machen was most encouraging. He began the letter "by relating that he held but the 'vaguest kind' of thoughts on the matter . . . of evidences." He then assured Van Til, "Your choice of topics is sure to be better than mine ever would be," to which Machen added this encouragement: "I wish I could take your course in Evidences. I need it, and I am sure it is greatly to the benefit of the Seminary that you are offering it."[2] Given this encouragement, Van Til was confident that he could

---

1. Van Til's critique of Princeton Seminary's apologetic approach was not a product simply of his reading. His initial discomfort came when he sat, as a student, in classes at Princeton in which were taught methods and ideas foreign to the Reformed theology that he had learned and affirmed. His critique, then, is not first of all that of a scholar of Old Princeton, but that of a student. It came out of his own experiences at Princeton.

2. John R. Muether, *Cornelius Van Til: Reformed Apologist and Churchman* (Phillipsburg, NJ: P&R Publishing, 2008), 70–71.

attempt, in this syllabus, to critique the method of apologetics that he had learned as a student at Princeton Seminary.

It is crucial to remember that there was a conscious and determined effort made by Machen, as he began Westminster Seminary, to maintain significant and substantial theological continuity between Old Princeton and the new school. Westminster was founded to continue the Reformed theological tradition that Princeton had squandered. In the area of apologetics, however, Van Til was convinced that there had to be significant *discontinuity* between the two institutions. With Machen's encouragement, Van Til set out to offer a new and radically consistent theological approach to the topic of evidences in apologetics.

It was clear to Van Til, then, as he began to prepare the second of two required apologetics courses in the curriculum at Westminster, that (1) a course on evidences was crucial and central to the training of men for pastoral ministry, and (2) he would need to reorient the topic in order to make it more consistent with the Reformed theology that was the trademark of Old Princeton and would continue at Westminster.

The apologetics training that Van Til had received at Princeton from William Brenton Greene, Jr., was not compatible with the theology that he had imbibed at Calvin College and then at Princeton Seminary. Taking his cue from Warfield and others, Greene's approach to apologetics at Princeton in the second decade of the twentieth century borrowed too heavily from an approach that was, at root, less than Reformed in its theological foundation. Van Til knew that his task as a new professor at this new seminary was to correct Princeton's approach.

It was this syllabus that began, in earnest, Van Til's Reformed reorientation and reformation of Christian apologetics. Although the syllabus was revised over several decades of teaching, the substance of it remained fundamentally unchanged, as Van Til set the topic of evidences within the context of the empiricism of David Hume and especially the evidential apologetic of Joseph Butler.[3]

3. The syllabuses available in the library of Westminster Theological Seminary (especially in the Van Til Archives) include one from 1935, a slightly altered syllabus from 1937, and others from 1944, 1947, 1951, 1961, and 1976. The two syllabuses from the 1930s are, understandably, the least developed and the most divergent from the rest, as illustrated in their table of contents: "Chapter I. 'Fact' and Fact; Chapter II. The Probability Argument; Chapter III. The Kinds of Evidence; Chapter IV. Idealism and Christian Theism; Chapter V. Possibility, Probability, and Actuality; Chapter VI. Evil and Evidence; the Part II, Chapter VII. Theological Evidences—Agnosticism; Chapter VIII. Theological Evidences—Creation and Providence; Chapter IX. Theological Evidences—Teleology and Theodicy; Chapter X. Anthropological Evidences—Evolution." By 1944, the table of contents, including the

GREENE AND HAMILTON

Although Van Til does not mention Greene in this syllabus, there can be no doubt but that it was written to correct Greene's approach—the approach that Van Til had been taught in Greene's class—in preparation for his new course at Westminster. It may be instructive to set this syllabus in the broader context of Van Til's own background, especially as a student at Princeton Seminary, in order to see more clearly why this work was, and remains, a central piece of Van Til's corpus.

Van Til rarely mentions Greene in his writing.[4] There are at least two reasons for this. First, Van Til considered Greene to be his "revered teacher" and mentions him as "the sainted William Brenton Greene, Jr."[5] His admiration and respect for his mentor no doubt caused him to deal gently with the ideas and method of Greene.

Second, while Van Til was critical of Greene's *apologetic method*, he was confident in, and complimentary of, Greene's *theology*, to the extent that it was consistent with the Reformed theology that Van Til had learned throughout his life, especially as a student at Calvin College and Princeton Seminary.

For example, after Greene died in 1928, Princeton underwent a reorganization, which would move it in a decidedly unorthodox, "modernist" direction. In light of that reorganization, John Kuizenga was appointed to be Greene's successor in apologetics at Princeton. In a critique of the "new apologetic" that was being taught by Kuizenga, Van Til shows Kuizenga's views to be seriously deficient, especially compared to the theology that was formerly in place there—the theology that was held and taught by Greene and others. After an initial critique of Kuizenga, Van Til notes,

> From these considerations it appears clearly that a new type of Apologetic is being taught at Princeton. One could not possibly

---

preface, had become much the same as in subsequent editions, including this one. In the 1930s, Van Til said much more about the problem of evil and about evolution than he did from the 1940s onward. However, in all of the syllabuses, the argumentation employed, including his method of critique, remained fundamentally the same. From the 1940s onward, he was more concerned to set out a focused critique of Butler and Hume and to include psychology, instead of evolution, as his example of anthropological evidences. In my view, it would have been helpful to keep the material from the 1930s syllabuses in the later ones, as much of that material continues to be relevant today. One could see that only in hindsight, however.

4. His most sustained critique of Greene can be found in Cornelius Van Til, *Defense of the Faith*, ed. K. Scott Oliphint, 4th ed. (Phillipsburg, NJ: P&R Publishing, 2008), 352–60.

5. Ibid., 368.

think of Professor Wm. Brenton Greene, formerly Professor of Apologetics at Princeton, speaking or writing in the way that Professor Kuizenga does. Professor Greene's Apologetics sought to be in harmony with the Systematic theology of the great Reformed theologians such as Charles Hodge and B. B. Warfield.[6] The numerous articles of Professor Greene all attest his anxiety to point out not only the distinctive character of orthodox theology but also the distinctive character of Reformed theology. He pointed out again and again that Christianity teaches while modern evolutionary philosophy denies that man was originally created perfect.[7]

Here, in the context of Kuizenga's approach and in contrast to it, Van Til makes it clear that the apologetic of his "revered teacher," Dr. Greene, "sought to be in harmony with the Systematic theology of the great Reformed theologians such as Charles Hodge and B. B. Warfield." He goes on to say, "No one could read the articles and lectures of Professor Greene and not know precisely what the difference is between Christianity and non-Christian types of thought." Furthermore, "Professor Greene contended boldly for the utter insufficiency of the 'naturalist' interpretation of human life and the complete sufficiency of the 'supernaturalist' interpretation."[8] These endorsements of Greene's approach are significant and should be read in light of Van Til's sincere and consistent appreciation of his former teacher. Whatever Greene's errors in apologetic method may have been, then, Van Til is convinced that they are errors of inconsistency—theological "blind spots"—and not of doctrine *per se*.

Not only so, but Van Til's critique of absolute idealism, which was the subject of his dissertation at Princeton University, and which would continue to be an important foil for his apologetic throughout his career, was itself informed, in part, by Greene.

6. Although Van Til affirms that Greene's approach "sought to be in harmony" with Reformed theology, he will reluctantly have to argue that Greene's approach compromised that theology in significant ways.

7. Cornelius Van Til and Eric H. Sigward, *The Articles of Cornelius Van Til*, electronic ed. (New York: Labels Army Company, 1997). This material comes from Cornelius Van Til, "A New Princeton Apologetic," *Christianity Today* 3 (January 1933): 12.

8. Van Til and Sigward, *The Articles of Cornelius Van Til*, electronic ed.

Indeed it was Professor Greene's constant concern to show clearly that the idealist type of philosophy, which speaks in terminology that resembles the terminology of Christianity, is often a greater enemy of Christianity than the crassest materialism just because the difference between Christianity and idealism is for the untrained mind difficult to detect.[9]

The critiques that Van Til offers of his Princeton mentors, therefore, should not be seen as critiques of their theology *per se*. Van Til was explicit in his support of his Princeton forebears, and it is clear that he prefers the method of Greene over that of the modernist Kuizenga. Instead, his critiques are attempts to incorporate Old Princeton's explicitly Reformed theology into a more theologically consistent *apologetic approach*, an approach which Princeton had failed consistently to take. This explains how and why Van Til could, on the one hand, defend Greene and others against the modernism that was characterizing Princeton's reorganization and, on the other hand, criticize the apologetic approach of Greene as well as of those who taught him (Warfield) and those who followed him (like Hamilton, discussed below).

As Van Til reflects on his development of a Reformed apologetic approach, he says,

Deciding, therefore, to follow the Reformers in theology, it was natural that I attempt also to do so in apologetics. I turned to such Reformed apologists as Warfield, Greene, and others. What did I find? I found the theologians of the "self-attesting Christ," defending their faith with a method which denied precisely that point![10]

Although Van Til recognized that, in places, "**Professor Greene virtually uses the argument from presupposition**" (and this would be expected, given Greene's theological commitments), his disappointment

---

9. Ibid. Van Til's concern to distinguish idealism was coincident with his (and Machen's) concern for the modernist takeover of Princeton. Later on in this article, Van Til says, "Now it is upon this confusion between idealism and Christianity that Modernism largely feeds today."

10. Cornelius Van Til, *The Reformed Pastor and the Defense of Christianity and My Credo* (Phillipsburg, NJ: Presbyterian and Reformed, 1980), 82.

lies in the fact that "Greene follows the traditional method of apologetics as worked out by Bishop Butler and others."[11] Greene's apologetic method was inconsistent with his Reformed theology. Greene's method, a method that was in agreement with Butler's approach, became the background for critique and analysis in Van Til's course on evidences. It could not be otherwise. Van Til notes, "It is this avowed insistence that apologetics must deal neutrally with such questions as the existence of God and the facts of Christianity that marks the old Princeton Apologetics."[12]

Given Van Til's concern over the initial content of this course on evidences, and given his commitment to teach this course and write this syllabus in a way that would correct what he had learned in apologetics at Princeton Seminary, it may help to note what Van Til's apologetics professor, William Brenton Greene Jr., understood to be the task and subject matter of apologetics. The "appeal to neutrality" that Greene incorporates can be illustrated in his junior year apologetics syllabus.[13] There Greene defines apologetics as "that branch of theological science setting forth to human *reason* the *proofs* that Xy is the supernat. and exclusive relig." (p. 3). This in itself might not be too troublesome; it depends on what Greene means by "human reason" and "proof," both of which he highlights for emphasis. Fortunately, he tells us what he means:

> The Reason = sum of man's rational, moral, and spiritual natures. Sometimes means "power of reasoning," understanding; sometimes intuition.—[McCosh's Cognitive and Motive Powers.] (p. 6)

It becomes clear, especially from Greene's reference here to McCosh,[14] that his view of reason was that which was set forth by common sense

11. Van Til, *Defense of the Faith*, ed. Oliphint, 353. Van Til notes that Greene recommends the apologetic approach set out in George Park Fisher's *The Grounds of Theistic and Christian Belief*, which does not offer a Reformed apologetic.

12. Ibid., 360.

13. The following quotations are from W. B. Greene Jr., *Outline Syllabus on Apologetics of Lectures* (Princeton: Barr & Stone, 1898–1899). Page numbers will refer to that syllabus.

14. James McCosh (1811–1894) was the eleventh president of the College of New Jersey (renamed Princeton University in 1896), and he had significant influence on its theology. According to www.scottishphilosophy.org, "McCosh differed from many of his contemporaries in being relatively uninfluenced by Kant. He was a 'Scottish' philosopher not only by training, but by his adherence to the tradition of Thomas Reid and other Scottish common-sense philosophers and his self-conscious articulation of that tradition. In 1875 he gave that tradition a more general self-consciousness and a higher profile by the publication of his book *The Scottish Philosophy*,—a chronologically order encyclopedia

realism and taught at Princeton by James McCosh. Among the principles of common sense realism, which Greene mentions in his syllabus, is that reason is assumed to be trustworthy because it includes intuitive self-knowledge, which "is self-evident, necessary and universally accepted" (p. 6). What this means for Greene is that "we must have rational basis for acceptance of supernat. revelation," which itself must be proved by way of reason because "reason is nearer and stronger to us than any external authority" (p. 8). Indeed, according to Greene, "outside the sphere of relig. Reason is supreme" (p. 8).

Greene supposes, therefore, that the way to defend Christianity is by reason alone, as it is able—self-evidently, necessarily, and universally—to intuitively understand who we are as human beings. When the topic is religion, says Greene, reason's role is "to prove rational truths as basis of Rev." and "to determine evidence of Rev." (p. 8). "We must," says Greene, "have rational basis for acceptance of supernat. revelation" (p. 8). Again, although Greene may have been inconsistent in his employment of common sense realism—such inconsistencies would be understandable in light of Greene's Reformed theology—he nevertheless taught that the foundation of his apologetic was the rational faculty, as that faculty had self-evident and universal application in and through all human beings.

Van Til was correct to detect serious problems in this apologetic method. Such a method is inconsistent with Reformed theology, as Richard Muller explains in his analysis of seventeenth-century Reformed prolegomena:

> While there is no foundational status given to natural theology in either the Reformed confessions or in the theology of the Reformers generally, both the confessions and the dogmatic systems acknowledge the presence of a revelation of God in the created order. What

---

of forty seven Scottish philosophers both major and minor. By using the term 'Scottish philosophy' (rather than 'School of Common Sense') McCosh established the intellectual agenda for later similar works—notably *Scottish Philosophy* by Andrew Seth (1885) and *Scottish Philosophy in its National Development,* by Henry Laurie (1902). McCosh's own most original work concerned the attempt to reconcile evolution and Christian beliefs. He argued that evolution, far from being inconsistent with belief in divine design, glorifies the divine designer. This aspect of his work found popularity among evangelical clergy, who found his arguments useful in their attempts to cope with scientific philosophy." Note also Geerhardus Vos's review of Herman Bavinck's *Gereformeerde Dogmatiek,* vol. 1, in *Redemptive History and Biblical Interpretation: The Shorter Writings of Geerhardus Vos,* ed. Richard B. Gaffin Jr. (Phillipsburg, NJ: Presbyterian and Reformed, 1980), 475–84. There Vos notes that Bavinck follows, to some extent, McCosh's method of common sense realism (p. 478).

is more, this revelation is recognized differently by the regenerate and the unregenerate: the unregenerate mind encounters the revelation of God in nature and fashions not a true description of God but blasphemies and idols; the regenerate or elect, however, see God clearly through the "spectacles" of Scripture, which make sure and certain their knowledge of God as Creator.[15]

And thus, says Muller,

No Reformed confession, therefore, views natural theology as a preparation for revealed theology, since only the regenerate, who have learned from Scripture, can return to creation and find there the truth of God.[16]

The problem with Greene's apologetic approach, then, is that it is out of accord with the theology of the Reformation, which he wholeheartedly confessed. In his apologetic method, Greene neglected to take into account the foundational and sweeping effects of sin on the mind of man—on *reason itself*—assuming instead that reason is intact and unaffected by sin with respect to its "common sense" beliefs.

There is something at work in the heart of man that is much deeper and more pervasive even than intuition, and Greene was surely aware of it. Especially after Calvin sought to make clear in his *Institutes* what Scripture teaches about "the twofold knowledge" of God and of man, the notion that all men live their lives as culpable knowers of God, a theological tenet that Greene would have held, should have been immediately and principially incorporated into Greene's apologetic. He should have recognized that the only knowledge that is self-evident to all men, by virtue of their creation in the image of God, is the clear and distinct knowledge of God—which, because given by God, is itself true, as it is always and everywhere present in and around them. Whatever beliefs men might hold in common, therefore, have to be seen in light of the true and common knowledge of God that is the ground and foundation of any other belief. Thus, one either responds to that universal knowledge in conformity to God's revelation, or one responds in idolatry (Rom. 1:23–25).

15. Richard A. Muller, *Post-Reformation Reformed Dogmatics: The Rise and Development of Reformed Orthodoxy, ca. 1520 to ca. 1725*, vol. 2: *Holy Scripture*, 2nd ed., 4 vols. (Grand Rapids: Baker Book House, 2003), 154.
16. Ibid.

In other words, realism in any variety—common sense, critical, etc.—can only properly affirm that which is "real" because it is the true knowledge of God, given and received through what is real, that comes to us by virtue of God's ever-present and constant revealing activity in us and in the world. There is, therefore, a revelational foundation that is necessary for realism to be what it is. Realism cannot be, because it cannot supply, its own foundation. In that sense, what is real should not be thought of as an "ism." Our revelational foundation, which is the universal knowledge of God in all people, can be understood and affirmed only by way of God's special revelation. God's natural revelation is properly seen and affirmed only in the context of an affirmation of God's special revelation, including an affirmation of the gospel in its biblical fullness. Apart from special revelation, reality can only be understood as devoid of intrinsic meaning (i.e., brute fact) and thus is fundamentally *mis*understood. Realism, apart from the affirmation of special revelation, takes its place among all other isms (except Christian theism) as an idol of human autonomy.

Consistent with Greene's approach is the direction that Floyd Hamilton takes in his own apologetic methodology.[17] Hamilton was a student of Greene's at Princeton Seminary. He wrote *The Basis of Christian Faith* as an exposition of the theology and apologetic he learned at Princeton. His mentor, Greene, critiqued the whole book and helped him to revise it prior to its publication. We can expect, therefore, that its content conforms, in the main, to Greene's views. Accordingly, Hamilton begins his book with this discussion of apologetics:

> Before we can attempt to prove the existence of God or discuss the truth of Christianity, we must show that the soul exists as something distinct from the body. We must show that our reasoning processes can be trusted, and that we have a valid right to reason from our sensations to the real world back of these sensations. And we must also show that when we attempt to deal with questions such as the existence of God and the possibility of His giving a revelation to man in a Book, we are dealing with questions which properly lie within the scope of the human reason. First of all, then, we must discuss the question of the existence of the soul.[18]

17. For a more complete assessment of Hamilton, see Van Til, *Defense of the Faith*, ed. Oliphint, 361–69.

18. Floyd E. Hamilton, *The Basis of Christian Faith: A Modern Defense of the Christian Religion* (New York: George H. Doran, 1927), 15, quoted in ibid., 361.

It is not difficult to see the influence of Greene on Hamilton's view of "human reason." The existence of God and of the possibility of God giving a revelation to man in a book are questions for human reason, in the first place. In this affirmation, there can be no question but that Hamilton, like Greene, affirms a neutral notion of reason and supposes that such questions as the existence of God and the possibility of a divine revelation are to be answered by way of that neutral reason. In other words, there cannot be, at this initial juncture in the discussion, an appeal to *Christian* truth; the topics under consideration must be accessible to anyone, believer or unbeliever.

Hamilton's entire apologetic rests on the presumed ability of human reason rightly to judge the evidence presented to it. Thus he reasons from the notion of causality to the external world, and then from the external world to God, who must have created the human soul. In his apologetic for the possibility of supernatural revelation, Hamilton says, "We approach the Bible as we would approach any other book."[19]

This apologetic method, Van Til rightly notes, is "**in line with Arminian and Romanist thinking.**"[20] Although the Princeton theologians and Hamilton were basically loyal to Reformed theology, "**it remains true that in their avowed apologetical procedure they embraced a method that resembled that of Bishop Butler, rather than that of Calvin.**"[21]

This notion of the neutrality of reason and of evidence was a problem that might have continued to plague Reformed theology had Van Til not sought to critique and correct it. No one else, at the time of the writing of Van Til's syllabus on evidences, had dealt such a deathblow to these notions. As Van Til makes clear, Kuyper certainly moved in the right direction. Bavinck was also more consistent than his Princeton peers in recognizing the reality of the antithesis. But even Bavinck had elements of a neutral notion of the real within his theology.[22] Van Til attempted, beginning in this syllabus, to excise all "isms" but Christian theism from Reformed theology

---

19. Hamilton, *The Basis of Christian Faith*, 134, quoted in Van Til, *Defense of the Faith*, ed. Oliphint, 366.

20. Van Til, *Defense of the Faith*, ed. Oliphint, 364.

21. Ibid., 368.

22. Note Van Til's critique of Bavinck's realism in Cornelius Van Til, *Introduction to Systematic Theology: Prolegomena and the Doctrines of Revelation, Scripture, and God*, ed. William Edgar, 2nd ed. (Phillipsburg, NJ: P&R Publishing, 2007), 94–95. For a defense and development of that critique, see K. Scott Oliphint, "Bavinck's Realism, the Logos Principle, and *Sola Scriptura*," *Westminster Theological Journal* 72 (2010): 359–90.

and apologetics. In this, he was a theological pioneer. As he used to put it, he stood on the shoulders of giants and could, therefore, see a bit farther.

THE COMMON (SENSE) PROBLEM[23]

The root of the problem in the Old Princeton apologetic (as well as in elements of Herman Bavinck's theology) was some version of the (Reidian) common sense realism that had gained some ascendency after the skepticism of David Hume had become obvious.[24]

In his excellent article, "The Collapse of American Evangelical Academia," George Marsden attempts to show the (partial) historical progression in which scholarship has divorced itself from Christianity, beginning in the eighteenth century and continuing in the nineteenth.[25] One of the key elements in this progression was the adoption and then failure of Thomas Reid's common sense philosophy in evangelical apologetics. The primary reason for this failure, according to Marsden, was that it was never able to provide a ground, or foundation, for its most basic principles; it was never able to account for its own understanding of "common sense."

As Marsden follows the historical progression up to the middle of the nineteenth century, he notes the inability of evangelical apologetics to deal with the destructive aspects of Darwinism. Marsden's central question, given such an inability, is this: "What . . . about this midnineteenth-century American evangelical apologetic made it particularly vulnerable to onslaughts of the scientific revolution associated with Darwinism?"[26] Now the "midnineteenth-century American evangelical apologetic" of which Marsden speaks is that promoted by, among others, Archibald Alexander, Charles Hodge, and B. B. Warfield. With regard to the approaches of these men, says Marsden, "Common-Sense philosophy was the starting point."[27]

An apologetic with its roots in Reid's common sense philosophy (such as we have seen in Greene's and Hamilton's views on the matter) begins with "immediate, noninferential beliefs . . . as Reid had proposed, such

---

23. Some of the material in this section is an edited version of material in K. Scott Oliphint, *Reasons for Faith: Philosophy in the Service of Theology* (Phillipsburg, NJ: P&R Publishing, 2006).

24. The primary proponent of common sense realism was Thomas Reid (1710–1796).

25. George Marsden, "The Collapse of American Evangelical Academia," in *Faith and Rationality: Reason and Belief in God*, ed. Alvin Plantinga and Nicholas Wolterstorff (Notre Dame, IN: University of Notre Dame Press, 1983), 219–64.

26. Ibid., 241.

27. Ibid., 235.

as the existence of the self, the existence of other personal and rational beings, the existence of the material world, the relationship of cause and effect, the continuity of past and present." These were called, by Reid, "principles of common-sense."[28] In defending Christianity, those who adopted this philosophy began by attempting to show how the basic truths and principles of Christianity could fit within the already established truths of common sense. In other words, they would argue, belief in God can fit the beliefs that we already have from common sense.

Without reproducing Marsden's penetrating article, we should note his analysis of the failure of the Reidian approach. As Hodge (following Reid) remarked in stating his assumptions, the truths of common sense were "given in the constitution of our nature." Having been so purposely designed, they could be relied on with confidence. This is true because, as Reid himself argued, it is possible to establish once for all the agreed-upon principles of common sense.[29] So, asserted Hodge, the design of nature involved the creation of a single, universal human nature. Since the principles of common sense were universal and unalterable, they provided the foundation for our defense of Christianity. It appears that Greene and Hamilton held the same view.

But Marsden notes serious problems with Reid's assumption. For example, when Darwinism came on the scene, one of its most serious challenges to the Christian faith was that it could retain its evolutionary principle without recourse to theism. The problem was not so much that Darwinism needed atheism, which would have been easier to deal with (because more explicit), but rather that Darwinism needed only agnosticism. In other words, it was not that Darwinism had to contend, "There is no God, but there is design," but only, "We see design in everything, though we are not sure whether or not God exists," which is far less radical (and thus more challenging) than blatant atheism. So Darwinism challenged Christian theism's contention that the existence of God was certain by postulating agnosticism, along with a thesis explaining the origin of apparent design. Those married to Reid's common sense realism could only respond that Darwin's position excluded an intelligent Designer, which was too obvious even to need asserting.[30] As Marsden points out, all that Hodge (for example) could do in the face of Darwinism was to assert that nearly everyone believed in an intelligent Designer. What, then, would

28. Ibid.
29. Ibid., 243.
30. Ibid., 243–44.

happen to this defense when the next generation would show a far less universal belief in an intelligent Designer? Darwinism and the growing opposition of science to Christian theism showed the fatal weakness of an apologetic based on common sense realism: "Common sense could not settle a dispute over what was a matter of common sense."[31]

Common sense philosophy, therefore, when tried in the fire of apologetic methodology, and thus also of epistemology, failed in its attempt to undergird the truth of Christianity in the face of a hostile science. In other words, the problem with a Reidian approach to epistemology is that there is no way to determine just what beliefs are common and what beliefs are not. One man's basic belief could easily be another man's irrationality.

Especially when such things as the existence of God and the authority of Scripture are in view, it is not the case that anyone who "looks at the evidence" in a reasonable way will reach the same conclusion. Although the evidence, objectively speaking, is the same for the Christian and the non-Christian, once that evidence is "taken" by the subject, it is inevitably understood according to that person's theological bent, either for or against God. What we believe about God is appropriated to our own understanding of the world around us. There can be, therefore, no compelling evidence for God's existence if the mind of man is hostile toward God (Rom. 8:7), unable to understand the world as God's world (1 Cor. 2:14), continually suppressing the truth that comes by way of the things that are made (Rom. 1:18ff.).

FROM PRINCETON TO PLANTINGA

The topic of evidences in this syllabus is as relevant today as it was when Van Til first wrote about it in 1930. Not only so, but the Reidian "common sense" approach to evidences, adopted by some at Princeton, has been given a significant and far-reaching push into prominence, especially with the new epistemological theory of Alvin Plantinga.

In his influential article, "Reason and Belief in God,"[32] Plantinga began, in earnest, to argue for the "proper basicality" of theistic belief.[33] His concern, generally, was that those who denied the rationality of belief

---

31. Ibid., 244.
32. Alvin Plantinga, "Reason and Belief in God," in *Faith and Rationality*, ed. Plantinga and Wolterstorff, 16–93.
33. This may not be completely accurate. Some would say that Plantinga began his argument in *God and Other Minds*. In any case, "Reason and Belief in God" was the beginning of a concerted effort to develop a new epistemological approach.

in God due to insufficient evidence had unduly placed requirements on that belief that they themselves did not maintain for their own beliefs. His more specific concern was that the rationality of belief in God had been illegitimately rendered suspect by too many. Those who demanded evidential proof for such a belief relaxed those same demands when it came to other, more "popular" beliefs that they themselves held.

Plantinga's project, in its initial stages, was to answer the evidential challenge to belief in God. The evidential challenge was expressed concisely by the late ethicist W. K. Clifford: "To sum up: it is wrong always, everywhere, and for anyone to believe anything upon insufficient evidence."[34] The link between a Reidian common sense approach and the so-called evidential challenge is this: the evidentialist claims that for any person's beliefs to be rational or rationally acceptable, those beliefs must be supported by some kind of evidence, be it empirical or propositional. Plantinga argues that many beliefs, including belief in God, can be included in the category of basic, common sense beliefs—what Plantinga calls "properly basic" beliefs.

The evidential challenge with respect to belief in God states, generally, that it is wrong to believe in God without sufficient evidence of his existence. Merold Westphal is helpful in his description of the problem:

> Evidentialism is the claim that religious belief is irrational, cognitively disreputable, a violation of our epistemic duties, unless supported by sufficient evidence or argument. Some theists have been willing to accept this assumption, assuming that sufficient evidence or adequate argument can be provided to render faith rational. But faith has not fared well in the empire of evidentialism, especially after the assault on theistic proofs by Hume and Kant; and Reformed epistemology rejects its rule as illicitly imperialistic, seeking to establish the counterclaim that belief in God is properly basic.[35]

---

34. Plantinga quotes this in numerous places, among which are "Rationality and Religious Belief," in *Contemporary Philosophy of Religion*, ed. Steven M. Cahn and David Shatz (New York: Oxford University Press, 1982), 258, and "Reason and Belief in God," 25. The quote itself comes from W. K. Clifford, "The Ethics of Belief," in *Lectures and Essays* (London: Macmillan, 1879), 186.

35. Merold Westphal, "A Reader's Guide to 'Reformed Epistemology,'" *Perspectives* 7, no. 9 (November 1992), 10.

As Westphal notes, most responses to this challenge have attempted to formulate evidential replies, showing that there is sufficient evidence for God's existence, and thus that belief in God is not irrational. But those responses have suffered at the hands of philosophical and theological challenges. In light of that plight, some have simply refused to admit that the challenges from Kant or Hume have anything important to say. That is one response—simply to dismiss the arguments. Others have attempted to strengthen the arguments for the existence of God, using more current literature or new discoveries. Oftentimes, however, these arguments have the effect of adding zeros to zero, since they neglect to deal with the assumptions behind the challenge to God's existence.

Plantinga proposes a different tack. He challenges the challenge itself, claiming that it cannot live up to its own criteria. What Plantinga sets out to investigate is what he calls the moderate evidentialist claim. It is (1) that it is irrational to accept theistic belief in the absence of sufficient evidence or reasons, and (2) that there is no, or at least insufficient, evidence or reason to support the proposition that God exists. Since the evidence for God is insufficient, unavailable, or inaccessible, the evidential conclusion is that belief in God is irrational.

Plantinga's response to the evidential challenge is to develop a new approach to epistemology along Reidian lines. He sets out to develop a response to the evidentialist that he initially calls "Reformed epistemology."[36] The project of Reformed epistemology, according to Nicholas Wolterstorff, is this:

> The project of Reformed epistemology is to answer the evidential-ist critique of Christianity. The project is not to say how religious beliefs are connected to each other. The project is not to say how religious beliefs are connected to experience. The project is not to say how religious beliefs are connected to life. The project is not to discuss how a religious way of life is taught. The project is not to explain what a religious way of life is. The project is not to offer a theory of the essence of religion. The project is not to consider what, if anything, can be said to an unbeliever to "bring him around." The project is not to discuss the role of argument

---

36. Plantinga, however, soon regretted the adjective "Reformed" and, for the most part, dropped it from his discussions in epistemology.

in religion. The project is not to discuss the role of reason in religion—to offer a theory of rationality in religion. The project is not to develop a whole philosophy of religion of a certain stripe. The project is to answer a certain criticism. Those who are Reformed epistemologists have views on many of the issues cited above; they have published some of those views. But, to say it one more time, the project of Reformed epistemology as such is to answer a certain criticism, a criticism not of Reformed epistemologists but rather of Christians in general, and of Jews and Muslims and all other theists: the evidentialist criticism. The project of Reformed epistemology is a polemical project.[37]

There is much to be said about Plantinga's project, and much that has been said, but at this juncture we need to stick closely to the topic at hand.[38] In his challenge to the evidential challenge, Plantinga argues that there is a Reformed objection to natural theology, and that such an objection has, at its root, a Reidian notion of belief in God as properly basic. That is, a belief in God need not be proved by demonstration; instead, it can be seen as properly basic.

Plantinga's suspicion concerning the evidential objection to belief in God was first expressed in *God and Other Minds*. In that book, Plantinga argues that belief in other minds and belief in God are on an epistemological par. That is, both beliefs can be rational, even if no argument is given for them.[39] Over against the evidential objection to belief in God, according to Plantinga, there are some very basic and universal beliefs, such as our belief in other minds, that are not deemed to be rational on the basis of argument. And yet, even so, they are rational beliefs. If that is the case, why not include belief in God among the set of rational, or properly basic, beliefs? In summarizing his argument, Plantinga says,

---

37. Nicholas Wolterstorff, "What Reformed Epistemology Is Not," *Perspectives* 7, no. 9 (November 1992), 15.

38. For a fuller analysis of Plantinga's epistemological project, see K. Scott Oliphint, "Plantinga on Warrant," *Westminster Theological Journal* 57 (1995): 81–102; idem, "Epistemology and Christian Belief," *Westminster Theological Journal* 63 (2001): 151–82; idem, "The Old New Reformed Epistemology," in *Revelation and Reason: New Essays in Reformed Apologetics,* ed. K. Scott Oliphint and Lane G. Tipton (Phillipsburg, NJ: P&R Publishing, 2007).

39. To be clear, the point is not that no argument *can* be given for such beliefs—perhaps they can. The point is that such beliefs are not in need of an argument in order to be held rationally.

I conclude that belief in other minds and belief in God are in the same epistemological boat; hence if either is rational, so is the other. But obviously the former *is* rational; so, therefore, is the latter.[40]

But Plantinga does not stop with a simple argument for parity, arguing that, since belief in other minds is rational without proof, so is belief in God. He argues as well that this kind of position has been held, with some consistency, in the Reformed tradition.

In his extended article that develops his new epistemology, Plantinga analyzes Calvin and Bavinck, among others, and concludes that each man argues that belief in God is justified, without a basis in argumentation. Calvin postulates a universal disposition to believe in God, the *sensus divinitatis*—an idea that will occupy a significant place in Plantinga's notion of a "proper function" epistemology. Bavinck similarly maintains that argument or proof is not the source of a believer's confidence in God. In other words, according to Plantinga, these Reformed thinkers agree that theistic proofs are not necessary for theistic belief. Calvin, Bavinck, and others set forth belief in God as that which either transcends argument or underlies it, or both.

Plantinga affirms Calvin's distrust of reason and concludes that Calvin's argument for the authority of Scripture is true also for the existence of God. That is, belief in either one comes not by argument but by the testimony of the Holy Spirit. He writes,

> From Calvin's point of view believing in the existence of God on the basis of rational argument is like believing in the existence of your spouse on the basis of the analogical argument for other minds— whimsical at best and unlikely to delight the person concerned.[41]

All of this suspicion of the arguments for God's existence adds up to this:

> What the Reformers held was that a believer is entirely rational, entirely within his epistemic rights, in *starting with* belief in God, in accepting it as basic, and in taking it as premise for argument to other conclusions.[42]

---

40. Alvin Plantinga, *God and Other Minds: A Study of the Rational Justification of Belief in God* (Ithaca, NY: Cornell University Press, 1990), xvi.
41. Plantinga, "Reason and Belief in God," 67–68.
42. Ibid., 72.

In other words, Plantinga argues that the Reformers took the same position that he does. He puts them within the foundationalist debate and attributes to them (and thus to at least a part of the Reformed theological tradition) the view that belief in God is properly basic. That is, a person is entirely within his epistemic rights, and is entirely rational, in believing in God, even if he has no argument for this belief and does not base it on any other beliefs that he holds. And in taking belief in God as properly basic, the Reformers were implicitly rejecting a whole epistemological structure, an entire picture of knowledge and rational belief, called classical foundationalism.

VAN TIL: FOUNDATIONS, *NOT* FOUNDATIONALISM

The question may immediately arise, and has arisen, as to the relationship of Plantinga's epistemology to that of Van Til.[43] Given that Plantinga is arguing that one may "start with" belief in God, isn't he arguing for a presuppositional approach to epistemology? Given what we have said above, the answer to this question is no.

Plantinga argues against classical foundationalism's three conditions for proper basicality (i.e., that a belief must be self-evident, incorrigible, and evident to the senses). But his argument is *not* that such conditions do not obtain; he is not arguing that foundationalism includes the *wrong* categories of properly basic beliefs. Rather, the problem with classical foundationalism is that there should be additional properly basic categories. Classical foundationalism, according to Plantinga, is suspect as an epistemological structure because it says too little. It has nothing to say, for example, to my belief that I was in Boston last year, or that I did not just appear at my desk five minutes ago, or that you, like me, are a person. Classical foundationalism's proper basicality is far too narrow and restrictive in its affirmation of common sense categories.

But classical foundationalism is also far too ambitious, and destructively so, according to Plantinga. Not only does it say too little, but it also says

---

43. D. Z. Phillips, for example, attempts to show that both Plantinga and Van Til are similar in their respective commitments to foundationalism. He is correct about Plantinga, but not about Van Til. See D. Z. Phillips, *Faith after Foundationalism* (London: Routledge, 1988). For a more helpful analysis of some coincidences between Plantinga and Van Til, see James Anderson, "If Knowledge Then God: The Epistemological Theistic Arguments of Alvin Plantinga and Cornelius Van Til," *Calvin Theological Journal* 40 (2005): 49–75.

too much. Consider Plantinga's formulated "fundamental principle" of classical foundationalism: "A proposition *p* is properly basic for a person *S* if and only if *p* is either self-evident to *S* or incorrigible for *S* or evident to the senses for *S*."[44] We have just noted Plantinga's problem with the "only if" aspect of this principle—it says too little—but now notice that it cannot cohere within its own criteria of rationality. It must either itself be a properly basic belief or it must be believed on the basis of some other, more basic belief(s). The classical foundationalist, believing this principle, must be able to support that belief by way of some beliefs that are either self-evident, incorrigible, or evident to the senses. But no such argument has been forthcoming from the classical foundationalists. Therefore, since this principle is not inferential, it must itself be properly basic in order to be believed rationally. But it cannot meet the condition of being evident to the senses, self-evident, or incorrigible. The fundamental principle of classical foundationalism, with its insistence on, and conditions of, proper basicality, is itself, as Plantinga likes to say, "self-referentially incoherent."[45] Foundationalism's own basic principles are insufficient to support the very position for which it seeks to argue.

So, even though Plantinga is critical of what he calls "classical foundationalism,"[46] his criticism is *not with the structure of foundationalism per se*, but rather that classical foundationalism is insufficiently narrow and is self-referentially incoherent. These two faults, argues Plantinga, render classical foundationalism untenable.

But this does not mean that Plantinga intends to move to another, more cogent epistemological structure. Instead, he argues that the categories of foundationalism must be enlarged and expanded to include a multitude of other beliefs that we rationally hold, and hold without the need for argumentation. Included in those categories, according to Plantinga, is theistic belief. Thus, for Plantinga, to "start with" belief in God means that we can rationally believe in God without argument, and that such belief can provide the foundation for other beliefs that we might hold inferentially. In other words, Plantinga moves from a narrower Reidian, common sense epistemology to a broader one, but it remains fundamentally Reidian;

44. Plantinga, "Reason and Belief in God," 59.
45. Ibid., 61. George Mavrodes seeks, among other things, to show that Plantinga's notion of self-referential incoherence is erroneous in "Self-Referential Incoherence," *American Philosophical Quarterly* 22 (January 1985): 65–72.
46. See, for example, Plantinga, "Reason and Belief in God," 48–63.

the "common sense" structure, both of classical foundationalism and of Plantinga's new foundationalism, remains the same.[47]

If this is the case, then foundationalism of any variety, in that it depends for its structure on some notion of common sense beliefs, will not be able to stand; it will sink, due to its insufficient strength. The foundation of any foundationalism is too weak to support it; common sense is not common enough to provide the strength needed to support the structure. Not only so, but epistemology, generally speaking, cannot stand on the ground of one's beliefs, no matter how common those beliefs might be. In epistemology, something more substantial, more solid, is needed than a mere human belief.

It is at this point that one can begin to appreciate Van Til's approach to evidences. Like Plantinga, Van Til is not content to answer evidential objections by piling on more and more evidence. Neither is he content with a method that seeks to prove or demonstrate theism by way of an evidential argument. In this, Plantinga and Van Til agree.

But Van Til is not content, either, to tout common sense realism, or any other kind of realism, as a solution to the evidential problem or as a sufficient structure for Christian apologetics. He says,

> Accordingly, when God did freely create something beside himself, this something, the universe, could never become a correlative to himself. *Least of all could man, who was one of the creatures of God, develop principles of interpretation or a method of reflective inquiry that could interpret life correctly without the presupposition of God.* Every fact and every law in the created universe is brought into existence by God's creation. Every fact and every law in the created universe continues to exist by virtue of the providence of God. Every fact and every law in the created universe accomplishes what it does accomplish by virtue of the plan or purpose of God. God foreordains whatsoever comes to pass, through his Son Jesus Christ. (p. 96, emphasis added)

47. In terms of structure, one author has likened foundationalism to a pyramid, according to which common sense beliefs are represented by the foundation of the pyramid and inferential beliefs correspond to its two sides. See Ernest Sosa, "The Raft and the Pyramid: Coherence versus Foundations in the Theory of Knowledge," *Midwest Studies in Philosophy: Studies in Epistemology* 5 (1980): 3–25. The foundation of the pyramid is too short in classical foundationalism, according to Plantinga; his epistemology aims to stay within the pyramid, but to lengthen its foundation.

When Van Til says that man could not develop principles of interpretation without the presupposition of God, he does not mean that we can begin our inquiry by "starting with" a generic belief in God. Instead, he means that our inquiry, to the extent that it is tenable, must presuppose the true and triune God and his revelation. Without such a presupposition, we are never able to give an adequate account of the very facts about which we mean to inquire. Any epistemological theory that begins without acknowledging and incorporating the reality of God and his revelation is doomed to fail; it cannot account for even one fact, or for any evidence.

> If we take the Scripture doctrines of God, of creation, of providence, and of the plan of God, we observe that we have a Christian philosophy of fact and a Christian methodology that is squarely opposed to the current philosophy of fact and the current scientific methodology. Scripture teaches that every fact in the universe exists and operates by virtue of the plan of God. There are no brute facts for God. (p. 96)

In seeking to critique standard approaches to "evidences," therefore, Van Til is not content to begin with that which may be "common" or "real" without first recognizing that, epistemologically speaking, every fact is what it is only by virtue of its place in, and interpretation by, the plan of God. The *real* is the *rational*, as Van Til liked to say, only because both—real and rational—have their foundation in the triune God.

Generally speaking, epistemology seeks to understand and analyze just how it is, *if* it is, that man can have knowledge. Historically, epistemology continues to tread that long and winding path without ever reaching its end. It has been unable to establish the credibility, or rationality, of any beliefs that we hold. For Van Til, epistemology must begin, not with *man's* beliefs, but with what *God* has said:

> If the universe is created by God and if it is maintained by God it is itself a revelation of God on a finite scale. (p. 141)

This revelation of God in the universe brings about, as the apostle Paul makes clear, *true* knowledge (Rom. 1:18–21, 32). Thus, to the extent that man is self-conscious, he is, at one and the same time, God-conscious. And this God-consciousness is not an ambiguous, obtuse feeling or a vague impression. Paul's argument is that all men are, by definition, *knowers* of God. The knowledge of God that we all have is *foundational* to every other thing that we know or believe. In that sense, it is knowledge that does not come by a process of believing, then of believing truly, then of being justified (or warranted) in that belief, then of knowledge. This is the standard way that knowledge is considered in much of philosophy and theology.

Instead, the connection between the knower and the known is given in God's revelational activity *through the things that are made* (Rom. 1:20), such that our knowledge of God entails a knowledge of creation. With respect to that knowledge of God, *God* is the author of it, *we* are the possessors of it, and it renders us inexcusable before God. So when Aristotle said that it was of the nature of man to know,[48] he was correct, but he had no idea why he was correct. He was correct because the "nature of man" is "image of God," and included in that image is true and incorrigible knowledge of God. Man is not one who simply begins his life and knowledge with common beliefs. Any beliefs that we have in common have their foundation in God's revelatory activity in, by, and through all of his creation. God, not man, is central to the process of knowing. So, as Van Til says,

> This does not mean that we hold creation or providence to be merely a matter of revelation in the sense that they are not *rationally defensible.* On the contrary, we hold that though we must, as sinners, get these doctrines from the Bible, they are indeed rationally defensible. With them it is as with the rest of the Bible teaching; unless they be true there can be no interpretation of anything without them. The world of facts would be utterly discrete. There would be no laws at all. There would be none to interpret the facts and the laws. We need them because we need the self-sufficient God as the presupposition of our experience. (p. 141, emphasis added)

This was Van Til's emphasis throughout his career, as he sought to be faithful to the self-attesting Christ of Scripture. This syllabus, indicative of the beginning of Van Til's long and fruitful ministry, is one of the most

---

48. See Aristotle, *Metaphysics*, ed. W. D. Ross (Oxford: Clarendon Press, 1924), Book I.

important examples of his approach, and it is as needful today as it was in the summer of 1930.

* * *

I would like to thank Sebastian Heck for his help in interpreting some of the German psychology terms used by Van Til. I would also like to express my deep appreciation to P&R Publishing, and to Amanda Martin, for their continued willingness to ensure that crucial—though perhaps not the most popular—publications, like this one, remain in print. The service to the church that such publications represent is, and has been, through P&R, surely substantial and significant, and indeed of incalculable value.

Except for some augmentation and correction of Van Til's source references, the additions (mainly here and in the notes) appear in the typeface you are now reading. Van Til's material, appearing in a more traditional text font, is otherwise almost untouched.

PREFACE

T he present study contains two parts. The first part was used by the author for a number of years as a class syllabus on Christian Evidences.[1] The main contention of this syllabus was to the effect that the traditional Butler-Analogy type of argument for the factual truthfulness of Christianity is basically defective.[2] Its basic defect is to be found in the fact that, with Arminian theology, it begins by assuming that the enemies of the gospel of Christ are right in holding that man is, or may be, self-explanatory, and that the facts of his environment are, or may be, purely chance-produced and directed.[3]

1. The catalogs of Westminster Theological Seminary indicate that Van Til taught a course entitled "Christian Evidences" from 1930 until the late 1950s. The topic of evidences was among the first he addressed in his teaching career.

2. Bishop Joseph Butler (1692–1752) was the most influential Protestant apologist of the eighteenth century. The book to which Van Til refers, entitled *The Analogy of Religion, Natural and Revealed, to the Constitution and Course of Nature* (1736), was a defense of Christianity against the deism of the day. Butler uses a double negative argument to argue from the natural religion of the deists to the probability of revealed religion as well. The basic thrust of Butler's argument is that this (observed) life and the (unobserved) afterlife, taken together, exhibit features that resemble known features of this life taken alone. For example, we can infer that this life is a training ground for the next life from the way in which the early years of this life are a training ground for the later years. Parenthetically, the reader should note that the term "analogy" is not used in the same way by Butler, Aquinas, and Van Til—which is one reason why confusion remains with respect to the term itself in apologetics.

3. When Van Til says that Butler, via Arminianism, "begins by assuming" the notion of man as self-explanatory and with facts as "purely chance-produced," he is not articulating what Butler (or Arminians) actually *say*, but is highlighting the inevitable conclusions of a system that begins with a supposedly neutral notion of probability and of rationality and a notion of man's freedom to which even God is subject.

A true method of Christian Evidences[4] must start with the interpretation of man and his universe as given to him on the absolute authority of Christ speaking in Scripture in order then to show that unless this is done man abides under the wrath of God and his speech is meaningless.[5]

The appendix contains a portion of a series of three lectures given at Calvin Theological Seminary in October 1968. It deals with essentially the same subject as the first part. Its argument is to the effect that the method of more recent non-Christian scientific methodology is bankrupt because it insists that man can know nothing of God and yet speaks in all its utterance about God. As a consequence recent scientists make an absolute separation between an abstract law of logic which is like a turnpike in the sky, and an infinite number of purely contingent facts, not one of which is distinguishable from another.[6]

4. By a "method of Christian Evidences," Van Til means a proper, Christian way of understanding, and appealing to, evidences, whether in science, apologetics, or any other discipline.

5. The dual consequence of "[abiding] under the wrath of God" and "meaningless" speech illustrates the deep, inextricable connection that Van Til rightly sees between man's covenantal status before God (wrath) and how that status affects everything that we do (including our speech and its proposed meaning). Van Til is not saying that the speech of unbelief is meaningless in that it cannot be understood or examined. He is saying that the unbeliever, due to his rebellion against God, is unable to make sense even of those things he articulates. God, as Van Til says repeatedly, is the only ground for meaningful predication.

6. A quotation elsewhere from Van Til on the relation of facts to logic may help the reader to understand him here: "But usually the traditional apologist is neither a pure inductivist nor a pure *a priorist*. Of necessity he has to be both. When engaged in inductive argument about facts he will therefore talk about these facts as proving the existence of God. If anything exists at all, he will say, something absolute *must* exist. But when he thus talks about what *must* exist and when he refuses even to admit that non-believers have false assumptions about their *musts*, let alone being willing to challenge them on the subject, he has in reality granted that the non-believer's conception about the relation of human logic to facts is correct. It does not occur to him that on any but the Christian theistic basis there is no possible connection of logic with facts at all. When the non-Christian, not working on the foundation of creation and providence, talks about *musts* in relation to *facts* he is beating the air. His logic is merely the exercise of a revolving door in a void, moving nothing from nowhere into the void. But instead of pointing out this fact to the unbeliever the traditional apologist appeals to this non-believer as though by his immanentistic method he could very well interpret many things correctly." See Cornelius Van Til, *Defense of the Faith*, ed. K. Scott Oliphint, 4th ed. (Phillipsburg, NJ: P&R Publishing, 2008), 262. As for his notion of logic as a "turnpike in the sky," Van Til was once asked what he meant by that, to which he replied, "I meant there is no way to get on it." See Cornelius Van Til, "At the Beginning, God: An Interview with Cornelius Van Til," *Christianity Today* 22 (December 30, 1977): 22.

The Butler type of argument is again shown to be helpless. It cannot apply the message of Christ as the Way and the Truth to this situation. Only on the presupposition of the truth of the words of the self-attesting Christ as available in the Scriptures can man, with his scientific enterprise, be saved.

GENERAL INTRODUCTION

The studies presented in this series are written with a view to the defense of the doctrine of the free grace of God through Christ as he testifies of himself in the Scriptures of the Old and New Testaments. They are written from the point of view of one who believes the Reformed Faith to be the most truly biblical expression of the Christian Faith. They are written from the point of view of one who believes that a world that lies in darkness needs, therefore, to hear about the Reformed Faith.

Moreover, if the world needs to hear the Reformed Faith, the statement of this Faith must be true to the historic Reformed creeds. The Reformed Faith, to be heard, must, therefore, be set over against Neo-orthodoxy.

These studies are merely student syllabi; they are not to be regarded as published books.[1]

These studies are produced under the auspices of the *Den Dulk Christian Foundation* of Ripon, California.

---

1. This is an important point to remember. Van Til's intent in writing this work was simply to produce a syllabus for a course he taught at Westminster Theological Seminary in Philadelphia.

INTRODUCTION

We preface our discussion in this course by a few general remarks about the nature and purpose of Christian evidences. Evidences is a subdivision of apologetics in the broader sense of the term. If we take apologetics in its broad sense we mean by it the vindication of Christian theism against any form of non-theistic and non-Christian thought.[1] This vindication of Christian theism has two aspects. In the first place, Christian theism must be defended against non-Christian science. It is this that we seek to do in the course in Christian evidences. Evidences, then, is a subdivision of apologetics in the broader sense of the word, and is coordinate with apologetics in the more limited sense of the word.

Christian-theistic evidences is, then, the defense of Christian theism against any attack that may be made upon it by "science." Yet it is Christian theism as a unit that we defend. We do not seek to defend theism in apologetics and Christianity in evidences, but we seek to defend Christian theism in both courses. Then, too, in the method of defense we do not limit ourselves to argument about facts in the course in evidences nor to philosophical argument in the course in apologetics. It is really quite impossible to make a sharp distinction between theism and Christianity and between the method of defense for each of them.[2]

1. This is a helpful, one-sentence explanation of what Christian apologetics is meant to be.
2. This statement needs to be kept in mind all along. There is no separation to be made between theism and Christian theism in apologetic methodology. If it is the *truth* that we are defending, it can be found only in *Christian* theism, not in a generic theism. Thus, apologetics is a defense of *Christianity* as a whole, not of a mere theism.

Nevertheless, in evidences it is primarily the factual question with which we deal. Christianity is an historical religion. It is based upon such facts as the death and resurrection of Christ. The question of miracle is at the heart of it. Kill miracle and you kill Christianity. But one cannot even define miracle except in relation to natural law.

Thus, we face the question of God's providence. And providence, in turn, presupposes creation. We may say, then, that we seek to defend the fact of miracle, the fact of providence, the fact of creation, and, therefore, the fact of God, in relation to modern non-Christian science.

We may as well say, therefore, that we are seeking to defend Christian theism as a fact. And this is really the same thing as to say that we believe the facts of the universe are unaccounted for except upon the Christian theistic basis. In other words, facts and interpretation of facts cannot be separated. It is impossible even to discuss any particular fact except in relation to some principle of interpretation. The real question about facts is, therefore, what kind of universal can give the best account of the facts. Or rather, the real question is, which universal can state or give meaning to any fact.[3]

Are there, then, several universals that may possibly give meaning to facts? We believe there are not. We hold that there is only one such universal, namely, the triune God of Christianity.[4] We hold that without the presupposition of the triune God we cannot even interpret one fact correctly. Facts without the triune God of Scripture would be brute facts.[5] They would have no intelligible relation to one another. As such they could not be known by man.

---

3. In this paragraph, Van Til is making it clear that, once man takes any fact and attempts to understand it, that understanding will be inextricably linked to his understanding of the way(s) in which that fact relates to other facts and to the world generally. Thus, every individual fact is thought to be what it is in relation to one's understanding of everything else. This "everything else" that pertains to the fact is what Van Til means by "universal."

4. Van Til speaks here of God as a "universal" only for pedagogical reasons. If one thinks that facts, to be meaningful, must be related to a universal, then the triune God is the only universal that can, ultimately, give meaning, definition, and understanding to any fact or to the relation of fact to fact.

5. That is, a fact that is related to nothing else, which is impossible, has no interpretation. A fact without an interpretation would be a "brute fact." But brute facts cannot exist, since every fact is what it is by virtue of God's plan in and for creation. Moreover, any fact that is given an interpretation that excludes the triune God and his plan is, to that extent, not known, in that its interpretation is false.

Suppose, then, that we take the "system" of Christian theism and think of the attacks that are made upon it by science. We may for convenience take the six divisions of systematic theology and note in turn the attacks that are made upon our doctrines of God, of man, of Christ, of salvation, of the church, and of the last things. Every attack upon one of these is an attack upon the whole system of truth as we hold it.[6] For that reason the answer to each attack must be fundamentally the same. We shall, in each case, have to point out that the explanations offered by non-Christian views are no explanations at all inasmuch as they cannot relate the facts discussed to all other facts that must be taken into account. Worse than that, these "explanations" spring from an ethical opposition to the truth as it is in Jesus, the self-attesting Christ. Yet, in order to work according to orderly procedure, we shall first notice the attacks made upon the doctrine of God, then those upon the doctrine of man, and so on till we come to the doctrine of the last things. Thus we have before us a broad outline picture of the road ahead.

It remains only to remark on the meaning of the scientific attack we have mentioned above. When we speak of evidences as the vindication or defense of Christian theism against science we take the word science in its current meaning. We think first of the results of science, real or imaginary. These results are before us in various fields. Physical science seems to have come to some definite conclusions about spiritual life. Social science seems to have come to some definite conclusions about the origin and nature of human society, and historical science seems to have come to some definite conclusions about the course of historical events. Even though there be much disagreement among modern scientists working within a given field, and among scientists working in different fields, there is a common negative attitude toward Christianity among them.

Together with thinking of the results of science as they are offered to us in various fields, we must think of the methodology of science. Perhaps there is greater agreement among scientists on the question of methodology than on the question of results. At any rate, it is quite commonly held that we cannot accept anything that is not consonant with the result of a sound scientific methodology.

6. This is the case because Christian theism is a coherent system, based upon the authority of Scripture, whose author is God himself (see Westminster Confession of Faith, 1.4).

With this we can as Christians heartily agree. It is our contention, however, that it is only upon Christian presuppositions that we can have a sound scientific methodology. And when we recall that our main argument for Christianity will be that it is only upon Christian theistic presuppositions that a true notion of facts can be formed, we see at once that it is in the field of methodology that our major battle with modern science will have to be fought. Our contention will be that a true scientific procedure is impossible unless we hold to the presupposition of the triune God of Scripture.[7] Moreover, since this question of methodology is basic to all the results of science, we shall have to devote our discussion largely to it. That is, we shall have to discuss it first so far as our systematic treatment of evidences is concerned. We shall, however, preface our systematic discussion with a brief survey of the history of evidences. From such a brief survey we may learn about much valuable material that we can use in our own defense of Christianity. We can also study the method of defense employed by apologists of the past.

Needless to say, the task that we have set before us in this preface is too great for us to accomplish with thoroughness. The field is too extensive. No scientist pretends to know the whole field of science with thoroughness. How much less can a layman pretend to do so? The discussion will, therefore, have to be largely general. Our hope is that a general discussion may not be false to the facts as experts know them. The chief major battle between Christianity and modern science is not about a large number of individual facts, but about the principles that control science in its work. The battle today is largely that of the *philosophy* of science.[8]

---

7. Note that Van Til speaks of a "true" scientific procedure. A scientific procedure cannot be "true" unless it acknowledges, and works within, the universe that God has made and that he controls.

8. This is crucial to keep in mind. No one would doubt that science can offer much that is useful with respect to the facts and their relations. The apologetic question, however, is to what extent non-Christian scientists can *account* for the methods and conclusions that they utilize.

CHAPTER 1

THE HISTORY OF EVIDENCES

BUTLER'S *ANALOGY*[1]

In this brief historical survey of evidences we cannot touch on all those who have written on the subject. We shall merely select for consideration some of the chief writers and more particularly Bishop Butler. The reason for this selection is obvious. Butler has virtually controlled the method of evidences in orthodox Protestant circles for two hundred years. His *Analogy of Religion Natural and Revealed to the Constitution and Course of Nature* was published in 1736. It was meant to be a defense of Christianity against the thought of the day, especially against deism.[2] Accordingly, a short summary of the argument of the *Analogy* is our first task.

In his Introduction, Butler tells us what he proposes to do. He begins by making the distinction between probable and demonstrative evidence. The former admits of degrees from mere

1. This chapter is meant to be a summary of Butler's argument, and thus it contains a series of quotations from Butler. Van Til is quoting Butler in order to show many of the salient points of his argument and to summarize the main points of his approach. It is important to catch the flow of Butler's work in this chapter in order to highlight the differences between his approach and Van Til's approach in coming chapters.

2. Butler's argument was not against atheists, but against deists. Thus, Butler attempts to use some of the tenets of deism to argue for Christianity.

presumption to moral certainty, while the latter brings immediate and absolute conviction.[3]

The degree of probability that a certain event will take place may increase in proportion to the number of times that we have seen a similar event take place in the past. "Thus a man's having observed the ebb and flow of the tide to-day, affords some sort of presumption, though the lowest imaginable, that it may happen again to-morrow: but the observation of this event for so many days, and months, and ages together, as it has been observed by mankind, gives us a full assurance that it will."[4]

It is this sort of probability that we must act upon in daily life:[5]

From these things it follows, that in questions of difficulty, or such as are thought so, where more satisfactory evidence cannot be had, or is not seen; if the result of examination be, that there appears upon the whole, any the lowest presumption on one side, and none on the other, or a greater presumption on one side, though in the lowest degree greater; this determines the question, even in matters of speculation; and in matters of practice, will lay us under an absolute and formal obligation, in point of prudence and of interest, to act upon that presumption or low probability, though it be so low as to leave the mind in very great doubt which is the truth. For surely a man is as really bound in prudence to do what upon the whole appears, according to the best of his judgment, to be for his happiness, as what he certainly knows to be so.[6]

But this is not enough. Butler goes on to point out that we must often act upon a chance of being right:

---

3. A demonstrative proof is one in which the conclusion flows inexorably from the premises. A probable demonstration, on the other hand, shows how certain evidences most likely point to a given conclusion. There is always room for error in a probable demonstration.

4. Joseph Butler, *The Works of Joseph Butler*, ed. W. E. Gladstone, 2 vols. (Oxford: Clarendon Press, 1896), vol. 1: *The Analogy of Religion, Natural and Revealed, to the Constitution and Course of Nature*, 3.

5. It is surely the case that probability plays a significant role in much of what we do on a daily basis. That is not the issue under scrutiny. The question we have before us is the apologetic question, that is, whether or not, *with respect to the truth of Christianity*, the best we have to offer is a probable demonstration.

6. Butler, *Analogy*, 6.

For numberless instances might be mentioned respecting the common pursuits of life, where a man would be thought, in a literal sense, distracted, who would not act, and with great application too, not only upon an even chance, but upon much less, and where the probability or chance was greatly against his succeeding.[7]

In these quotations we have the heart of the probability concept upon which the *Analogy* is based. We are to argue that Christianity has at least a practical presumption in its favor. We are to be very modest in our claims. Even if there were only a mere chance that Christianity is true we ought to act upon its precepts. And if we act upon a mere chance of the truth of Christianity we are acting upon the same principle that we frequently act upon in daily life with respect to ordinary matters of experience.[8]

But Butler does not mean that there is no more than a chance of Christianity's being true. He thinks there is a considerable degree of probability that it is true. We shall see this in what follows. For the moment we must note on what basis such a probability rests. Probability in daily life rests upon analogy.

That which chiefly constitutes probability is expressed in the word likely, i.e. like some truth, or true event; like it, in itself, in its evidence, in some more or fewer of its circumstances. For when we determine a thing to be probably true, suppose that an event has or will come to pass, it is from the mind's remarking in it a likeness to some other event, which we have observed has come to pass. And this observation forms, in numberless daily instances, a presumption, opinion, or full conviction, that such event has or will come to pass; according as the observation is, that the like event has sometimes, most commonly, or always so far as our observation reaches, come to pass at like distances of time, or place, or upon like occasions.[9]

7. Ibid., 7.
8. As we will see, the problem here is not that we do not act on probability; the problem is that Butler wants to include the facts of Christianity within the parameters of our everyday probable decisions. This serves to put Christianity on a par with the probable facts of our ordinary experience.
9. Butler, *Analogy*, 4.

This passage indicates something of what Butler means by "analogical reasoning." It is reasoning about unknown possibilities from the known "constitution and course of nature." This "constitution and course of nature" is our starting point as far as the facts from which we reason are concerned.[10] We take for granted that God has made and controls the "constitution and course of nature."[11]

The application of analogical reasoning to the question of the truth of Christianity as made by Butler can perhaps be best illustrated by quoting what he himself remarks about Origen:[12]

Hence, namely from analogical reasoning, Origen has with singular sagacity observed, that he who believes the scripture to have proceeded from him who is the Author of nature, may well expect to find the same sort of difficulties in it, as are found in the constitution of nature. And in a like way of reflection it may be added, that he who denies the scripture to have been from God upon account of these difficulties, may, for the very same reason, deny the world to have been formed by him. On the other hand, if there be an analogy or likeness between that system of things and dispensation of Providence, which revelation informs us of, and that system of things and dispensation of Providence, which experience together with reason informs us of, i.e. the known course of nature; this is a presumption, that they have both the same author and cause.[13]

---

10. Van Til quite rightly highlights the fact that, for Butler, we are meant to found and ground our argument for Christianity on the basis of an analogy to an agreed upon notion of the natural world. Thus, argues Butler, just as the deist thinks "x" of the natural world, it is not beyond question that one could, *analogously*, think "x" of a supernatural world as well.

11. Butler, *Analogy*, 18.

12. Origen was born in Alexandria sometime around A.D. 185 and died around 254. He was one of the most prolific of the Eastern church fathers. Eusebius of Caesarea, the "father of church history," collected many of Origen's writings and wrote (with Pamphilus) an *Apology for Origen*. For more on Origen, see William Edgar and K. Scott Oliphint, eds., *Christian Apologetics: Past and Present; A Primary Source Reader*, vol. 1 (Wheaton, IL: Crossway Books, 2009), 157–72.

13. Butler, *Analogy*, 9–10.

REASON

These words of Butler really state the whole case. It will clarify matters fully, however, if we quote still further with respect to the place of human reason in the argument. Butler explains what use he makes of human reason by contrasting the position of Descartes[14] to his own:

Forming our notions of the constitution and government of the world upon reasoning, without foundation for the principles which we assume, whether from the attributes of God, or any thing else, is building a world upon hypothesis, like Descartes. Forming our notions upon reasoning from principles which are certain, but applied to cases to which we have no ground to apply them, (like those who explain the structure of the human body, and the nature of diseases and medicines from mere mathematics without sufficient *data*,) is an error much akin to the former: since what is assumed in order to make the reasoning applicable, is hypothesis. But it must be allowed just, to join abstract reasonings with the observation of facts, and argue from such facts as are known, to others that are like them; from that part of the divine government over intelligent creatures which comes under our view, to that larger and more general government over them which is beyond it; and from what is present, to collect what is likely, credible, or not incredible, will be hereafter.[15]

It is not always easy to ascertain in detail just what place Butler assigns to reason, but in general it is plain. Broadly speaking, Butler

14. René Descartes (1596–1650) was born in Tours, France. At the age of ten, he was sent to boarding school, where he studied, among other things, Aristotelian philosophy for about nine years. When he was twenty-two, having earned a law degree, he became interested in mathematics. For him, mathematics was a discipline that truly bore the name *scientia*, since in it was the kind of certainty which Aristotelian philosophy could not provide. During the course of his travels in Europe, he determined in 1619 to found a new philosophy or philosophical system. Descartes is sometimes called the founder of the modern age, or of modern philosophy. His famous dictum, "I think, therefore I am" (*Cogito, ergo sum*), displays his rationalistic methodology.

15. Butler, *Analogy*, 10–11.

is an adherent of the empiricist school of John Locke.[16] Locke's *An Essay concerning Human Understanding* had appeared in 1690, two years before Butler's birth. In his early life Butler had taken careful notice of Samuel Clarke's attempt to give a demonstrative proof of the existence of God by the way of Descartes' *a priori* reasoning.[17] Butler found Clarke unconvincing. "Ever afterwards he was chary of Clarke's mathematical methods in philosophy, veering sharply toward the doctrines of empiricism and probabilism which he found in the study of Locke."[18]

It is of basic importance to understand the function of reason as Butler conceives it. We may learn more about the matter by turning to chapter 5 of his book. In this chapter he argues that even if by abstract reasoning we should be driven to the position of fatalism,[19] we should not be justified in rejecting the commands of religion. The reason for this is that we have a *practical experience of freedom.* The notion of necessity is "not applicable to practical subjects."[20] But if this be then interpreted as a reflection upon the powers of reason, Butler hastens to add:

> Nor does this contain any reflection upon reason: but only upon what is unreasonable. For to pretend to act upon reason, in opposition to practical principles, which the Author of our nature gave us to act upon; and to pretend to apply our reason to subjects, with regard to which, our own short views,

16. John Locke (1632–1704) is known as the founder of empiricism and of political liberalism. He was the son of a Protestant lawyer and landowner, John Locke Sr., and a Protestant mother, Agnes. From the age of fourteen, he was educated at Westminster School. In 1652, he went to Christ Church, Oxford, where he graduated in 1656. In 1683, because a number of Whigs were being arrested and because he was a known follower of the Earl of Shaftesbury, Locke fled to Holland, where he put his *Essay concerning Human Understanding* into final form. His last completed work was *Paraphrase and Notes on the Epistles of St. Paul.* He is considered to be one of the three main empiricists, along with George Berkeley and David Hume.

17. Samuel Clarke (1675–1729) was an English philosopher and Anglican minister. His cosmological argument followed more along the lines of Thomas Aquinas's third way, an argument from contingency to necessity. Clarke, however, made more explicit use of the principle of sufficient reason in his argument. In his college days, Butler began to correspond with Clarke.

18. Ernest Campbell Mossner, *Bishop Butler and the Age of Reason* (New York: Macmillan, 1936), 1.

19. In whatever form, fatalism holds that the "constitution and course of nature" is all predetermined, such that there can be no real meaning to our actions and choices.

20. Butler, *Analogy,* 146–47.

and even our experience, will show us, it cannot be depended upon, and such, at best, the subject of necessity must be; this is vanity, conceit, and unreasonableness.[21]

With the empiricists in general Butler wishes to make a certain reasonable use of reason.[22] Butler is severe on the Cartesian a priorism,[23] it seems, inasmuch as it ventures far beyond known fact, and inasmuch as it ventures to draw conclusions which he thinks are *contrary to fact.* When Clarke seeks to give a demonstrative proof of God he reasons, according to Butler, far *beyond* fact. When the fatalists argue against free will they reason, according to Butler, *contrary* to fact. But in putting the matter in this way we have not put it quite correctly. Butler does not really object to Clarke's reasoning beyond facts to the existence of God, but to Clarke's contention that such reasoning is demonstrative. Clarke's reasoning was supposed to be *demonstrative* because it was *a priori.* Thus it was likely to be contrary to fact because it was reasoning that disregarded facts or possible facts.[24]

The point with respect to the freedom of the will is basic to the whole matter.[25] Freedom is said to be a fact of experience. All reasoning must adjust itself to this and other facts. This constant necessity of returning to the facts clips the wings of reason. No reasoning can be absolutely conclusive except when it deals with the purely abstract. On the other hand, it "must be considered just to join abstract reasoning with the observation of facts." That is, we are justified because of the observed constitution and course of nature and because of the assumption of the "Author of nature," to reason from the known to the unknown.

21. Ibid., 147.

22. We should remember here that empiri*cism* does not negate the use of reason; it only seeks to argue that our knowledge has its foundation in experience, rather than in rational principles.

23. That is, "Butler is severe" on Descartes' rationalism, which sought to ground knowledge in a priori (i.e., rational) principles.

24. In other words, because Clarke attempted to reason from that which is contingent (and observable) to that which is necessary (and thus a priori and not observable), (1) he thought he was proposing a *demonstrative proof* (and not a probable conclusion) of God's existence, and (2) he was reasoning beyond observable facts (to that which is necessary).

25. By "freedom of the will" here, Van Til means, roughly, that one does have and must always have the power of contrary choice. So, to choose "x" entails that, in any and every circumstance, one could also have chosen "y," and that one could also choose "not x." It should be noted that even God does not have such freedom (cf. 2 Tim. 2:13).

11

When Butler applies these principles of reasoning to the question of Christianity he makes a twofold use of them. He makes, first, a positive use of them. It is based upon the idea that we can legitimately make conclusions about the unknown, assuming that it will be *like* the known.[26] In the second place, he makes negative use of them. The unknown, though we may expect it will be like the known, may also be *unlike* the known. When such a phenomenon as Christianity presents itself, we are, according to Butler, in a position to believe it is *like* the constitution and course of nature. There is a real continuity between nature and Christianity. But when men make objection to Christianity on the ground that it is so unlike what we know of nature, we fall back upon the argument from ignorance. We should expect, Butler would say, that the unknown will be to a considerable extent unlike the known, even when it is also like the known.

In order to make plain the meaning of these principles, and especially the function of reason according to Butler, we quote what he holds the place of reason to be with respect to the Scriptures and their content. In reply to certain objections made against Christianity, Butler says:

And now, what is the just consequence from all these things? Not that reason is no judge of what is offered to us as being of divine revelation. For this would be to infer, that we are unable to judge of any thing, because we are unable to judge of all things. Reason can, and it ought to judge, not only of the meaning, but also of the morality and the evidence, of revelation. First, it is the province of reason to judge of the morality of the scripture; i.e. not whether it contains things different from what we should have expected from a wise, just, and good Being; for objections from hence have been now obviated: but whether it contains things plainly contradictory to wisdom, justice, or goodness; to what the light of nature teaches us of God. And I know nothing of this sort objected against scripture, excepting such objections as are formed upon suppositions, which would equally conclude, that the

26. Here "like the known" means "analogous to the known."

constitution of nature is contradictory to wisdom, justice, or goodness; which most certainly it is not. . . .[27] Secondly, Reason is able to judge, and must, of the evidence of revelation, and of the objections urged against that evidence: which shall be the subject of a following chapter.[28]

A little later, when speaking of the credibility of a Mediator's coming into the world he adds:

Let reason be kept to: and if any part of the scripture account of the redemption of the world by Christ can be shown to be really contrary to it, let the scripture, in the name of God, be given up: but let not such poor creatures as we go on objecting against an infinite scheme, that we do not see the necessity or usefulness of all its parts, and call this reasoning; and, which still further heightens the absurdity in the present case, parts which we are not actively concerned in.[29]

These are the main principles of reasoning as employed by Butler. By the use of these principles he proceeds to prove the reasonableness of both *natural* and *revealed* religion. We cannot follow him into the subdivisions of the argument. A selection from the section dealing with natural religion and a selection from the section dealing with revealed religion must suffice.

A Future Life

In the section dealing with natural religion, Butler devotes a good deal of space to the question of a future life. The argument hinges largely on the significance of the fact of death. Is death likely to be the end of all? To find out, we must turn to experience and reason from analogy. Although we have in our lifetime undergone much change, we have still survived. Therefore, it is likely that we shall also survive death. Butler says:

27. Butler, *Analogy*, 238–39.
28. Ibid., 240.
29. Ibid., 275.

But the states of life in which we ourselves existed formerly in the womb and in our infancy, are almost as different from our present in mature age, as it is possible to conceive any two states or degrees of life can be. Therefore, that we are to exist hereafter in a state as different (suppose) from our present, as this is from our former, is but according to the analogy of nature; according to a natural order or appointment of the very same kind, with what we have already experienced.

We know we are endued with capacities of action, of happiness and misery: for we are conscious of acting, of enjoying pleasure and suffering pain. Now, that we have these powers and capacities before death, is a presumption that we shall retain them through and after death; indeed a probability of it abundantly sufficient to act upon, unless there be some positive reason to think that death is the destruction of those living powers: because there is in every case a probability, that all things will continue as we experience they are, in all respects, except those in which we have some reason to think they will be altered. This is that *kind* of presumption or probability from analogy, expressed in the very word *continuance*, which seems our only natural reason for believing the course of the world will continue to-morrow, as it has done so far as our experience or knowledge of history can carry us back. Nay, it seems our only reason for believing, that any one substance now existing will continue to exist a moment longer; the self-existent substance only excepted.[30]

This passage affords an excellent illustration of the principle of likeness or *continuity*[31] on which Butler rests his reasoning from the known to the unknown. His positive argument for a future life depends upon the observed principle of continuity. In the immediately following section he deals with the main objections against the idea of a future life. In meeting these objections he uses his celebrated argument from unlikeness or *discontinuity*. The objections against the idea of a future life must spring, he says, either "from *the reason of the thing*, or from *the analogy of nature*." As to the former, he adds:

30. Ibid., 22–23.
31. Butler's word "analogy" is what Van Til means by "likeness" and "continuity."

But we cannot argue from *the reason of the thing*, that death is the destruction of living agents, because we know not at all what death is in itself; but only some of its effects, such as the dissolution of flesh, skin, and bones.[32]

And as for the analogy of nature, Butler asserts:

Nor can we find any thing throughout the whole *analogy of nature*, to afford us even the slightest presumption, that animals ever lose their living powers; much less, if it were possible, that they lose them by death: for we have no faculties wherewith to trace any beyond or through it, so as to see what becomes of them. This event removes them from our view. It destroys the *sensible* proof, which we had before their death, of their being possessed of living powers, but does not appear to afford the least reason to believe that they are, then, or by that event, deprived of them.[33]

We might stop at this point to ask whether Butler, in view of his empiricism, is entitled to make the distinction he does make between the "reason of the thing" and the "analogy of nature," but we are just now engaged in the nature of his argument from ignorance or discontinuity. Butler says that there is a strong probability for the general notion of continuance of the course of nature. We seek to find specific reasons for thinking it will not continue in the future as it has in the past. But we cannot find such specific reasons because we are in the dark about that future. This mode of reasoning is typical of Butler. For our positive contentions we rest on general probation raised against our positive contentions, we fall back on what he thinks of as legitimate ignorance.

In this connection it should be noted that Butler makes his ignorance or discontinuity apply not only to future events, but to present events as well. He extends the principle in these words:

And besides, as we are greatly in the dark, upon what the exercise of our living powers depends, so we are wholly ignorant

---

32. Butler, *Analogy*, 24–25.
33. Ibid., 26.

what the powers themselves depend upon; the powers themselves as distinguished, not only from their actual exercise, but also from the present capacity of exercising them; and as opposed to their destruction: for sleep, or however a swoon, shows us, not only that these powers exist when they are not exercised, as the passive power of motion does in inanimate matter; but shows also that they exist, when there is no present capacity of exercising them: or that the capacities of exercising them for the present, as well as the actual exercise of them, may be suspended, and yet the powers themselves remain undestroyed. Since, then, we know not at all upon what the existence of our living powers depends, this shows further, there can be no probability collected from the reason of the thing, that death will be their destruction: because their existence may depend upon somewhat in no degree affected by death: upon somewhat quite out of the reach of this king of terrors. So that there is nothing more certain, than that *the reason of the thing* shows us no connection between death, and the destruction of living agents.[34]

It becomes apparent from such an argument as this that it is the *bruteness or dumbness of the facts that is of basic importance for Butler.*[35] With it he meets the argument for fatalism; with it he also meets all objections to general morality and Christianity. His principle of unlikeness or discontinuity is based upon the idea of pure contingency as pervasive of all reality.[36]

We now have the main trend of the argument of Butler before us. There is one detail that we would instance in passing. It has to do with the relation of man to the animal. Butler himself voices an objection to his argument from ignorance by saying that according to it animals as well as man might be immortal. To this objection he replies by saying that natural immortality in animals would not

---

34. Ibid., 25–26.

35. For Van Til, "bruteness" or "dumbness" of the facts means that, for Butler, facts do not testify of the existence of God; they do not testify of *anything.* This assumes that facts are there for the interpreting, and are not pre-interpreted (because created) by God.

36. That is, there is discontinuity because there is no way to determine what the future will be. It is all a matter of contingency, or chance, and thus necessarily indeterminate.

imply rationality. But suppose it did, even that would be no argument against our own future life. In this connection he makes a statement that sounds very modern:

> There was once, prior to experience, as great presumption against human creatures, as there is against the brute creatures, arriving at that degree of understanding, which we have in mature age. For we can trace up our own existence to the same original with theirs. And we find it to be a general law of nature, that creatures endued with capacities of virtue and religion should be placed in a condition of being, in which they are altogether without the use of them, for a considerable length of their duration; as in infancy and childhood. And great part of the human species go out of the present world, before they come to the exercise of these capacities in any degree at all.[37]

At this point we recall that Butler presupposes an "Author of nature." We may find this presupposition inconsistent with his statement that there was prior to experience as great presumption against man's attaining to mature rationality as against the animal, but we should not forget that Butler himself does believe in God. He does not pretend to argue for the existence of God in this volume. He takes God's existence for granted.[38] Still he gives us at one or two places a fairly clear idea as to what he thinks an argument for the existence of God should be like. We quote:

> . . . taking for proved, that there is an intelligent Author of nature, and natural Governor of the world. For as there is no presumption against this prior to the proof of it: so it has been often proved with accumulated evidence; from this argument of analogy and final causes; from abstract reasonings; from the most ancient tradition and testimony; and from the general consent of mankind. Nor does it appear, so far as I can find,

---

37. Butler, *Analogy*, 37–38.
38. Again, Butler takes the existence of God for granted because he is arguing against deists, who themselves believe in a god.

to be denied by the generality of those who profess themselves dissatisfied with the evidence of religion.[39]

To this passage another similar in nature may be added:

Indeed we ascribe to God a necessary existence, uncaused by any agent. For we find within ourselves the idea of infinity, i.e. immensity and eternity, impossible, even in imagination, to be removed out of being. We seem to discern intuitively, that there must, and cannot but be somewhat, external to ourselves, answering this idea, or the archetype of it. And from hence (for *this abstract*, as much as any other, implies a *concrete*) we conclude, that there is and cannot but be, an infinite, an immense eternal Being existing, prior to all design contributing to his existence, and exclusive of it. And from the scantiness of language, a manner of speaking has been introduced, that necessity is the foundation, the reason, the account of the existence of God. But it is not alleged, nor can it be at all intended, that *every thing* exists as it does, by this kind of necessity; a necessity antecedent in nature to design: it cannot, I say, be meant that every thing exists as it does, by this kind of necessity, upon several accounts; and particularly because it is admitted, that design, in the actions of men, contributes to many alterations in nature.[40]

For the moment it is not necessary to analyze these passages that speak of the argument for the existence of God. We merely call attention to the fact that they present us with a problem. The question cannot be avoided whether the argument for God as thus briefly outlined by Butler rests upon the same foundation as, for instance, does the argument for a future life. We know that Butler says he "supposes," i.e., presupposes, the "Author of nature." We now see that he "supposes" it because he thinks God's existence can be established by a reasonable argument. On exactly what then does this reasonable argument rest? Is there another foundation beside experience and observation from which we can reason from the

---

39. Butler, *Analogy*, 12.
40. Ibid., 141.

known to the unknown? If there is, why may we not use that other foundation as a starting point for our reasoning with respect to a future life? If there is not, is not our argument for the existence of God of just as great or just as little value as our argument for a future life? What meaning is there then in the idea that we "suppose" an "Author of nature"? Are we not then for all practical purposes ignoring him? In other words, if God is presupposed, should not that presupposition control our reasoning? And in that case can we be empiricists in our method of argument?

CHRISTIANITY

We come now to Butler's discussion of Christianity, and note at the outset something of his general approach to the question of the evidence for Christianity.

The first question to be asked in this connection is why there should be any Christianity at all. On this point Butler says:

And indeed it is certain, no revelation would have been given, had the light of nature been sufficient in such a sense, as to render one not wanting and useless.[41]

According to Butler we are to consider Christianity:

. . . first, as a republication, and external institution, of natural or essential religion, adapted to the present circumstances of mankind, and intended to promote natural piety and virtue: and secondly, as containing an account of a dispensation of things not discoverable by reason, in consequence of which, several distinct precepts are enjoined us.[42]

By reason is revealed the relation, which God the Father stands in to us. Hence arises the obligation of duty which we are under to him. In scripture are revealed the relations, which the Son and Holy Spirit stand in to us. Hence arise the obligations of duty, which we are under to them.[43]

41. Ibid., 185.
42. Ibid., 188.
43. Ibid., 197.

The essence of natural religion may be said to consist in religious regards to *God the Father Almighty*: and the essence of revealed religion, as distinguished from natural, to consist in religious regards to *the Son*, and to *the Holy Ghost*.[44]

Speaking further of our relations to Christ and the Holy Spirit, he adds:

And these relations being real, (though before revelation we could be under no obligations from them, yet upon their being revealed,) there is no reason to think, but that neglect of behaving suitably to them will be attended with the same kind of consequences under God's government, as neglecting to behave suitably to any other relations made known to us by reason.[45]

These quotations give us considerable information as to what Butler means by Christianity and as to why he thinks revelation is necessary. But we must go back of what he says at this point to an earlier section of his book. In chapter 5 Butler discusses the question, "Of a State of Probation, as Intended for Moral Discipline and Improvement." In this chapter he gives expression to his views about man's original estate. We should know what he says on this subject in order to understand what he means by the necessity of revelation.

Having previously proved the moral government of God, Butler tells us at the outset of the fifth chapter that we are placed in this world "that we might qualify ourselves, by the practice of virtue, for another state which is to follow it. . . . The known end then, why we are placed in a state of so much affliction, hazard, and difficulty, is, our improvement in virtue and piety, as the requisite qualification for a future state of security and happiness."[46]

Naturally the point that interests us here is whether we are really placed, as Butler says, in this estate of affliction and hazard. Were we created perfect and then fell into sin? If we were created perfect and then fell into sin afterward, was there anything in the nature

44. Ibid., 198.
45. Ibid., 200.
46. Ibid., 106.

of things that made it difficult for us not to fall into sin? On these points Butler does not leave us in the dark. He says:

> Mankind, and perhaps all finite creatures, from the very constitution of their nature, before habits of virtue, are deficient, and in danger of deviating from what is right: and therefore stand in need of virtuous habits, for a security against this danger.[47]

This general statement really affords us sufficient information about Butler's position on man's original estate. Yet, since it is a matter of extreme importance, we quote him more fully on this point. He tells us that originally man had certain propensions that were not subject to virtue.

> For, together with the general principle of moral understanding, we have in our inward frame various affections towards particular external objects. These affections are naturally, and of right, subject to the government of the moral principle, as to the occasions upon which they may be gratified; as to the times, degrees, and manner, in which the objects of them may be pursued: but then the principle of virtue can neither excite them, nor prevent their being excited. On the contrary, they are naturally felt, when the objects of them are present to the mind, not only before all consideration, whether they can be obtained by lawful means, but after it is found they cannot. For the natural objects of affection continue so; the necessaries, conveniences, and pleasures of life, remain naturally desirable; though they cannot be obtained innocently: nay, though they cannot possibly be obtained at all. And when the objects of any affection whatever cannot be obtained without unlawful means; but may be obtained by them: such affection, though its being excited, and its continuing some time in the mind, be as innocent as it is natural and necessary; yet cannot but be conceived to have a tendency to incline persons to venture upon such unlawful means: and therefore must be conceived as putting them in some danger of it.[48]

47. Ibid., 120.
48. Ibid., 120–21.

Against this danger that we as finite creatures are in because of these propensions to external objects, we have a remedy in the cultivation of the habit of virtue.

Thus the principle of virtue, improved into an habit, of which improvement we are thus capable, will plainly be, in proportion to the strength of it, a security against the danger which finite creatures are in, from the very nature of propension, or particular affections.[49]

In reading this argument, one might still be in doubt as to whether Butler is offering the fact of our "natural propensions" as an explanation for the original fall of man, though it is difficult to see how he could avoid doing it. But he tells us in so many words that he does explain the fall of man by the above considerations.

From these things we may observe, and it will further show this our natural and original need of being improved by discipline, how it comes to pass, that creatures made upright fall; and that those who preserve their uprightness, by so doing, raise themselves to a more secure state of virtue.[50]

It appears, then, that Butler takes an essentially Arminian position with respect to the fall of man. Arguments similar in nature to that given by Butler may be found, e.g., in Watson's *Theological Institutes*[51] and in Miley's *Systematic Theology*,[52] *sub voce*.[53]

For Butler the very idea of finite perfection includes the idea of "propensions" to particular objects, which, if gratified, mean sin. He tells us that we cannot explain the fall of man simply by stating that man was made free.

---

49. Ibid., 122.

50. Ibid., 123.

51. Richard Watson (1781–1833) was a Methodist (Arminian) minister and teacher. His *Institutes* were influential in establishing Arminian theology in the Wesleyan tradition and were originally entitled *Theological Institutes or, A View of the Evidences, Doctrines, Morals, and Institutions of Christianity*. He began to publish the *Institutes*, which were the first attempt to systematize Wesley's theology, in 1823. His *Institutes* are dependent in places on Butler's arguments.

52. John Miley (1813–1895) was a Methodist (Arminian) minister and educator. His two-volume *Systematic Theology*, published in 1892, was used for decades to train Methodist ministers.

53. *Sub voce*, i.e., "under the respective heading," in this case, of the fall of man.

To say that the former [the fall of man] is accounted for by the nature of liberty, is to say no more, than that an event's actually happening is accounted for by a mere possibility of its happening.[54]

Continuing from that point he adds:

But it seems distinctly conceivable from the very nature of particular affections or propensions. For, suppose creatures intended for such a particular state of life, for which such propensions were necessary: suppose them endued with such propensions, together with moral understanding, as well including a practical sense of virtue, as a speculative perception of it; and that all these several principles, both natural and moral, forming an inward constitution of mind, were in the most exact proportion possible; i.e. in a proportion the most exactly adapted to their intended state of life: such creatures would be made upright, or finitely perfect. Now particular propensions, for their very nature, must be felt, the objects of them being present; though they cannot be gratified at all, or not with the allowance of the moral principle. But if they can be gratified without its allowance, or by contradicting it; then they must be conceived to have some tendency, in how low a degree soever, yet some tendency, to induce persons to such forbidden gratification. This tendency, in some one particular propension, may be increased, by the greater frequency of occasions naturally exciting it, than of occasions exciting others. The least voluntary indulgence in forbidden circumstances, though but in thought, will increase this wrong tendency; and may increase it further, till, peculiar conjunctures perhaps conspiring, it becomes effect; and danger of deviating from right, ends in actual deviation from it: a danger necessarily arising from the very nature of propension; and which therefore could not have been prevented, though it might have been escaped, or got innocently through. The case would be, as if we were to suppose a strait path marked out for a person, in which such a degree of attention would keep him steady: but

54. Butler, *Analogy*, 123.

if he would not attend in this degree, any one of a thousand objects, catching his eye, might lead him out of it.[55]

We see from this that finite perfection is to be thought of, according to Butler, as a matter of proportion between natural and moral principles. According to this manner of thinking the fall is something that comes by degrees.

> Now it is impossible to say, how much even the first full overt act of irregularity might disorder the inward constitution; unsettle the adjustments, and alter the proportions, which formed it, and in which the uprightness of its make consisted: but repetition of irregularities would produce habits. And thus the constitution would be spoiled; and creatures made upright, become corrupt and depraved in their settled character, proportionably to their repeated irregularities in occasional acts.[56]

Butler's position with respect to man's original estate corresponds to his empiricism in general. The "Author of nature" finds certain facts with characteristics of their own when he creates the world. He cannot fashion a perfect man except in so far as he can manipulate these facts. These facts have from the outset an independent influence upon the course of history. In their own nature they constitute a source of danger to the moral principle in man. On this point, too, the position here taken by Butler is similar to that taken by the Arminian theologians and to that of Roman Catholicism.[57]

Man's Ability

Corresponding to what from the Reformed point of view must be called a low view of the original estate of man, is Butler's teaching on man's ability to do what God wishes him to do, after the fall. After

55. Ibid., 123–24.
56. Ibid., 124.
57. There is a formal agreement between Butler (and with him Arminianism) and Roman Catholicism in that both theologies posit something wrong in man even before the fall. Thus, it was not the case that everything God created was "good"; rather, man was either in need of something else (the *donum superadditum* in Roman Catholicism) or was inclined toward sin ("propension" in Butler) even before the entrance of sin in the world.

telling us that as men we do not seem to be situated as fortunately as we might be, he adds that we have no reason for complaint.

> For, as men may manage their temporal affairs with prudence, and so pass their days here on earth in tolerable ease and satisfaction, by a moderate degree of care: so likewise with regard to religion, there is no more required than what they are well able to do, and what they must be greatly wanting to themselves, if they neglect.[58]

This statement of Butler's may be compared with that of the Westminster Larger Catechism, Question 25: "The sinfulness of that estate whereinto man fell, consisteth in the guilt of Adam's first sin, the want of original righteousness wherein he was created, and the corruption of his nature, whereby he is utterly indisposed, disabled, and made opposite unto all that is spiritually good, and wholly inclined to all evil, and that continually; which is commonly called original sin, and from which do proceed all actual transgressions." The contrast between Butler's view and that of the Westminster divines is basic.

Butler knows of no "corruption of man's nature." According to him man's reason is now virtually what it was when it was created, and man's will, though weakened by the habit of sin, is yet inherently as much inclined to the good as it ever was. Accordingly, Christianity need be no more than a "republication" of what was originally God's requirement, plus such requirements as the second and third Persons of the Trinity have seen fit to add to those of the first. From what we can learn of Butler, the first Person of the Trinity seems to have changed his relation to men very little, if any, on account of sin. At any rate, Butler definitely says that revelation speaks only of the Son and of the Spirit. Reason, even after the entrance of sin, continues to be able to know what needs to be known about the Father. Still further, there is no mention of the need of regeneration anywhere in Butler's *Analogy*. Butler limits the content of Christianity to the objective facts of the redemptive works of Christ. Man can accept this or he can refuse to

---

58. Butler, *Analogy*, 102.

25

accept of his own power. Here, too, Butler's point of view must be contrasted with that of the Reformed Faith. The latter holds that Christianity includes the subjective factors of regeneration and faith as well as the objective factors of the incarnation, death, and resurrection of Christ.

The Remedy for Sin

To understand clearly what Butler thinks Christianity is we must now consider briefly his discussion of the work of the Mediator. He finds that the idea of a Mediator is in analogy with what we may expect from the constitution and course of nature. All the bad natural consequences of man's actions do not always follow such actions. The "Author of nature" has afforded reliefs for many of the ills of natural evil. Thus there are several instances not only of severity, but also of "indulgence" in nature. We might conceivably think of a constitution and course of nature in which there would be no redress from evil at all. But, as a matter of fact, nature has a certain compassion. We quote:

> But, that, on the contrary, provision is made by nature, that we may and do, to so great degree, prevent the bad natural effects of our follies; this may be called mercy or compassion in the original constitution of the world: compassion, as distinguished from goodness in general. And, the whole known constitution and course of things affording us instances of such compassion, it would be according to the analogy of nature, to hope, that, however ruinous the natural consequences of vice might be, from the general laws of God's government over the universe; yet provision might be made, possibly might have been originally made, for preventing those ruinous consequences from inevitably following: at least from following universally, and in all cases.[59]

In this passage there lies before us what may be called the Arminian equivalent to the Reformed doctrine of common grace.[60]

59. Ibid., 256.
60. For Van Til's extended discussion of common grace, see Cornelius Van Til, *Common Grace and the Gospel*, ed. K. Scott Oliphint (Phillipsburg, NJ: P&R Publishing, 2015).

On it Butler is soon to build a more specific argument for the necessity of a Savior. Before doing that, he investigates the question as to whether we could possibly save ourselves. He concludes that it is unlikely that we could. People often ruin their fortunes by extravagance. Yet sorrow for such extravagance and good behavior ever after will not suffice to erase the evil consequence of their deeds. Then, too, their natural abilities by which they might help themselves are often impaired. All this being the case, Butler asks:

> Why is it not supposable that this may be our case also, in our more important capacity, as under his perfect moral government, and having a more general and future interest depending? If we have misbehaved in this higher capacity, and rendered ourselves obnoxious to the future punishment, which God has annexed to vice: it is plainly credible that behaving well for the time to come may be—not useless, God forbid—but wholly insufficient, alone and of itself, to prevent that punishment; or to put us in the condition, which we should have been in, had we preserved our innocence.[61]

Upon this foundation Butler now proceeds to bring in the revelation about a Savior:

> Revelation teaches us, that the unknown laws of God's more general government, no less than the particular laws by which we experience he governs us at present, are compassionate, as well as good in the more general notion of goodness: and that he hath mercifully provided, that there should be an interposition to prevent the destruction of human kind; whatever that destruction unprevented would have been. *God so loved the world, that he gave his only begotten Son, that whosoever believeth*, not, to be sure, in a speculative, but in a practical sense, *that whosoever believeth in him should not perish*: gave his Son in the same way of goodness to the world, as he affords particular persons the friendly assistance of their fellow-creatures; when, without it, their temporal ruin would be the certain

61. Butler, *Analogy*, 259–60.

consequence of their follies: in the same way of goodness, I say: though in a transcendent and infinitely higher degree.[62]

Still further, Butler finds an analogy in nature for the vicarious suffering of Christ:

And when, in the daily course of natural Providence, it is appointed that innocent people should suffer for the faults of the guilty, this is liable to the very same objection, as the instance we are now considering. The infinitely greater importance of that appointment of Christianity, which is objected against, does not hinder but it may be, as it plainly is, an appointment of the very same kind, with what the world affords us daily examples of.[63]

Finally, if the objector should still continue to bring in further points that seem to him to be strange in the economy of Christianity, Butler falls back on the argument from ignorance.

Lastly, That not only the reason of the thing, but the whole analogy of nature, should teach us, not to expect to have the like information concerning the divine conduct, as concerning our own duty.[64]

From the passages cited the nature of the argument for Christianity employed by Butler appears clearly. Little needs to be added on the question of miracles, which was, after the attack on them by Hume, to occupy such an important place in Christian evidence. The real defense of miracle rests upon the defense of Christianity as a whole. After having defended the concept of Christianity as a whole, Butler goes on to give the historical evidence for miracle, and meets the objection brought against them. He seeks to prove that the witnesses who gave testimony to the happening of miracles were trustworthy, that they had no cause for deceit, etc. All this is familiar.

62. Ibid., 261–62.
63. Ibid., 272.
64. Ibid., 275.

Yet there is one point to which we wish to call special attention. After having discussed several arguments for Christianity from prophecy fulfilled and miracle performed, Butler seeks to bring all of these arguments together into one whole. He says:

> I shall now, secondly, endeavor to give some account of the general argument for the truth of Christianity. . . . For it is the kind of evidence, upon which most questions of difficulty, in common practice, are determined: evidence arising from various coincidences, which support and confirm each other, and in this manner prove, with more or less certainty, the point under consideration. And I choose to do it also: first, because it seems to be of the greatest importance, and not duly attended to by every one, that the proof of revelation is, not some direct and express things only, but a great variety of circumstantial things also; and that though each of these direct and circumstantial things is indeed to be considered separately, yet they are afterwards to be joined together; for that the proper force of the evidence consists in the result of those several things, considered in their respects to each other, and united into one view: and in the next place, because it seems to me, that the matters of fact here set down, which are acknowledged by unbelievers, must be acknowledged by them also to contain together a degree of evidence of great weight, if they could be brought to lay these several things before themselves distinctly, and then with attention consider them together; instead of that cursory thought of them, to which we are familiarized.[65]

Butler then proceeds to bring all the evidence for Christianity and natural religion together into one argument. He supposes a person who is wholly ignorant of Christianity. Such a person is to be shown how largely natural religion is corroborated by Scripture, and how the two blend together. If this is done there will be no danger that such a person will see conflict between reason and revelation, "any more than the proof of Euclid's Elements is

---

65. Ibid., 328–29.

destroyed, by a man's knowing or thinking, that he should never have seen the truth of the several propositions contained in it, nor had these propositions come into his thoughts, but for that mathematician."[66]

After reviewing this argument as a whole Butler remarks as follows:

> This general view of the evidence for Christianity, considered as making one argument, may also serve to recommend to serious persons, to set down every thing which they think may be of any real weight at all in proof of it, and particularly the many seeming completions of prophecy: and they will find, that, judging by the natural rules, by which we judge of probable evidence in common matters, they amount to a much higher degree of proof, upon such a joint review, than could be supposed upon considering them separately, at different times; how strong soever the proof might before appear to them, upon such separate views of it. For probable proofs, by being added, not only increase the evidence, but multiply it.[67]

The nature of Butler's argument is clear. Butler thinks that he has done more than he need have done to make the practice of Christianity reasonable.

> And that the practice of religion *is* reasonable, may be shown, though no more could be proved, than that the system of it *may be* so, for ought we know to the contrary: and even without entering into the distinct consideration of this.[68]

If therefore there were no more than a presumption in favor of the truth of Christianity, men should act upon it. But Butler has shown, he thinks, that there is more than a presumption. He has shown that there is a great positive probability for the truth of Christianity. And that is all that reasonable men should require. If they require more they forget that satisfaction "in this sense, does not belong to such a creature as man."[69]

66. Ibid., 339.
67. Ibid., 350–51.
68. Ibid., 362.
69. Ibid., 364.

But the practical question in all cases is, Whether the evidence for a course of action be such, as, taking in all circumstances, makes the faculty within us, which is the guide and judge of conduct, determine that course of action to be prudent. Indeed, satisfaction that it will be for our interest or happiness, abundantly determines an action to be prudent: but evidence almost infinitely lower than this, determines actions to be so too; even in the conduct of every day.[70]

Toward the end of the book Butler makes a point of telling us again exactly what his mode of procedure has been. He has sometimes, as in the case of fatalism, argued upon the principles of his opponents. Then, too, he has omitted the consideration of the "moral fitness and unfitness of actions, prior to all will whatever," and the principle of liberty itself.

Now these two abstract principles of liberty and moral fitness being omitted, religion can be considered in no other view, than merely as a question of fact: and in this view it is here considered.[71]

What Butler says here is simply a restatement of his disregard of *a priori* reasoning. At an earlier point he absolutely rejected the validity of *a priori* reasoning. At the conclusion he seems to say that he, though admitting its validity, has simply omitted the use of it. He explains the difference between the two types of reasoning at this point in the following words:

To explain this: that the three angles of a triangle are equal to two right ones, is an abstract truth: but that they appear so to our mind, is only a matter of fact.[72]

At any rate, it is plain that the argument for Christianity as set forth by Butler is an argument that wishes to make its appeal to fact, first of all. After it has been shown that miracle and fulfilled prophecy are facts, that is, that such things as have been recorded

70. Ibid., 365.
71. Ibid., 367–68.
72. Ibid., 368.

have actually taken place, these facts must be shown to be in analogy with the facts as we observe them in the "constitution and course of nature." The tool with which we do the work of comparing one "fact" with another "fact" of a different nature is the "faculty of reason, which is *the candle of the Lord within us.*"[73]

With this we may conclude our summary of Butler's *Analogy* in order to see something of what later generations have done about its argument.

73. Ibid., 375.

CHAPTER 2

HUME'S SCEPTICISM[1]

T he argument of Butler's *Analogy* was directed against the deists. The "Deist Bible," i.e., Matthew Tindal's book *Christianity as Old as Creation: Or, The Gospel, a Republication of the Religion of Nature*, appeared in 1730.[2] The deists believed, generally speaking, in the following points: (1) that there is one supreme God, (2) that he ought to be worshiped, (3) that virtue and piety are the chief parts of divine worship, (4) that we ought to be sorry for our sins and repent of them, (5) that divine goodness dispenses rewards and punishments both in this life and after it.

1. David Hume (1711–1776) was, to some, "one of the most important philosophers to write in English" ("David Hume," Stanford Encyclopedia of Philosophy, last modified May 21, 2014, http://plato.stanford.edu/entries/hume/). Hume was the last of the three most influential empiricists (after John Locke and George Berkeley). Many believe that an attempt to be more radically consistent as an empiricist led Hume from empiricism to utter skepticism. His philosophy provides a helpful example of the implications of basing one's philosophy or science only on evidences, facts, or sense experience. Some see Hume as the precursor to today's philosophical naturalism.

In this chapter, Van Til uses the very arguments of Hume in order to show how and why empirical arguments cannot sustain a claim to knowledge. When Van Til argues that empiricism is an illegitimate foundation for knowledge, he is reiterating what Hume and others themselves have argued.

2. Matthew Tindal (1657–1733) argued that no special revelation is needed as a source for Christianity; all that is needed is "the religion of nature" and the right use of reason. Tindal's argument was highly influential for the propagation of deism in England and beyond.

It will be observed that Butler did not need to oppose the deists on what they believed, but only on what they did not believe. He argued that if they could believe what they believed, they ought also be willing to believe Christianity.

Before long, however, the reasoning and the conclusion of both Butler and the deists were subjected to radical criticism. The question is sometimes asked: Who won the deistic controversy, Butler or the deists? The answer is often given that the sceptics won it.

David Hume published his *Treatise of Human Nature* anonymously 1739–40. He is said to have had a high regard for Butler. He tried to get Butler to read the manuscript before publication, as appears from a letter he wrote to Lord Kames:[3]

> Your thoughts and mine agree with respect to Dr. Butler, and I would be glad to be introduced to him. I am at present castrating my work, that is, butting off its nobler parts; that is, endeavoring it shall give as little offence as possible, before which, I could not pretend to put it into the Doctor's hands.[4]

Hume did not meet Butler, but we may look at what later fell into Butler's hands when the *Treatise* appeared.

The high regard of Hume for Butler was due in part to the "judicious" character of Butler's writings. Hume hated all "enthusiasm." But more than that it was the common opposition they shared against all *a priori* reasoning that drew Hume toward Butler.[5] Both had learned from Locke. Both hated "innate ideas."[6] The only difference between Hume and Butler was that Hume was not willing to accept any positive construction of knowledge even to the extent

---

3. Henry Home (1696–1782), who took the title Lord Kames when he became a judge in the Scottish Court, was a central figure in the Scottish Enlightenment. He wrote a number of works on philosophy, history, and other topics related to the Enlightenment, including *Elements of Criticism* and *Sketches on the History of Man*. Lord Kames corresponded both with David Hume and with Thomas Reid.

4. David Hume to Henry Home (later Lord Kames), December 2, 1737, in Ernest Campbell Mossner, *Bishop Butler and the Age of Reason* (New York: Macmillan, 1936), 156.

5. In other words, both Hume and Butler thought knowledge to be grounded in the empirical, the *a posteriori*, rather than in rational, *a priori* laws of thought.

6. The notion of "innate ideas" had been proposed by the rationalist Descartes. Locke argued that man came into the world as a *tabula rasa*, a blank slate, which experience alone could fill.

of reasonable probability. The carefully prepared argument of the *Analogy* seemed to Hume to be invalid.

KNOWLEDGE BASED ON SENSATION

Basic to all of Hume's opposition to Christianity and to theism is his conception of knowledge as derived from the senses. His objections to miracles as well as his objections to natural religion are based upon his theory of knowledge. He marched right up to the very citadel of his opponents in order to attack them there.

All the perceptions of the human mind resolve themselves into two distinct kinds, which I shall call IMPRESSIONS and IDEAS. The difference betwixt these consists in the degrees of force and liveliness, with which they strike upon the mind, and make their way into our thought or consciousness. Those perceptions, which enter with most force and violence, we may name *impressions*; and under this name I comprehend all our sensations, passions and emotions, as they make their first appearance in the soul. By *ideas* I mean the faint images of these in thinking and reasoning; such, as, for instance, are all the perceptions excited by the present discourse, excepting only those which arise from the sight and touch, and excepting the immediate pleasure or uneasiness it may occasion.[7]

In this opening sentence of the *Treatise* we have the gist of the matter. All knowledge comes from sensation; that is basic to Hume's theory of knowledge.[8] We have no ideas which are not faint copies of previous impressions. Ideas, as copies of sensations, Hume argues, are discrete. He is in entire agreement with Berkeley that "all general ideas are nothing but particular ones, annexed to a

7. David Hume, *A Treatise on Human Nature, Being an Attempt to Introduce the Experimental Method of Reasoning into Moral Subjects,* and *Dialogues concerning Natural Religion,* ed. T. H. Green and T. H. Grose, 2 vols. (London: Longmans, Green, 1874), 1:311.

8. To be more precise, other philosophers (e.g., Kant) claimed that knowledge of any fact had to begin with experience. What made Hume more radical in his empiricism is that he argued that knowledge of facts could have *only* an empirical foundation; nothing else could be added to, or synthesized with, our sense experience in order for us to claim to know.

certain term."[9] He holds that Berkeley's "discovery" of this point is "one of the greatest and most valuable discoveries that has been made of late years in the republic of letters."[10]

The far-reaching significance of Hume's point of view appears at a glance. Since all knowledge is of sensation there is no *a priori* reasoning. To be sure, in the field of algebra, when we are merely concerned with the manipulation of figures, we may speak of *a priori* knowledge, but when we pretend to deal with factual knowledge, *a priori* reasoning is taboo.

But what of the *a posteriori* reasoning such as Butler has employed in his *Analogy*? Granted we are willing to forego the certainty and universality that *a priori* reasoning was supposed to bring, can we not at least depend upon probability? May we not reasonably expect that the "constitution and course of nature" will continue in the future as it has in the past? Such questions, though not asked by Hume with direct reference to Butler, are yet asked by him with respect to the type of argument used by Butler.

The answer to such questions, says Hume, depends upon the nature of the connection between our various ideas. One particular idea simply recalls another particular idea. It is thus that we obtain our general ideas. There is no necessary connection between our various particular ideas. There is no systematic relation between them. There is no systematic relation between them because there is no systematic relation between our sensations.

It will be observed that in this way there is no basis for the notion of cause and effect. There is no "impression, which produces an idea of such prodigious consequence."[11] Yet all ideas must come from impressions. My impressions are simply of contiguity and succession. Hence my ideas too are merely of contiguity and succession.

> Tho' the mind in its reasonings from causes or effects carries its view beyond those objects, which it sees or remembers, it must

---

9. George Berkeley (1685–1753) was an Irish-born philosopher and Anglican minister. Along with Hume and Locke, he is considered one of the most prominent empiricists of his day. His empiricism, however, is less radical than Hume's and is more deeply embedded in theology. Berkeley's main apologetic work, entitled *Alciphron*, in which he attempted to defend his Anglican faith against the "free thinkers," was written while he was in America (1730).

10. Hume, *Treatise on Human Nature*, ed. Green and Grose, 1:325.

11. Ibid., 377.

never lose sight of them entirely, nor reason merely upon its own ideas, without some mixture of impressions, or at least of ideas of the memory, which are equivalent to impressions. When we infer effects from causes, we must establish the existence of these causes; which we have only two ways of doing, either by an immediate perception of our memory or senses, or by an inference from other causes; which causes again we must ascertain in the same manner, either by a present impression, or by an inference from *their* causes, and so on, till we arrive at some object, which we see or remember. 'Tis impossible for us to carry on our inferences *in infinitum*; and the only thing, that can stop them, is an impression of the memory or senses, beyond which there is no room for doubt or enquiry.[12]

Absolutely all our reasoning about cause and effect goes back to sensation, and sensations are discrete. To this basic point Hume returns again and again.

'Tis therefore by EXPERIENCE only, that we can infer the existence of one object from that of another. The nature of experience is this. We remember to have had frequent instances of the existence of one species of objects; and also remember, that the individuals of another species of objects have always attended them, and have existed in a regular order of contiguity and succession with regard to them. Thus we remember, to have seen that species of object we call *flame*, and to have felt that species of sensation we call *heat*. We likewise call to mind their constant conjunction in all past instances. Without any farther ceremony, we call the one *cause* and the other *effect*, and infer the existence of the one from that of the other.[13]

From the mere repetition of any past impression, even to infinity, there never will arise any new original idea, such as that of a necessary connexion; and the number of impressions has in this case no more effect than if we confin'd ourselves to one only.[14]

12. Ibid., 384.
13. Ibid., 388.
14. Ibid., 389.

It is easy to sense the implication of all this for the argument of Butler. Butler holds that we may reasonably expect the course and constitution of nature to remain the same in the future as it has been in the past. Hume says that if we expect this it is because of custom only.[15] *There is simply no logical relation between the past and the future.*

To see this point clearly we may follow Hume still further when he enters upon a discussion of probability.

PROBABILITY

Continuing from the passage we have just quoted, Hume says:

Since it appears, that the transition from an impression present to the memory or senses to the idea of an object, which we call cause or effect, is founded on past *experience,* and on our remembrance of their *constant conjunction,* the next question is, Whether experience produces the idea by means of the understanding or imagination; whether we are determin'd by reason to make the transition, or by a certain association and relation of perceptions. If reason determin'd us, it would proceed upon that principle, *that instances, of which we have had no experience, must resemble those, of which we have had experience, and that the course of nature continues always uniformly the same.* In order therefore to clear up this matter, let us consider all the arguments, upon which such a proposition may be suppos'd to be founded; and as these must be deriv'd either from *knowledge* or *probability,* let us cast our eye on each of these degrees of evidence, and see whether they afford any just conclusion of this nature.

15. Hume's radical commitment to sensation as the only source of knowledge requires, he argues, that we give up on any necessary connection between our various discrete ideas. So, to use an example from Hume, we may strike one billiard ball, watch it move along the table and strike another billiard ball, and watch the second ball move. Hume's argument is that what we have in this circumstance are discreet impressions—one billiard ball moving, it striking another, and the second one moving. We do not have cause and effect because there is no *necessity* in the second ball moving. For various reasons, it might have remained where it was. Thus, sensation cannot establish the cause-and-effect relationship. If we posit such a relationship, Hume notes, we do so only by "habit and custom," not because we know that such a relationship actually exists in reality.

Our foregoing method of reasoning will easily convince us, that there can be no *demonstrative* arguments to prove, *that those instances, of which we have had no experience, resemble those, of which we have had experience.* We can at least conceive a change in the course of nature; which sufficiently proves, that such a change is not absolutely impossible. To form a clear idea of any thing, is an undeniable argument for its possibility, and is alone a refutation of any pretended demonstration against it.

Probability, as it discovers not the relations of ideas, consider'd as such, but only those of objects, must in some respects be founded on the impressions of our memory and senses, and in some respects on our ideas. Were there no mixture of any impression in our probable reasonings, the conclusion wou'd be entirely chimerical: And were there no mixture of ideas, the action of the mind, in observing the relation, wou'd, properly speaking, be sensation, not reasoning. 'Tis therefore necessary, that in all probable reasonings there be something present to the mind, either seen or remember'd; and that from this we infer something connected with it, which is not seen nor remember'd.

The only connexion or relation of objects, which can lead us beyond the immediate impressions of our memory and senses, is that of cause and effect; and that because 'tis the only one, on which we can found a just inference from one object to another. The idea of cause and effect is deriv'd from *experience*, which informs us, that such particular objects, in all past instances, have been constantly conjoin'd with each other: And as an object similar to one of these is suppos'd to be immediately present in its impression, we thence presume on the existence of one similar to its usual attendant. According to this account of things, which is, I think, in every point unquestionable, probability is founded on the presumption of a resemblance betwixt those objects, of which we have had experience, and those, of which we have had none; and therefore 'tis impossible this presumption can arise from probability. The same principle cannot be both the cause and effect of another; and this is, perhaps, the only proposition concerning that relation, which is either intuitively or demonstratively certain.[16]

BUTLER'S INCONSISTENCIES

This passage deals with the central concept of Butler's *Analogy*, namely, that of the presumption that the constitution and course of nature will be the same in the future as we have seen it to be in the past. Hume finds no justification for this presumption except in custom. It is important to note that his argument here is, if sound, as destructive of Butler's reasoning as it is of *a priori* reasoning. To be sure, his argument appears to be primarily against the idea of a necessary connection of an *a priori* sort. Yet his argument is equally opposed to the idea of a presumptive rational connection of a probable sort. The whole point of Hume's argument is that there is no rational presumption of any sort about future events happening in one way rather than in another. We may expect that they will, but if we do, we do so on non-rational grounds. Our reasoning is based upon past experience. Past experience is nothing but an accumulation of brute facts which have been observed as happening in a certain order. Why should not the events of the future be entirely different in nature from the events of the past?

Could Butler have escaped the argument of Hume? It does not seem so. Butler appealed to brute fact. To brute fact Hume forced him to go. Butler sought to defend Christianity and theism upon an "empirical" basis. Hume tested his system by a *consistent empiricism.* Butler's empiricism was not consistent. It was inconsistent at two points. It had in it a mixture of *a priori* reasoning as well as *a posteriori* reasoning. We have seen in the previous chapter that Butler sometimes appeals to "the reason of the thing" and to "intuition." His main assumption, that the constitution and course of nature may be expected to remain in the future what it has been in the past, rests upon an uncritical remnant of a priorism. The "reasonable use of reason" that Butler held to, his "joining of abstract reasoning with facts," which he said must be allowed to be just, was entirely uncritical. Butler gives evidence of halting between two opinions. Butler should have justified his procedure. If one

---

16. Hume, *Treatise on Human Nature,* ed. Green and Grose, 1:389–91.

expects to defend the Christian religion by the use of clear-cut *a priori* reasoning, it is well. If one expects to defend the Christian religion by a clear-cut use of *a posteriori* reasoning, it is well. This, too, is well if one will tell us the exact nature of the combination between the *a priori* and the *a posteriori* that he has in mind. Butler did none of these things.[17]

The second point on which Butler's empiricism was inconsistent was in its relation to his conception of the "Author of nature." We have hinted at this point in the previous chapter. The matter may be put as follows: If an "Author of nature" is really presupposed it will control the nature of reasoning that one employs. If we may presuppose an "Author of nature," the facts are created by him. That means we cannot be empiricists, in the sense in which Butler takes empiricism and in the sense in which Hume takes empiricism. If an "Author of nature" is presupposed, all the facts of the "course and constitution of nature" are bound together by the mind of God. Then human minds are made by God. This means that we can never be a priorists in the Cartesian sense of the term.[18] Our minds can never legislate future possibility and probability because this future possibility and probability lies in the control of God. Yet it means that human minds may speak of universal connection between ideas and things. There is an entirely reasonable expectation that the constitution and course of nature will be the same in the future as it has been in the past because of the rationality of God that is back of it. Even so it should be remembered that God may at any time send His Son to change the constitution and course of nature. The point is that only that will happen in the future which will be in accord with the program of God. We can contrast this position with that of Hume by saying that for Hume the basic concept of thought is bare possibility, while for one who holds to an "Author of nature" the basic concept of thought should be God's complete rationality. *Butler failed to see this basic alternative.* We may agree with him when he rejects a priorism of the Cartesian

---

17. In other words, Van Til is chiding Butler both for his inconsistency (where Hume was consistent with his empiricism) and for neglecting to justify his apologetic method. Butler assumed what he should have explained.

18. If God created the world, then all facts are, in the beginning, his interpretation, and are in no way simply products of the human mind. For Descartes, *a priori* facts are what they are simply by virtue of who *man* is, not by virtue of who God is.

sort, but we cannot agree with him when he substitutes for it an empiricism of an uncritical sort.

Hume's empiricism was far more critical and consistent than that of Butler. We proceed to see what happens to the conception of probability on the basis of Hume's empiricism. If all knowledge is based upon experience, and experience is interpreted without the presupposition of the "Author of nature" as Hume claims it is, we cannot expect that one thing rather than another will happen in the future. From the point of view of logic, one thing as well as another might take place in the future. But why is it then that we expect the course and constitution of nature to remain the same? "*Wherein consists the difference betwixt incredulity and belief?*" asks Hume.[19] The answer is once more that it is in nothing but custom and feeling.

> Now as we call every thing CUSTOM, which proceeds from a past repetition, without any new reasoning or conclusion, we may establish it as a certain truth, that all the belief, which follows upon any present impression, is deriv'd solely from that origin.[20]

Custom gives vividness to an idea, and the vividness of the idea is the source of our belief in the existence of the object of the idea. "Thus all probable reasoning is nothing but a species of sensation. 'Tis not solely in poetry and music, we must follow our taste and sentiment, but likewise in philosophy."[21]

FUTURE LIFE

In this connection Hume applies these principles to the question of a future life:

> As belief is an act of the mind arising from custom, 'tis not strange the want of resemblance shou'd overthrow what custom has establish'd, and diminish the force of the idea, as

19. Hume, *Treatise on Human Nature*, ed. Green and Grose, 1:395.
20. Ibid., 403.
21. Ibid.

much as that latter principle encreases it. A future state is so far remov'd from our comprehension, and we have so obscure an idea of the manner, in which we shall exist after the dissolution of the body, that all the reasons we can invent, however strong in themselves, and however much assisted by education, are never able with slow imaginations to surmount this difficulty, or bestow a sufficient authority and force on the idea. I rather choose to ascribe this incredulity to the faint idea we form of our future condition, deriv'd from its want of resemblance to the present life, than to that deriv'd from its remoteness. For I observe, that men are everywhere concern'd about what may happen after their death, provided it regard this world; and that there are few to whom their name, their family, their friends, and their country are in any period of time entirely indifferent.

And indeed the want of resemblance in this case so entirely destroys belief, that except those few, who upon cool reflection on the importance of the subject, have taken care by repeated meditation to imprint in their minds the arguments for a future state, there scarce are any, who believe the immortality of the soul with a true and establish'd judgment; such as is deriv'd from the testimony of travellers and historians. This appears very conspicuously wherever men have occasion to compare the pleasures and pains, the rewards and punishments of this life with those of a future; even tho' the case does not concern themselves, and there is no violent passion to disturb their judgment. The *Roman Catholicks* are certainly the most zealous of any sect in the Christian world; and yet you'll find few among the more sensible people of that communion who do not blame the *Gunpowder-treason*, and the massacre of *St. Bartholomew*, as cruel and barbarous, tho' projected or executed against those very people, whom without any scruple they condemn to eternal and infinite punishments. All we can say in excuse for this inconsistency is, that they really do not believe what they affirm concerning a future state; nor is there any better proof of it than the very inconsistency.[22]

22. Ibid., 413–14.

In these passages we have the answer from a pure empiricist to the argument for a future life as set forth in Butler's *Analogy*. There is no doubt but that the criticism of Hume is sound.[23] A pure empiricism can give no presumption for anything to happen in the future. A pure empiricism would require us to be entirely neutral as to the future. Hume develops the point in this immediate connection. It is well that we look at it carefully inasmuch as it brings before us the whole problem of the law of chances, which has played so large a part in later works on evidences.

In order to bring this question before us as clearly as possible, Hume distinguishes between three kinds of reason, viz., "*that from knowledge, from proofs, and from probabilities.*"[24] Explaining these three kinds of reason he says:

> By knowledge, I mean the assurance arising from the comparison of ideas. By proofs, these arguments, which are deriv'd from the relation of cause and effect, and which are entirely free from doubt and uncertainty. By probability, that evidence, which is still attended with uncertainty. 'Tis this last species of reasoning, I proceed to examine.[25]

Thereupon he divides reasoning from "conjecture" into two parts, namely, reasoning from chance and reasoning from causes. The first one is now before us. We quote from Hume at length on this subject:

THE LAW OF CHANCES

> The idea of cause and effect is deriv'd from experience, which presenting us with certain objects constantly conjoin'd with each other, produces such a habit of surveying them in that relation, that we cannot without a sensible violence survey them in any other. On the other hand, as chance is nothing

23. Van Til does not mean that Hume's philosophical empiricism is sound. What he means is that Hume's argument against Butler is sound in that, if Butler wants to be an empiricist, he cannot count on the "constitution and course of nature," or on some notion of the future life, to make his arguments. Such things cannot be established empirically.

24. Hume, *Treatise on Human Nature*, ed. Green and Grose, 1:423.

25. Ibid., 423–24.

real in itself, and, properly speaking, is merely the negation of a cause, its influence on the mind is contrary to that of causation; and 'tis essential to it, to leave the imagination perfectly indifferent, either to consider the existence or non-existence of that object, which is regarded as contingent. A cause traces the way to our thought, and in a manner forces us to survey such certain objects, in such certain relations. Chance can only destroy this determination of the thought, and leave the mind in its native situation of indifference; in which, upon the absence of a cause, 'tis instantly re-instated.

Since therefore an entire indifference is essential to chance, no one chance can possibly be superior to another, otherwise than as it is compos'd of a superior number of equal chances. For if we affirm that one chance can, after any other manner, be superior to another, we must at the same time affirm, that there is something, which gives it the superiority, and determines the event rather to that side than the other: That is, in other words, we must allow of a cause, and destroy the supposition of chance; which we had before establish'd. A perfect and total indifference is essential to chance, and one total indifference can never in itself be either superior or inferior to another: This truth is not peculiar to my system, but is acknowledg'd by every one, that forms calculations concerning chances.

And here 'tis remarkable, that tho' chance and causation be directly contrary, yet 'tis impossible for us to conceive this combination of chances, which is requisite to render one hazard superior to another, without supposing a mixture of causes among the chances, and a conjunction of necessity in some particulars, with a total indifference in others. Where nothing limits the chances, every notion, that the most extravagant fancy can form, is upon a footing of equality; nor can there be any circumstance to give one the advantage above another. Thus unless we allow, that there are some causes to make the dice fall, and preserve their form in their fall, and lie upon some one of their sides, we can form no calculation concerning the laws of hazard. But supposing these causes to operate, and supposing likewise all the rest to be indifferent and to be determin'd by chance, 'tis easy to arrive at a notion of a superior combination of chances. A dye that has four sides mark'd with a certain number of spots, and only two with another, affords us an obvious and easy instance of this superiority. The mind is here limited by the causes to such a precise number and quality of the events; and at the same time is undetermin'd in its choice of any particular event.

Proceeding then in that reasoning, wherein we have advanc'd three steps, *that* chance is merely the negation of a cause, and produces a total indifference in the mind; *that* one negation of a cause and one total indifference can never be superior or inferior to another; and *that* there must always be a mixture of causes among the chances, in order to be the foundation of any reasoning: We are next to consider what effect a superior combination of chances can have upon the mind, and after what manner it influences our judgment and opinion. Here we may repeat all the same arguments we employ'd in examining that belief, which arises from causes; and may prove, after the same manner, that a superior number of chances produces our assent neither by *demonstration* nor *probability*. 'Tis indeed evident, that we can never by the comparison of mere ideas make any discovery, which can be of consequence in this affair, and that 'tis impossible to prove with certainty, that any event must fall on that side where there is a superior number of chances. To suppose in this case any certainty, were to overthrow what we have establish'd concerning the opposition of chances, and their perfect equality and indifference.

Shou'd it be said, that tho' in an opposition of chances 'tis impossible to determine with *certainty*, on which side the event will fall, yet we can pronounce with certainty, that 'tis more likely and probable, 'twill be on that side where there is a superior number of chances, than where there is an inferior: Shou'd this be said, I wou'd ask, what is here meant by *likelihood* and *probability*? The likelihood and probability of chances is a superior number of equal chances; and consequently when we say 'tis likely the event will fall on the side, which is superior, rather than on the inferior, we do no more than affirm, that where there is a superior number of chances there is actually a superior, and where there is an inferior there is an inferior; which are identical propositions, and of no consequence.

The question is, by what means a superior number of equal chances operates upon the mind, and produces belief or assent; since it appears, that 'tis neither by arguments deriv'd from demonstration, nor from probability.[26]

Grant an infinite number of possibilities, to begin with, as an absolutely pure empiricism must presuppose, then there is an infinite number of improbabilities to cancel every infinite number of probabilities.[27] That is, there is no probability at all. Such is Hume's argument. Hume is right when he says again and again that "an entire indifference is essential to chance." The idea of a law of chances is, strictly speaking, a contradiction in terms. *It is to this position of total indifference with respect to the future that anyone embracing a pure empiricism is driven.* By Hume's argument Butler would be driven to accept a pure empiricism with the consequences now before us, or to accept the "Author of nature" as a real and effective principle of interpretation.

A PRIORISM FACES THE SAME DIFFICULTY

At this point some one may argue that Butler would not necessarily be driven to this alternative, because he is not a consistent empiricist. He may, therefore, fall back upon the a priorism in his thought in order to escape the sceptical conclusions of Hume. But apart from the fact that Butler himself rests the whole of his argument upon the empirical fact, we may point out that any sort of non-Christian a priorism would eventually also be placed before Hume's alternative. Those who seek to prove the existence of God by an *a priori* argument of the non-Christian sort, prove too much. If they prove the necessary existence of God, they also prove the necessary existence of everything else that exists.[28] The necessary

26. Ibid., 424–26.
27. That is, "an absolutely pure empiricism," as Hume was trying to set forth, can make no pronouncement on what *must* be the case, since experience cannot produce laws. It can produce, perhaps, an expectation of some kind of regularity, but even that cannot be guaranteed. So, with every probability must be included an improbability as well.
28. That is, if one seeks to conclude that the existence of God is necessary, *based on the contingent existence of man*, that necessity is dependent on the contingent in order for it to be defined as necessary. The two poles, therefore, of necessity and contingency mutually entail each other. That is, if G (the existence of God) is a sufficient reason for C (the existence of creation), then G must entail C. But a necessity cannot entail a contingency,

existence of God is said to be implied in the finite existence of man. That is taken to mean, in effect, that necessary existence is a correlative to relative existence. But this in turn implies that relative existence is a correlative to necessary existence. Thus God comes into existence by the hypostatization of man.[29] Temporal things together with the evil in them are then taken as correlative to God. This is destructive of God's unchangeability. God as well as man is in this way made subject to change.[30] Thus we are back at chance as the most fundamental concept in philosophy. *A priori* reasoning on non-Christian assumptions, no less than *a posteriori* reasoning upon non-Christian assumptions, leads to the apotheosis[31] of chance and thus to the destruction of predication.

Hume's main criticism is now before us. It is destructive of both aspects of Butler's reasoning. On an empirical basis there can be no positive presumption that the future will be like the past and the unknown like the known. Neither, on the other hand, can we use the argument from ignorance with respect to the future and unknown in general. To say that we are justified in expecting that the future will in a measure be unlike the past or that God will, in his dealings with the universe, act in a measure differently from ourselves, presupposes our ability first to show that the future and God will be in a large measure like the present and like ourselves. The validity of the negative aspect of Butler's argument presupposes the validity of the positive aspect of his argument. And in both cases the "unknown causes" working in the field of chances are taken for granted.

OBJECTION TO MIRACLES

The real character of Hume's objection against miracles now appears. His objection against miracles is built upon the section

---

so everything, in this construal, must be necessary. This view has deep theological and philosophical errors imbedded in it.

29. By this Van Til means that God's existence is affirmed, based on the personality ("hypostatization") of man, as one reasons *from* man *to* God.

30. The reason that God and man are subject to change is that, if both are not necessary, then both are aspects of the contingent. God's necessity is determined, in terms of this way of reasoning, by the reality of the contingent. Thus, the contingent, which by definition is always subject to change, is the determining factor for anything else that we conclude.

31. I.e., "deification."

about belief in general. The whole point of the objection to miracle is that "a weaker evidence [numerically considered] can never destroy a stronger."[32] We have so many times in the past experienced that certain phenomena follow certain other phenomena that we cannot accept the evidence from testimony for events that are out of accord with what we have experienced in the past.[33]

It is well to observe what Hume signifies by the term "miracle." He sometimes speaks of it simply as that which happens out of the ordinary course of nature. Yet he realizes that he needs to give a more exact definition of miracle. A more careful definition of miracle, according to Hume, is that it is something that happens by a particular volition of the deity. *The real point of Hume's opposition to miracle is, accordingly, that there is no reason to think that a God who could work miracles can be proved to exist.* As to particular miracles that are said to have happened, Hume seeks to discount the testimony with respect to them by urging that: (a) it is among barbarous people that such claims for the miraculous abound, (b) the passions of surprise and wonder to which the idea of miracle appeals are agreeable emotions, (c) the miracles of one religion cancel the miracles of another religion.[34] After all is said and done, however, the real point by which Hume seeks to destroy the conception of miracle is by the destruction of a valid argument for the existence of God. For suppose, on an empiricist basis, that all of the evidence with respect to the miracles that are said to have taken place in connection with the establishment of Christianity were proved to have taken place, it would simply be that much more experience of the strangeness of natural events. Hume need not have worried too greatly to destroy the validity of the evidence for miracles. Granted the evidence for the validity to miracles was incontestable. Granted that it could be proved by undeniable

---

32. Norman Kemp Smith, "Introduction," in *Hume's Dialogues concerning Natural Religion*, ed. Smith (Oxford: Clarendon Press, 1935), 59, n. 1. Smith quotes Hume and adds the words in brackets.

33. This is Hume's empiricism applied to the notion of miracle. If a miracle is an "abnormality" in our normal experience, then, by definition, the probability of its happening are extremely low. Since experience alone establishes our expectations, anyone who assumes that a miracle has occurred assumes what experience cannot confirm, so it must be an illegitimate assumption. As Van Til makes clear in the following paragraph, however, Hume did not need to worry about miracle, given that his system, based as it is on chance, could accommodate such anomalies without regarding them as anything more than strange occurrences.

34. Smith, "Introduction," in *Hume's Dialogues*, 62.

historical evidence that Christ has been raised from the grave; this would, on the basis of his empiricism, prove no more than that our custom with respect to what we expect from the womb of chance would have to change.[35]

CHRISTIANITY IN GENERAL

What holds for miracles in particular holds with respect to the truth of Christianity in general. If one seeks to make an empirical defense of Christianity as Butler seeks to make, the real and most fundamental question at issue is not the historicity of the events that have taken place in connection with the introduction of Christianity. If these were all assumed to have taken place, it would still be possible for Hume to undermine the foundation of the whole structure built on empirical foundations.

With this we might conclude the matter of Hume's criticism of the type of argument as set forth by Butler. Because of the prevalence of Butler's type of argument down to the present day, however, we may trace in somewhat greater detail the argument that Hume urges against the foundations of Christianity. This argument appears most fully in his *Dialogues Concerning Natural Religion*. Three persons are introduced in this dialogue: Demea, Cleanthes, and Philo. There has been much debate concerning whom or what these three persons represent. Mossner thinks he is justified in saying that Demea represents Samuel Clarke and his a priorism, that Cleanthes represents Butler and his *a posteriori* argument for Christianity, while Philo represents Butler[36] and his *a posteriori* argument for Christianity, while Philo's position is best set forth by

---

35. In other words, even if Hume's method *were* able to confirm a miracle, it would only be a strange phenomenon, given the ultimacy of chance. It could not be interpreted properly apart from biblical revelation.

36. This should read, "while Philo represents Hume," not "Butler." There is an error in this section that serves to confuse. Mossner actually says, "The three interlocutors on the subject of Natural Religion, Cleanthes, Demea, and Philo, may be identified respectively as the school of Locke, represented by Butler; the common or *a priori* school, represented by Samuel Clarke; and the skeptical school, represented by Hume himself." Mossner, *Bishop Butler and the Age of Reason*, 164. Clearly, then, Van Til meant to agree with Mossner that Philo represents Hume. Furthermore, Smith argues that "Cleanthes can be regarded as Hume's mouthpiece only in those passages in which he is explicitly agreeing with Philo." Smith, "Introduction," in *Hume's Dialogues*, 76. This is what Van Til means when he says, "Philo's position is best set forth by Cleanthes."

Cleanthes. Still others maintain that Hume's position appears from the general outcome of the argument as a whole.[37] We need not enter upon this discussion. It matters not to us what Hume's personal beliefs were. We are concerned merely with the objections he raises in one form or another to Christianity. These objections are certainly most fully set forth, as far as the present dialogue is concerned, by Philo.

THE ARGUMENT FROM DESIGN

The main point in dispute in these dialogues is the argument from design. Cleanthes sets forth this argument at various stages. We quote from his first statement of the case:

> Not to lose time in circumlocutions, said CLEANTHES, addressing himself to DEMEA, much less in replying to the pious declamations of PHILO; I shall briefly explain how I conceive this matter. Look round the world: contemplate the whole and every part of it: You will find it to be nothing but one great machine, subdivided into an infinite number of lesser machines, which again admit of subdivisions, to a degree beyond what human senses and faculties can trace and explain. All these various machines, and even their most minute parts, are adjusted to each other with an accuracy, which ravishes into admiration all men, who have ever contemplated them. The curious adapting of means to ends, throughout all nature, resembles exactly, though it much exceeds, the productions of human contrivance; of human designs, thought, wisdom, and intelligence. Since therefore the effects resemble each other, we are led to infer, by all the rules of analogy, that the causes also resemble; and that the Author of Nature is somewhat similar to the mind of man; though possessed of much larger faculties, proportioned to the grandeur of the work, which he has executed. By this argument *a posteriori*, and by this argument alone, do we prove at once the existence of a Deity, and his similarity to human mind and intelligence.[38]

37. See Smith, "Introduction," in *Hume's Dialogues*, 75.
38. Hume, *Dialogues concerning Natural Religion*, ed. Green and Grose, 2:392 (part 2).

In part 4 he says much the same thing in these words: "The whole chorus of Nature raises one hymn to the praises of its creator."[39]

The main question here is, What is the nature of the criticism that Philo brings against this sort of argument?

The first point Philo raises in opposition to Cleanthes is that by *a posteriori* method Cleanthes can never hope to prove the existence of an absolute deity. He can at best prove the existence of a finite God.

It is not easy, I own, to see, what is gained by this supposition, whether we judge of the matter by *Reason* or by *Experience*. We are still obliged to mount higher, in order to find the cause of this cause, which you had assigned as satisfactory and conclusive.[40]

Or a little later he adds:

How therefore shall we satisfy ourselves concerning the cause of that Being, whom you suppose the Author of Nature, or, according to your system of Anthropomorphism, the ideal world, into which you trace the material? Have we not the same reason to trace that ideal world into another ideal world, or new intelligent principle? But if we stop, and go no farther; why go so far? Why not stop at the material world? How can we satisfy ourselves without going on *in infinitum*? And after all, what satisfaction is there in that infinite progression? Let us remember the story of the INDIAN philosopher and his elephant. It was never more applicable than to the present subject. If the material world rests upon a similar ideal world, this ideal world must rest upon some other; and so on, without end. It were better, therefore, never to look beyond the present material world.[41]

In this argument Hume questions the power of analogy to carry us to a region in any way different from that of our experience.[42]

---

39. Ibid., 410 (part 4).
40. Ibid., 407 (part 4).
41. Ibid., 408 (part 4).
42. In this argument from design, in other words, based as it is on experience, there is no way to move from the finite to the infinite, especially since no one has had experience of

We can at most discover a God who is, like ourselves, subject to limitations. He carries this type of criticism still farther when he says that the God whose existence could be proved by the method of Cleanthes should have evil in him as well as good. Such a God must in every major aspect of his being resemble us. There is no good reason to hold that God resembles us in the good that is in us and differs from us with respect to the evil that is in us. There had been many attempts on the part of Christian apologists to show that the good of the world outweighs the evil. To this sort of attempt Philo makes reply as follows:

> But allowing you, what never will be believed; at least, what you never possibly can prove, that animal, or at least, human happiness, in this life, exceeds its misery; you have yet done nothing: For this is not, by any means, what we expect from infinite power, infinite wisdom, and infinite goodness. Why is there any misery at all in the world? Not by chance surely. From some cause then. Is it from the intention of the Deity? But he is perfectly benevolent. Is it contrary to his intention? But he is almighty. Nothing can shake the solidity of this reasoning, so short, so clear, so decisive; except we assert, that these subjects exceed all human capacity, and that our common measures of truth and falsehood are not applicable to them; a topic, which I have all along insisted on, but which you have, from the beginning, rejected with scorn and indignation.[43]

We recognize this argument. Xenophanes[44] in ancient times said that cows would make gods in their own image. Hume in a similar vein speaks of a world of spiders that would make a spider god. Speaking of the spider who weaves a web from its own substance, Philo adds: "Why an orderly system may not be spun from the

---

the infinite. Not only so, but, as Van Til will note, based on experience we should conclude that God is both good and evil.

43. Hume, *Dialogues concerning Natural Religion*, ed. Green and Grose, 2:442–43 (part 10).

44. Xenophanes (c. 570–c. 475 B.C.) was a pre-Socratic poet and philosopher. In his *Fragments*, he says, "But if <horses> or cows or lions had hands to draw with their hands and produce works of art as men do, horses would draw the figures of gods like horses and cows like cows, and they would make their bodies just as the form which they each have themselves."

belly as well as from the brain, it will be difficult for him to give a satisfactory reason."[45]

THE ARGUMENT FROM ANALOGY FAILS

All the objections of Philo, we note, are alike in nature and spring from the same source. Analogy cannot carry us into the unknown; that is the burden of them.[46] Analogy is based upon experience. Experience cannot predict the future nor look into the unknown above us. But granted it could, then that which is above us or in the future must in every respect resemble us. We cannot positively prove the existence of God, but if we could, he would have to resemble us in being finite and evil as well as good. Plato would say that there are somehow ideas of "mud and hair and filth" in the ideal world.[47]

We are anxious to know what Cleanthes has to say for himself after this attack of Philo. Will he accept the offer of Demea to fall back on the *a priori* proof for God's existence? Demea feels that Philo's strictures have been to the point only if one should seek to establish the existence of God by *a posteriori* proof. But he is equally confident that one can demonstrate God's existence by the *a priori* method.

> But if so many difficulties attend the argument *a posteriori*, said DEMEA; had we not better adhere to that simple and sublime argument *a priori*, which, by offering to us infallible demonstration, cuts off at once all doubt and difficulty? By this argument, too, we may prove the INFINITY of the divine attributes, which, I am afraid, can never be ascertained with certainty from any other topic.[48]

45. Hume, *Dialogues concerning Natural Religion*, ed. Green and Grose, 2:425 (part 7).

46. When Van Til writes of "analogy" here, he is referring to Butler's use of it in his *Analogy of Religion*. Butler argues that the truths of supernatural religion can be shown to be probable based on similar truths accepted by deists.

47. Parmenides broached to Socrates the realities of "mud and hair and filth," questioning whether such things exist in the ideal world. Plato had a difficult time categorizing such "vile and paltry" things, given that the ideal world was meant to be the world of perfection. Some argue, and Van Til believes, that Plato changed his mind on the Forms. See Plato, *Parmenides*, 130.

48. Hume, *Dialogues concerning Natural Religion*, ed. Green and Grose, 2:430–31 (part 9).

Demea, we note, agrees that the *a posteriori* argument can do nothing but prove at best a finite deity. Will Cleanthes accept his offer to fall back on the *a priori* proof? Not for all the world. In reply to the *a priori* proof offered by Demea, he says:

I shall begin with observing, that there is an evident absurdity in pretending to demonstrate a matter of fact, or to prove it by any arguments *a priori*. Nothing is demonstrable, unless the contrary implies a contradiction.[49] Nothing, that is distinctly conceivable, implies a contradiction. Whatever we conceive as existent, we can also conceive as non-existent. There is no being, therefore, whose non-existence implies a contradiction. Consequently there is no being, whose existence is demonstrable. I propose this argument as entirely decisive, and am willing to rest the whole controversy upon it.

It is pretended that the Deity is a necessarily-existent being; and this necessity of his existence is attempted to be explained by asserting, that, if we knew his whole essence or nature, we should perceive it to be as impossible for him not to exist as for twice two not to be four. But it is evident, that this can never happen, while our faculties remain the same as at present. It will still be possible for us, at any time, to conceive the non-existence of what we formerly conceived to exist; nor can the mind ever lie under a necessity of supposing any object to remain always in being; in the same manner as we lie under a necessity of always conceiving twice two to be four. The words, therefore, *necessary existence*, have no meaning; or, which is the same thing, none that is consistent.[50]

But farther; why may not the material universe be the necessarily-existent Being, according to this pretended explication of necessity? We dare not affirm that we know all the qualities of matter; and for aught we can determine, it may

---

49. This refers to Hume's notion of analytic propositions; an analytic proposition obtains when its negation is self-contradictory. So, "All bachelors are married," which is the negation of "All bachelors are unmarried," proves this latter statement to be analytic.

50. That is, "necessary existence" has no meaning because it cannot be conceived. All existence of which we can conceive includes the fact that we can conceive of its nonexistence.

contain some qualities, which, were they known, would make its non-existence appear as great a contradiction as that twice two is five. I find only one argument employed to prove, that the material world is not the necessarily-existent Being; and this argument is derived from the contingency both of the matter and the form of the world. "Any particle of matter," 'tis said, "may be *conceived* to be annihilated; and any form may be *conceived* to be altered. Such an annihilation or alteration, therefore, is not impossible." But it seems a great partiality not to perceive, that the same argument extends equally to the Deity, so far as we have any conception of him; and that the mind can at least imagine him to be non-existent, or his attributes to be altered. It must be some unknown, inconceivable qualities, which can make his non-existence appear impossible, or his attributes unalterable: and no reason can be assigned, why these qualities may not belong to matter.[51] As they are altogether unknown and inconceivable, they can never be proved incompatible with it.[52]

When Cleanthes has thus delivered himself of his ultimatum against all *a priori* reasoning for the existence of God, Philo cannot refrain from adding many similar words. He too argues that the idea of necessary existence would have to rest upon something in such an existence that is entirely unknown to us. But if that is the case, who knows but that the material universe may harbor such unknown powers as to be necessarily existent? Philo asks us to look at the fact of the numerical relationship. A superficial glance might make us think that this relationship rests upon nothing but chance. A skillful algebraist will, however, conclude that this relationship rests on necessity. Thereupon he asks:

> Is it not probable, I ask, that the whole economy of the universe is conducted by a like necessity, though no human algebra

---

51. If, for example, we ascribe infinity or eternity to a deity, even though we can conceive of neither, what prevents us from assigning the same attributes to the universe? Only that which is conceivable could be rendered unreasonable.

52. Hume, *Dialogues concerning Natural Religion*, ed. Green and Grose, 2:432–33 (part 9).

can furnish a key, which solves the difficulty? And instead of admiring the order of natural beings, may it not happen, that, could we penetrate into the intimate nature of bodies, we should clearly see why it was absolutely impossible, they could ever admit of any other disposition? So dangerous is it to introduce this idea of necessity into the present question! and so naturally does it afford an inference directly opposite to the religious hypothesis![53]

Thus, there appears upon the horizon a very strange phenomenon. Demea the devotee of the *a priori*, agrees with Philo the sceptic that *a posteriori* reasoning leads to pure irrationality or diversity. On the other hand, Cleanthes, the devotee of the *a posteriori*, agrees with Philo the sceptic that *a priori* reasoning leads into blank identity. In this manner do the shades of Heraclitus and of Parmenides control us from their urns.[54] It only remains for us to say that all three of the participants in the debate were right in what they affirmed by way of objection to their opponents. But this will occupy us in the sequel. We limit ourselves just now to pointing out that Cleanthes, whose argument resembles that of Butler in its main outline, virtually admits that he cannot prove the existence of God. He not only admits that there is uncertainty in the proof, for uncertainty he was gladly willing to admit because it was involved in the very nature of his argument, but what is more, he virtually admits that the only God he can prove to exist would be a finite God, a God whose being is essentially penetrable by the mind of man. In reply to the contention of Demea that God can be proved to exist by an *a priori* argument, Cleanthes affirms that such a God would be a pure blank. Thereupon, he adds:

53. Hume, *Dialogues concerning Natural Religion*, ed. Green and Grose, 2:434 (part 9).

54. For Van Til, the non-Christian principle of continuity is best exemplified by the monism of Parmenides (fifth century B.C.). For Parmenides, all that is, is Being. Anything else would be non-Being, and thus would not "be." The non-Christian principle of discontinuity is best exemplified by Heraclitus (535–475 B.C.). Heraclitus taught that everything is in flux, and thus one never steps into the same river twice. So the principle of continuity has its focus on unity, whether metaphysical or epistemological, and the principle of discontinuity has its focus on diversity, whether metaphysical or epistemological.

For though it be allowed, that the Deity possesses attributes, of which we have no comprehension; yet ought we never to ascribe to him any attributes, which are absolutely incompatible with that intelligent nature, essential to him. A mind, whose acts and sentiments and ideas are not distinct and successive; one, that is wholly simple, and totally immutable; is a mind, which has no thought, no reason, no will, no sentiment, no love, no hatred; or in a word, is no mind at all. It is an abuse of terms to give it that appellation; and we may as well speak of limited extension without figure, or of number without composition.[55]

Then, at the conclusion of the whole discussion, when Philo has urged his alternative with respect to evil, namely, that either we must hold to an infinite God and hold him responsible for evil, or else we must drop to a lower level and be content with a finite God, Cleanthes once more refuses the services of Demea and says:

Thus, in the present subject, if we abandon all human analogy, as seems your intention, DEMEA, I am afraid we abandon all religion, and retain no conception of the great object of our adoration. If we preserve human analogy, we must for ever find it impossible to reconcile any mixture of evil in the universe with infinite attributes; much less can we ever prove the latter from the former. But supposing the Author of Nature to be finitely perfect, though far exceeding mankind; a satisfactory account may then be given of natural and moral evil, and every untoward phenomenon be explained and adjusted. A less evil may then be chosen, in order to avoid a greater; Inconveniencies be submitted to, in order to reach a desirable end: And in a word, benevolence, regulated by wisdom, and limited by necessity, may produce just such a world as the present.[56]

55. Hume, *Dialogues concerning Natural Religion*, ed. Green and Grose, 2:407 (part 4).
56. Ibid., 444 (part 11).

The upshot of the whole dialogue is, therefore, that the representative of Butler's type of thought virtually admits defeat. He will not give up his mode of appeal to fact. Yet he realizes that with this mode of appeal to fact he cannot prove anything more than a finite god. In fact, though he does not admit it, he really cannot prove anything. On the basis of brute fact no predication is possible.[57]

57. The notion of "brute fact" is one that has been misunderstood in Van Til's thought. It is sometimes thought that Van Til's point is that, since there are no brute facts, all facts are so by virtue of our interpretation of them. This, however, has more to do with postmodern relativism and has nothing to do with Van Til's view of fact. As we have said, for Van Til, a brute fact is a mute fact. That is, it is a fact that does not "say" anything; it has no meaning, unless and until a person gives meaning to it. Thus, according to Van Til, there are no brute facts—but not because every fact carries *our* interpretation with it. To think that way is to fall prey to relativism. For Van Til, there are no brute facts because every fact is a *created* fact. As created, every fact carries with it *God's* own interpretation. God speaks the facts into existence, and he speaks through that which he has created.

CHAPTER 3

IDEALISTIC RECONSTRUCTION

B utler's *Analogy* continued to have great influence after his death. It is no great marvel that this should have been the case. Butler expressed the temper of the age. The tendency in theology was in the direction of Arminianism. Wesley and Butler differed in their characters, but in their theology there was a large measure of agreement. Mossner says: "Yet theologically the two leaders were not disparate, both being Arminian in principle."[1] If there is to be any philosophical apologetics for Arminianism, it must be of the sort that Butler furnishes. Arminianism will not allow that "whatsoever comes to pass" comes to pass in accord with the counsel of God. Philosophically expressed, this means that Arminianism begins with "brute facts" and with the human mind as the final interpreter of those facts. God is excluded from the outset. This being the case, Arminianism can turn only to some form of non-theistic reasoning. Of these forms of non-theistic reasoning, it is the *a posteriori* reasoning that fits in with the genius of Arminianism rather than the *a priori* form of reasoning. When Arminianism flourishes in the field of theology we may be certain that Butler's method will flourish in apologetics and evidences.[2]

---

1. Ernest Campbell Mossner, *Bishop Butler and the Age of Reason* (New York: Macmillan, 1936), 166–67.
2. This is a central point, sometimes overlooked, in Van Til's overall approach. As we have emphasized, Van Til's apologetic method is what it is by virtue of the theology

Butler's method has two points that at first sight seem to commend it to us. If we use it we have common ground with our opponents on the question of "fact." We do not have to raise the knotty problem of the philosophy of fact. Non-believers and believers alike are ready to appeal to facts in order to settle their differences. In the second place, believers and non-believers can in Butler's method use the same method of procedure in going to the facts. The knotty question of scientific methodology does not have to be raised.[3]

To this a third point must be added. In addition to similarity on the question of starting point and method, there is not too great a difference in the conclusions to which the believers and non-believers come. Arminianism does not ask unbelievers to accept the doctrine of a sovereign or absolute God. A finite God is really all that it asks men to accept. And with a finite God goes a conception of man as having original powers next to God, and a conception of the sinner as able to judge of good and evil without the necessity of regeneration.[4]

It is no wonder, then, that Butler's *Analogy* continues to be popular. The really amazing thing is that it has been and still is popular in some Reformed circles as well as in Arminian circles. But of this we shall speak later.

It is impossible and unnecessary to trace the influence of Butler in detail. Those interested in the details of the matter can find fuller discussion in Mossner's book. We only observe that, though there was some recognition on the part of Butler's followers that his argument needed to be corrected in some respects, the main concepts of the *Analogy* were not altered by them. William Paley's "Natural Theology" presents an argument for theism similar to that of Butler for Christianity.[5] Paley's argument, like Butler's, contains a

that grounds it. Such is the case with any apologetic method. So, one who holds to an Arminian theology could not countenance Van Til's approach. That could be done only if one's theology were Reformed.

3. To see an example of what Van Til means by an argument that begins with brute fact and a presumably neutral stance, see K. Scott Oliphint, *Covenantal Apologetics: Principles and Practice in Defense of Our Faith* (Wheaton, IL: Crossway, 2013), 110–13. To see how to reconfigure such a proof according to Reformed theology, see pp. 117–22.

4. Once one allows, as Arminianism does, that man's presumably autonomous will trumps God's meticulous, sovereign control, then God is no longer the *a se*, sovereign God of Scripture. Like man, he is limited, and therefore man has the power to bring about totally new facts.

5. The most popular treatment of the argument from design is found in William Paley's *Natural Theology*, published in 1802. Paley (1743–1805) was the one who offered the "watch implies watchmaker" argument. Paley wrote several books on philosophy and Christianity,

negative and a positive aspect. In the negative aspect of his argument Paley reasons against the rationalists, and in the positive aspect of his argument, he reasons against the sceptics. The attributes men ascribe to God, Paley argues, are negative ideas.[6] " 'Eternity' is a negative idea, clothed with a positive name. . . . 'Self-existence' is another negative idea, namely, the negation of a preceding cause, as of a progenitor, a maker, an author, a creator."[7] This negative argument would lead Paley straight into scepticism. It implies that man knows nothing at all of a transcendent God. It is the idea of pure equivocation in reasoning.[8] To prevent this sceptical conclusion Paley argues that we can assert something about the attributes of God if only we "do not affect more precision in our ideas than the subject allows of" and confine our explanation to "what concerns ourselves."[9] Here a bit of univocal reasoning is supposed to cure the pure equivocation to which his negative argument led him.[10] Pure equivocation which leads straight to scepticism and pure univocation which leads straight to the identification of man with God are combined to form what is called analogical reasoning. Both Paley's and Butler's methods are similar to that of Thomas Aquinas.[11] And what is true of Paley is generally true of other, though less known, writers on evidences and natural theology.

---

which proved very influential. His 1794 book, *A View of the Evidence of Christianity*, was required reading at Cambridge University until the twentieth century. His most influential contribution to biological thought, however, was his *Natural Theology: or, Evidences of the Existence and Attributes of the Deity, Collected from the Appearances of Nature.* In this book, Paley laid out a full exposition of natural theology, the belief that anyone can understand the nature of God simply by reference to his creation, the natural world.

6. This is sometimes called "apophatic" theology (from the Greek *apophēmi,* "to deny"). We state something about God by saying what he is *not.* For example, in order to say that God is *not* finite, we say that he is infinite.

7. William Paley, *Natural Theology* (New York: American Tract Society, n.d.), 289.

8. In other words, if we want to ascribe attributes like eternity to God, we simply have no idea what we mean by such words. "Pure equivocation" results because there is no content possible in using words of this kind. Whatever we might want to say about God, we simply cannot know anything of him.

9. Paley, *Natural Theology,* 287.

10. The way out of pure equivocation, according to Paley, is to affirm univocism, which means that words used of God and of man must coincide. We can meaningfully predicate something of God only if our predication is embedded in our own concepts and ideas. Thus, God's being is, in some ways, just like man's, except "bigger."

11. Aquinas rejected both equivocation and univocism, arguing for analogical reasoning. Van Til's point is that analogy, for Thomas, was nothing more than a combination of the equivocal and the univocal. For more detail on Thomas's view, see K. Scott Oliphint, "Bavinck's Realism, the Logos Principle, and *Sola Scriptura,*" *Westminster Theological Journal* 72, no. 2 (Fall 2010): 365–69.

FIDEISM[12]

All this does not mean that there were no believers in Christianity who observed the sceptical tendency of Butler's and Paley's arguments. On the contrary, there were many of these. We may perhaps place them into two categories. There were, in the first place, those who deemed Hume's criticism of Butler's argument as conclusive not only against Butler, but as conclusive against any intellectual argument for Christianity. Thinking that Butler's type of argument is the only type of argument conceivable, they gave up all hope when they saw their hero defeated by Hume. They saw no way of harmonizing the facts of the Christian religion with the "constitution and course of nature." They gave up the idea of a philosophical apologetics entirely. This fideistic attitude comes to expression frequently in the statement of the experiential proof of the truth of Christianity. People will say that they know that they are saved and that Christianity is true no matter what the philosophical or scientific evidence for or against it may be. And this is done not only by those who have had no opportunity to investigate the evidence for Christianity, but also by those who have.

But, in thus seeking to withdraw from all intellectual argument, such fideists have virtually admitted the validity of the argument against Christianity. They will have to believe in their hearts what they have virtually allowed to be intellectually indefensible.

A second and less consistent class of fideists, though denying the validity of any philosophical argument for Christianity, turns to arguments taken from archaeology, biological science, etc., hoping in this way to show that the spade corroborates the Bible. This class of fideists approaches very closely to those who profess to follow the method of Butler. They seek a scientific or factual defense for Christianity. In fact, we may say that there is only a difference of degree between the three groups spoken of: (a) the direct followers of Butler, (b) the more consistent fideists, and (c) the less consistent fideists. There is in all of them an emphasis upon the appeal to "brute facts," whether those facts be external or internal. They differ only in respect to the relative faith they have in their ability

---

12. Fideism, in the way Van Til is using the term here, refers to a belief that has no foundation or basis in knowledge. It is empty faith.

to unite the "facts" in which they believe into a rational whole that will be able to withstand attack on the part of modern science and philosophy. The followers of Butler think that there is a defense of the Christian experience before the bar of philosophy as well as before the bar of science. The consistent fideists hold that no defense of any sort is possible. The inconsistent fideists contend that Christianity may be scientifically, but cannot be philosophically, defended.[13]

RECONSTRUCTION

In distinction from the three classes enumerated there are those who see that Hume's criticism has destroyed the validity of Butler's argument, but who think that Hume may be answered and a better argument for Christianity constructed. The reconstruction attempted has usually been built with the help of the thought patterns of Immanuel Kant. When we say this, we do not think of that large host of modern theologians who have sought to combine Christianity and modern thought by reducing Christianity to something hazy and subjective. We are thinking only of the orthodox theologians who really wish to preserve the central concepts of historic Christianity. Of these there are two classes who have depended on Kant.

There are first, those who have sought help from Kant by dividing, as he did, the field between science and religion. Kant claims to have made room for faith by giving to it the whole of the *noumenal* realm, reserving for science only the *phenomenal* realm.[14] It

13. Van Til terms all three approaches "fideist" because, he says, they all appeal to brute fact. As such, the extent of corroboration between the faith one has and the "facts" is relative. In all three, it is impossible for one's faith to find its ground in knowledge. Thus, corroboration can provide, at best, another "brute fact" testimony to one's faith; it cannot provide a ground for it.

14. Immanuel Kant (1724–1804) is one of the most influential philosophers in the history of philosophy. In his development of a transcendental approach, he thought that reality consisted of the "phenomenal" realm, which is the realm of scientific law and empirical facts, and the "noumenal" realm, in which are those things that must be posited, but which cannot be known, such as God. Kant also regarded the objects of this world as essentially unknowable and thus as noumenal. Kant's now famous phrase in the preface to the second edition of his *Critique of Pure Reason* is, "I have therefore found it necessary to deny knowledge in order to make room for faith" ("*Ich mußte also das Wissen aufheben, um zum Glauben Platz*"). See Immanuel Kant, *Critique of Pure Reason*, trans. Norman Kemp Smith (New York: St. Martin's Press, 1958), 28.

appears, however, that such a division is based upon the idea of an appeal to brute fact. We are free in the noumenal realm, though determined in the phenomenal realm. According to science, there is no rational cosmology, but we feel and are morally certain that the world was created by God. According to science, there is no argument for the existence of God, but we feel that there is a God. That is, we feel the truth of the existence of freedom, immortality, and God because these are *regulative concepts.*[15] They are not altogether irrational, but seem in some way to be implied in our rational understanding of the universe. There is once again a vague *probability* which ought to make us act *as if.*[16] The presumption seems to be in favor of the existence of God. This position resembles that of Butler.[17] The only difference is that this position has granted the validity of Hume's and Kant's criticism on the positive analogy argument of Butler. We can at best come to the idea of a finite God only, by the process of analogy, say Hume and Kant, and strictly speaking we must end with a neutral attitude on the question of God's existence. On Kant's basis we may believe in Christianity as "practically true" even though intellectually it cannot even be shown to be probably true.[18]

Kant's phenomenalism is the typically modern expression of the philosophy of the would-be autonomous man. This man virtually makes the man the measure of reality. He boldly claims that only that is significantly real which he can categorize.

Kant's phenomenalism is but the natural out-growth of ancient philosophy. Once man assumes the virtual identity of his intellect with that of God he is driven to maintain with even greater clarity that all rationality is purely formal and that, correspondingly, all differentiation is purely non-rational. Aristotle virtually maintained

15. That is, those things that are noumenal, though they cannot be known, nevertheless are meant to provide some kind of conceptual "balance" to the things that are phenomenal and thus determined. The existence of God cannot be known, but it is, to use Van Til's term, "felt" because we cannot imagine that everything is determined.

16. Van Til may be referring here to the famous Kantian philosopher Hans Vaihinger, whose book on Kant was entitled *Die Philosophie des Als Ob* ("the philosophy of the 'as if'"). One is to act *as if* God exists, though his existence cannot be proved.

17. The resemblance is in the fact that, in Butler's method, we accept the "phenomenal" and then posit a probable "noumenal" god, given what we know of the phenomenal facts.

18. This summarizes the conclusions to Kant's *Critique of Pure Reason* and his *Critique of Practical Reason.*

this, and Thomas Aquinas followed him.[19] It remained for Kant and his followers to assert the exhaustive correlativity of *pure* logic and *pure* fact, thus banishing the God of Christianity from any intellectually ascertainable contact with the universe.

THE IDEALISTIC RECONSTRUCTION

There are others, however, who use Kant in order to refute Hume, and then seek to refute Kant with the help of Kant. These men think, and we believe think correctly, that every appeal made to bare fact is unintelligible. Every fact *must stand in relation to other facts* or it means nothing to anyone. We may argue at length whether there is a noise in the woods when a tree falls even if no one is there to hear it, but there can be no reasonable argument about the fact that even if there be such a noise, it means nothing to anyone.[20] There is, therefore, a necessary connection between the facts and the observer or interpreter of facts.

It was in this way that Kant met the criticism of the causality concept by Hume. It is by the use of Kant's arguments that Professor James Orr,[21] e.g., seeks to reply to the criticism of Hume in general. His book *David Hume* tells us how he hopes to accomplish his purpose. After having spoken of minor criticisms that Kant makes of Hume, Orr goes on to say:

> But Kant goes deeper. It is essential to Hume's theory of the derivation of the causal judgment, that, prior to the possession of the idea of causality, we should observe successions of

19. In other words, what is consistent in much of secular philosophy is that thought must be only "formal"; it cannot include the differentiation of changing facts. For Aristotle, and Thomas following him, the intellect abstracts the form from the matter, and thus knows only the form. The matter cannot be known. So also for Kant, except that for Kant the "formal" is the application of intellectual, innate categories to the otherwise unknowable experience of the world. There are differences in nuance between these thinkers, but the conclusions are identical with respect to the existence of the Christian God.

20. Van Til is referring to a famous statement, likely introduced by the empiricist George Berkeley (1685–1753), who asked whether a sound is made by a falling tree when no one is there to hear it. It is not certain whether Berkeley himself utilized the question in his philosophy or whether it is an objection to it. The question did take on a life of its own after Berkeley.

21. James Orr (1844–1913) will be discussed by Van Til later on. In some ways, his views correspond more directly with Van Til's. In other ways, Orr is beholden to a Kantian paradigm.

phenomena in a fixed order. It is from observation of their regular conjunctions that the idea is supposed to be obtained. It is here that Kant strikes in with his penetrating criticism. In assuming the existence of an objective world, and of orderly succession in that world, you have, he argues, already implicitly supposed the operation of that causal principle which you imagine yourself to obtain from your experience of it. For what is meant by speaking of objects, and of a succession of objects, in the natural world? To speak of a thing as object at all, is, as shown in the last chapter, to give that thing a place in an order or system which has a subsistence, coherence, and connection of parts, irrespective of the course of our ideas of it. It implies an order in which the parts are definitely related to each other, in which each has its place fixed by relation to the other parts. But such an order already involves—is constituted for our thought and experience through—this very principle of causation which we are proposing to derive from it.[22]

In reflecting on this passage, we may distinguish two points. There is first, the method of the argument, and there is second, the conclusion drawn from it. With Orr we hold that *the form of the argument is in its form essentially sound.* By that we mean that it is impossible to reason on the basis of brute facts. Every one who reasons about facts comes to those facts with a schematism into which he fits the facts. The real question is, therefore, into whose schematism the facts will fit. As between Christianity and its opponents the question is whether our claim that *Christianity is the only schematism into which the facts will fit,* is true or not. Christianity claims that unless we presuppose the existence of God, in whom, as the self-sufficient One, schematism and fact, fact and reason apart from and prior to the existence of the world, are coterminous, we face utterly unintelligible "brute fact." We do not intend to develop this point here. We mention it merely to indicate that we can be in a large measure of agreement with Orr when he uses this aspect of Kantian methodology in order to meet the brute facts of Hume and Butler.

22. James Orr, *David Hume and His Influence on Philosophy and Theology* (Edinburgh: T. & T. Clark, 1903), 136–37.

The second question we must ask, however, is whether the particular schematism of Kant itself avoided landing us once more into the realm of chance or brute fact. And here, too, we are happy to be in agreement with Orr when he seeks to go beyond Kant. It is apparent that the whole realm of the noumenal as Kant conceives it is a realm of brute facts. And since that noumenal realm surrounds the phenomenal realm and has a possible influence on it, the result is that the phenomenal realm is really also a realm of chance and brute fact. Kant's phenomenal realm is but an island, and that a floating island on a bottomless and shoreless sea. After all, the human mind can furnish at most a finite schematism or *a priori*. We do not admit that the human mind can furnish any *a priori* at all unless it is related to God. But suppose for a moment that it could, such a schematism could never be comprehensive. Even Kant himself, besides setting his noumenal realm over against the phenomenal, admits that those facts for which the human mind furnishes the *a priori* arc at the outset says Kant. This, he should have argued, points to the need of God in whom there is no correlative relation between percepts and concepts, because his concept includes all possible percepts of his creatures.[23]

Orr has sensed something of this. This appears in the book of which we are speaking, and in *The Christian View of God and the World*. He has made use of the later Hegelian or idealist argument in order to overcome the limitation of the position of Kant. In the book on Hume he quotes frequently with approval from the famous idealist criticism made on Hume by Thomas Hill Green.[24] Green has criticized Hume from the Hegelian point of view. Going beyond Kant, he says it is not enough to bring the schematism of the human mind to bear upon the brute facts of Hume and empiricism. We need back of the human mind an absolute mind. Without such an absolute mind the human mind and the facts it seems to coordinate would still be nothing but brute facts. In line with this sort of argument Orr says:

23. Van Til is referring to Kant's statement that is meant to synthesize the best of rationalism with the best of empiricism: "Concepts without percepts are empty; percepts without concepts are blind." In other words, rationalism needs experience (percepts), even as experience needs concepts (rationalism).
24. Thomas Hill Green (1836–1882) was a theologian and a leading British idealist.

When all is said, it must be granted that an ultimate inexplicability attaches to this act in which, under sense conditions, a world which is not ourselves enters as a real factor into our knowledge. How is this possible? Only, it may be replied, on the hypothesis that the distinction between ourselves who know and the world we know is not after all final—that there is a deeper ground and ultimate unity, that the universe, including ourselves, is a single system the parts of which stand in reciprocal relation through the spiritual principle on which in the last resort the whole depends. Here, however, we enter a transcendental region which leaves Hume far behind, and into which, in this connection, we need not travel further.[25]

It will be necessary for us, however, to travel much further along the road on which Orr has taken us. Orr represents a tendency in orthodox apologetics to utilize the idealist argument for the defense of Christianity. We shall have to see whether it is legitimate to do this.

We may agree at the outset that idealism is right as over against empiricism in claiming that bare facts are in themselves unintelligible. We may also rejoice in the fact that Hegelian idealism has outgrown the eighteenth century rationalism in that it has recognized the fact that an *a priori* that stands in no relation to the facts is unintelligible. All this Kant taught idealism. He sought "*die Bedingungen die die Erfahrung möglich machen*," i.e., "the presuppositions that make learning by experience possible."[26] He held that we could not recognize or individuate objects without an *a priori* equipment furnished by the mind. That was the death blow to empiricism. On the other hand, he recognized as over against Leibniz that individuation is not by minute description, but by space-time coordinates. On this point Kant agreed with Hume. Brute facts occupies as fundamental a place in the philosophy of Kant as in that of Hume. And Kant's philosophy is, in consequence, fully as sceptical as that of Hume. Retaining the idea of brute fact,

---

25. Orr, *David Hume*, 163–64.

26. See Edgar A. Singer, Jr., "Experience and Reflection," chap. 2, p. 5, mimeographed. Singer's book of this title was published posthumously in 1959. Apparently CVT obtained a copy of this work in unpublished form, probably as Singer used it in his classroom (at the University of Pennsylvania, 1909–943).

or pure chance differentiation, he was driven to reduce the idea of absolute rationality to that of a merely contingent rationality *for us*. He "saved" universality by subjectivising it. He "saved" causality within the world by denying God as the creator of the world. That is to say, from the Christian point of view he destroyed rather than saved universality.

We must go on briefly to note the nature of the idealistic development that went beyond Kant. Hegelian idealism is usually called objective idealism inasmuch as it is by *inclusion* rather than by *exclusion* of the "facts" that it seeks to interpret experience. It looks for a "concrete" rather than an "abstract" universal.[27] It wishes to bring the phenomenal and the noumenal world of Kant into one world explained by one principle of interpretation. That is the principle of dialecticism.[28]

Kant's view, valuable as it was, would, if tested by its own standard, defeat itself. We quote the admirable statement of Singer on this point:

> But no sense of the cogency of the reasons driving Kant to the doctrine of *a priori* science should blind one to the difficulties facing this philosophy. . . . The following objections are as obvious as they are serious: The sciences to which *a priori* knowledge is confined are (1) such science as enables us to order our experience in space-time coordinates—the science of geometry, and (2) such as furnish us with the concepts by means of which we recognize an object as an object—the science of logic. Since we bring these abilities to experience, we must in some sense bring to experience the sciences not to possess which is to lack such abilities. But we all know—and Kant was willing to concede, even to insist on the point—that these sciences are the possession of none but the mature,

27. Van Til has been criticized for referring to God as a "concrete universal." The term itself comes from Hegelianism, which, in reaction to Greek and Kantian notions of an abstract universal, posited a universal that is embedded in reality and is in dialectic tension (between Being and Nonbeing). A concrete universal in Hegel's thought is that which is real and which includes everything in its scope. Thus, facts are "included," not "excluded," because they are no longer relegated to a Kantian noumenal realm.

28. The "principle of dialecticism" is that there are two opposing principles that are in need of synthesis. For Hegel, history is a series of thesis, antithesis, and synthesis. The synthesis, in the historical process, then became another thesis, set over against another antithesis, and on the process goes.

which is to say, the highly experienced mind. We might even go farther and maintain that no human mind has yet won a complete insight into the ways of either geometry or logic. The technical journals are filled with patient efforts to put science in more masterful possession of these disciplines: one would not be risking much in predicting that if this cooling planet ever comes to its last day, and if in that day there still appear technical journals, their tables of contents will continue to include such titles as 'On the axioms of Geometry,' 'On the Postulates of Logic.' How then and in what sense can that science which is beyond the grasp of a Euclid or of an Aristotle be the possession of a newborn babe? Or to render the matter still more preposterous, does it not seem that a Euclid or an Aristotle must have spent his life in a none too successful struggle to possess himself of a science the possession of which was the condition of his beginning the struggle?[29]

The point of difficulty to which Singer calls attention is our old friend *hard* or *brute fact*. Kant was not willing to go with the rationalists in identifying the particular facts with the *infima species*,[30] i.e., in individuating by minute description. His principle of individuation was non-rational. The space-time coordinates by which facts are brought into contact with the rational principles of the mind are themselves non-rational; they are intuitions.[31] Thus, the rational principle of the mind, i.e., the *a priori*, is still set abstractly over against the non-rational facts. The result is that the hard facts are still with us. The *Ding an sich selbst*[32] escapes us. Hume has not really been answered; his criticism on Butler still stands.

In order to overcome the weakness of Kant's position the idealist school boldly advanced the idea that the real is the rational and the rational is the real.[33] Hegel and his successors felt that Kant's

29. Singer, "Experience and Reflection," chap. 4, p. 5.
30. I.e., the lowest species.
31. This is the point that Kant makes in the first section of his *Critique of Pure Reason*. Space and time can only be intuited, and never known by reason.
32. This refers to the "thing in itself," which, along with God and the soul, Kant relegated to the "as if" of the noumenal realm.
33. This statement was made famous by Georg W. F. Hegel (1770–1831). In his *Phenomenology of Spirit*, Hegel argues that the Absolute (as Absolute Mind or Spirit— Geist), which is in the process of self-development, is real. Furthermore, all that is *real*, since it is the culmination of the historical, dialectical process of consciousness, is *rational*.

thought had to be supplemented by an appeal to an absolute mind. The rationalists were basically right in asserting that unless reason can comprehend all facts it does not really understand one fact. For one fact to be known truly, it must be known in all of its relations to all other facts. But since man cannot have such comprehensive knowledge, we must introduce the notion of the Absolute or God. Only an *a priori* principle that is wide enough to sweep the whole universe would vanquish the spectre of brute fact.[34]

On the other hand, the idealists also felt that Kant was right as over against the rationalists in holding that the *a priori* must not stand abstractly over against brute facts.[35] In that case, too, brute facts would still be independent of the rational principle. Idealism was not willing to give up the space-time coordinates as the principle of individuation. Idealism sought to bring Kant's intuitions of sense into closer contact with the categories of understanding than Kant himself had done.[36]

Idealism sought to bridge the gap between Plato's world of sense and of Ideas, and between Kant's phenomena and noumena. For Plato the world of sense had *somehow participated in* or *imitated the world of Ideas.* Plato sought but could not find a rational connection between the two worlds. Aristotle wanted to correlativize form and matter in order to bring them together. Kant went much further in the same direction. Even so, pure form or rationality still stood abstractly over against pure matter.[37] What Plato, Aristotle, and Kant looked for but could not find, Hegel found. Or so he thought.

---

34. This is the reason that Van Til will sometimes say, in agreement with Hegel, that the real is the rational and the rational is the real. Van Til's point, though, is necessarily antithetical to Hegel's and the idealism that Hegel incorporated. Since God is fully self-conscious, in that he lacks nothing, in him the real is identical with the rational. In other words, God is what he thinks and thinks what he is. Given the self-exhaustive character of God and his knowledge, the "specter of brute fact" can be avoided only by affirming the ontological Trinity as the presupposition behind any and all facts.

35. That is, the rationalists attempted to ground knowledge in *a priori* laws of thought, over against the empirical. In that way, they thought, knowledge can have some constancy that the changing world cannot provide.

36. This is a technical point, but the gist of it is that idealism sees too great a separation between Kant's understanding of *intuition*, which is the faculty that alone can affirm space and time, and the *understanding*, which is the faculty that synthesizes the categories of thought with experience. Later idealism attempts to bring intuition and understanding closer together.

37. This is Van Til's summary of dimensionalism in philosophy. In each case—Plato, Aristotle, Kant—there is an attempt to bring together that which transcends experience

He found the rational connection between fact and principle, the one and the many, the Ideal and the Real, with the help of the concept of the dialectic. The meaning of this concept will become apparent to an extent if we contrast it with Plato's concept of absolute affirmation. For Plato the ideal world, the world of Reality, was the fully known world. That ideal world was fully known without any reference to the sense world.[38] The ideal world would affirm itself without setting over against itself the world of non-being as a correlative. Affirmation was there, independent of negation. In that world there was individuation by pure description, if there was individuation at all.

At opposite ends of this ideal world was the world of pure non-being, and pure ignorance. The sense world lay somewhere between these two. In his earlier dialogues Plato tended simply to identify reality with the world of ideas. At a later stage Plato sought a solution to his problem by toning down something of the independence of the ideal world. It was no longer to stand over against the world of non-being in a self-sufficient spirit. The world of non-being was to contribute the element of diversity, and the ideal world was to contribute the element of identity in the knowledge situation (see *The Sophist*). The ideal world was to admit that its pure affirmation was in itself as meaningless as the pure negation of the world of non-being. They simply were unintelligible without each other. The idea of a husband disappears without the idea of a wife, and the idea of a wife disappears without the idea of a husband. So the ideal world and the world of non-being were to recognize the need of each other.[39]

But we have really put too much of Hegel into Plato. We can really say no more than that Plato felt that it was somehow in this direction that the solution was to be found. Hegel now made this

---

with experience itself. For Plato, the transcendent is the world of Forms. For Aristotle, the world of forms is resident in the matter. For Kant, the noumenal is necessary in order to "guide" the phenomenal.

38. In other words, for Plato, the world of Forms is real, though separate from the world of material objects.

39. Plato recognized that the world of Forms, as real, needed the "lesser" material world, in which forms were only imperfectly present, in order to posit the perfection of the Forms. "Dogginess" can be the perfect Form of dog only as we recognize it exemplified, in a limited and imperfect way, in individual dogs.

idea of the correlativity of the principle of identity and diversity the foundation of his system. The ideas of *pure being* and *pure non-being*, he said, were interchangeable because empty. It is only if brought into contact with one another that they have meaning. And this contact must be established by the principle of dialectic. Both pure being and pure non-being, or pure affirmation and pure negation are to give up their isolation and seek to interpenetrate one another. By interpenetration only can they live. *Sein* and *Nicht-Sein* found their common reality and meaning in *Werden* (*Hegel's Logic*).[40]

In this way Hegel sought to establish a rational connection between fact and principle. By rational connection he did not mean the same thing that the Rationalists meant. He did not hold to his *a priori* at the expense of the facts, but he held to his *a priori* with the help of the facts. Without the diversity offered by the factual, there would be no meaning in the rational.

F. H. Bradley and Bernard Bosanquet[41]

Since the matter is of utmost importance, it is well that a short survey of the idealist conception of judgment be introduced at this point.[42] Hegel held that it was of the essence of human judgment or predication that there be an equal ultimacy of the principle of identity and diversity. F. H. Bradley and Bernard Bosanquet have worked this idea out in their great works on logic.

Both Bradley and Bosanquet have made much of the point that we need to have a comprehensive *a priori* if we are to have knowledge

40. As we have mentioned, Hegel's dialectic was supposed to "solve" the problem of Kant's abstract noumenal realm. It was supposed to be *concrete*, not abstract. Hegel argued that history is a process of Being (*Sein*), as thesis, over against Nonbeing (*Nicht-Sein*), as antithesis, which is synthesized as Becoming (*Werden*), which itself then becomes Being, and so the historical process continues, until it culminates in the Absolute.

41. Bernard Bosanquet (1848–1923) and F. H. Bradley (1846–1924) were Absolute idealists with whom Van Til interacted in many of his writings. The Absolute idealists were opposed to logical methods such as linear inference, insisting that all inference must necessarily presuppose some universal system.

42. The notion of "judgment" in idealistic philosophy is deep and complex. For Kant, judgment is the activity of the mind in imposing categories on the raw data of sense experience. For Hegel, judgment is more concrete than it is for Kant. Judgment, in Hegel's thought, is a matter of synthesizing the data of history. Bosanquet was thought to be one of the most Hegelian of the British idealists. He did, however, think of judgment more holistically than did Hegel, arguing that it consists of the influence of the whole on the particular fact.

at all.[43] The idea of a brute fact, they say, is unintelligible. We simply can do nothing with brute facts in and by themselves. We cannot even count them. If we are to count them we must think of a number scheme as a whole. Says Bradley: "The main point is this, that all counting presupposes and depends on a qualitative Whole, and that the Collective Judgment asserts a generic connection within its group. Hence no mere particulars can be counted."[44] Similarly Bosanquet tells us: "The hope of complete enumeration is the justification of counting."[45] Or again, when speaking of demonstrative judgments, he says: "Except in view of a finite goal, number does not help us, does not tell us anything, grounds no ratio of parts to whole."[46]

The point with respect to this matter of counting is that unless there were a numerical system as a whole we could not tell one number from another. If we are to add information to our store of knowledge, we need the system of knowledge in order to relate a new fact to the system of facts already known. We cannot think of an infinite series without thinking of a system. "The idea of numerical infinity arises from neglecting the continuous nature of the unit, and therefore omitting the element which alone arrests computation at one number rather than at another."[47]

In this way Bosanquet seeks to meet the challenge of empiricism. The charge against all forms of rationalism by the empiricists has always been that on a rationalistic basis one can know only abstractions; one cannot know the particular in its unique character. To this Bosanquet makes reply by saying that "the more marked an individuality is the more it depends on internal proportion."[48] Naturally, if individuality is dependent upon internal proportions, then individuality cannot be observed except in relation to other

43. As Van Til will illustrate, the Absolute idealists, in seeking to solve the impasse between the *a priori*, or unifying principle, so prevalent in rationalism, and the *a posteriori*, or principle of diversity, so present in empiricism, argued that any fact, or any number of facts, is what it is by virtue of its relation to the whole. A "2" can be what it is only because "1," "3," and so on, are what they are. A "2," as a brute fact, means nothing. One can begin to see how Van Til takes these theories of idealism and argues that they can be true only if they are properly incorporated into Christianity.

44. F. H. Bradley, *The Principles of Logic*, 2nd ed., 2 vols. (London: Oxford University Press, 1922), 1:368–69, n. 2.

45. Bernard Bosanquet, *Logic, or The Morphology of Knowledge*, 2 vols. (Oxford: Clarendon Press, 1888), 1:176.

46. Ibid.

47. Ibid., 175.

48. Ibid., 137.

facts, and that to all other facts. True, as human beings we cannot in any instance observe all the relations of one fact to all other facts, but it is enough if we know that they are so related. Then we can at least see something of the nature of individuality; without that knowledge we could see nothing of it. So runs the argument.

The question we must ask at this point is whether Hume has now been answered. Has the idealist insistence that we must presuppose an absolute system if we are to have knowledge of any fact, met the challenge of Hume? It would at first glance seem that it has. Kant had shown that for universals, such as cause and effect, to have any significance, we must presuppose them, the Hegelian idealism has shown that this presupposition must be all-inclusive. And it would seem that thus we are at the same time very close to the Christian position. Have we not presupposed the idea of God and shown that without this presupposition we could not know so much as a single fact?

It would seem, too, that in this way we have outgrown the weaknesses of Butler's *Analogy*. The basic weakness of the *Analogy* was its appeal to bare fact. The positive argument for the probable truth of Christianity, no less than the negative argument from ignorance was based upon the appeal to brute fact. But now brute facts seems to have been vanquished.[49] Accordingly, we can now show that the positive probability presupposes the actual existence of that which is supposed to be proved. Without the existence of God as a system[50] there would be no probable relation between any set of facts, none even between two facts. But with the presupposition of God's existence you have more than probability, you have absolute necessity.[51] The indispensable character of the presupposition of God's existence is the best possible proof of God's actual existence. If God does not exist, we know nothing. For Descartes' formula, "I

49. Van Til is agreeing here, but only formally, with the construal of the Absolute idealists. It is the case, as a matter of fact, that brute facts are meaningless, nonsense, and of no value, in that their meaning, sense, and value must be found in the "system" in which they exist. Once they are "vanquished," Butler's appeal to brute fact is vanquished as well. So, as Van Til argues in the rest of this paragraph, in transcendental fashion, the only real way to make sense of facts is to understand them in terms of the Christian system of thought.

50. The phrase "without the existence of God as a system," as the context here indicates, means "without the presupposition of God and his revelation to us"—that is, without the Christian system of truth.

51. There is "absolute necessity" in that, apart from that presupposition, facts and "systems" are themselves reduced to nothing.

think, therefore I am," we now substitute, "God thinks, therefore I am." The actuality of God's existence is the presupposition of the intelligibility of the concepts of possibility and probability.[52]

IDEALISM BOWS TO BRUTE FACT[53]

But now we come to the other side of the story. Above we noted that Plato attributed to the sense world an original, non-created existence. When he sought to bring the ideal world and the world of non-being into one whole he took for granted that each was to make an original contribution to the union. Each was to recognize its insufficiency without the other. In a similar fashion the Hegelian logicians hold that the principle of diversity is the original contribution of pure time as the principle of identity is the original contribution of the world of pure reason. The history of idealistic logic shows that the originality and ultimacy of the contribution made by the world of diversity has been increasingly stressed as time went on. We cannot trace this history in detail; a few observations must suffice.

In his book *Hegelianism and Personality*, A. S. Pringle-Pattison[54] contended that Bradley and Bosanquet had been unfair to the world of diversity. He was afraid that in their philosophy God had swallowed up man.[55] He contended for the *imperviousness of the human individual*. In a similar way James Ward[56] contended that

---

52. This statement is even more relevant today, given the upsurge in modal logic and modal semantics in philosophy. Possibility (and probability) has to have its roots in, and is always guided by, our understanding of God and his revelation.

53. Keep in mind in this section that Van Til is working through idealistic constructions of the Absolute and its relationship to diversity, or experience. In each case, either the Absolute trumps diversity, in which cases experience and facts are swallowed up by a rationalistic construct, or the Absolute is correlative to diversity, in which cases it cannot really be Absolute. Van Til's analysis of Absolute idealism was the subject of his doctoral dissertation, "God and the Absolute" (Princeton, 1927). His critique is designed to show why and how our presupposition of the ontological Trinity alone provides for an Absolute that is truly absolute, as well as for the reality and coherence of experience and diversity.

54. A. S. Pringle-Pattison (1856–1931) was a Scottish idealist philosopher, originally named Andrew Seth, but who became Pringle-Pattison because of a bequest. He saw both Absolute idealism (especially of the F. H. Bradley variety) and empiricism as deficient. The work to which Van Til refers was his Balfour Philosophical Lectures, given at the University of Edinburgh in 1887.

55. That is, Pringle-Pattison, over against Bradley and others, did not want to see the self as swallowed up in the Absolute system of idealism.

56. James Ward (1843–1925) was a contemporary of Pringle-Pattison and was an English philosopher and psychologist.

the ideal world should not presume to supply to us both principles, diversity as well as identity. In that case the world of sense would be reduced to a slave of the ideal world. "In whatever sense you say absolute in that sense you cannot say many."[57] For that reason he urges that we cannot begin with God in our reasoning. "We cannot begin from God and construct the universe."[58] He insists on complete correlativity between God and the world. "If we attempt to conceive of God apart from the world there is nothing to lead us on to the idea of creation."[59]

Yet it is not from strict correlativity that idealists wish to start. It is, says Ward, "from the reality of the world that we start."[60] If we conclude to the existence of God, such a God must live in accordance with the conditions of the universe. "As immanent in this world God must, it would seem, so far be conceived as subject to its fundamental conditions."[61] He says that much of the talk about the transcendence of God is based upon a violation of the categories of experience. "If the categories of substance and cause are only valid *within* experience, they cannot be applied to experience as a whole. Whatever implications experience may involve, it surely cannot involve that of transcending itself. Such miscalled transcendence, if it have any validity, must really be immanence at bottom."[62, 63]

This criticism of the absolute idealism of Bradley and Bosanquet made by Pringle-Pattison and Ward is typical of that made by others. The contention of these critics is that according to the logic of idealism itself, we are not entitled to a really transcendent God. When Bosanquet spoke much of God as the "Beyond," he was entitled by his own logic to mean no more than the "higher aspect" of the universe. In fact, man must begin with his own experience and count that as the ultimate starting point of his philosophy.

57. James Ward, *The Realm of Ends, or Pluralism and Theism* (Cambridge: University Press, 1920), 37.

58. James Ward, *Naturalism and Agnosticism*, 2 vols. (New York: Macmillan, 1899), 2:120.

59. Ward, *Realm of Ends*, 309.

60. Ibid., 245.

61. Ibid., 194.

62. Ward, *Naturalism and Agnosticism*, 2:129.

63. In other words, transcendence cannot be had by way of experiences or by way of experience as a whole. Thus, it must be rejected, and the notion of God is that of pure immanence. For this reason, Pringle-Pattison and Ward were thought to be panentheists—a view in which God is wholly immanent, interpenetrating all aspects of reality.

But this places idealism before a dilemma. The very purpose of introducing the concept of God was that in terms of God our experience might be explained. It was found that Kant's *a priori* which was the *a priori* contributed by the mind of mankind, was not comprehensive of all facts. For that reason idealists had turned to a divine mind which should be comprehensive of all facts. But if the universe is a non-created, ultimate reality, the plurality and the evil that characterize it are ultimate too. This means that there will be once more ideas of "mud and hair and filth" in the ideal world. The ideal world cannot be offered as the explanation of the sense world, since it is from the outset, by definition, conceived of as no more than a correlative of the sense world.[64]

G. Watts Cunningham,[65] in his book *The Idealistic Argument in Recent British and American Philosophy*, sets this dilemma before us in the course of his argument. The gist of his argument against idealism is, in effect, that it has not lived up to its own view of experience. To quote:

> The whole matter may perhaps be put briefly. If the Absolute is to grow logically out of what is "within our own experience," then it must be conceived so as to leave room for finite centers of experience standing in their integrity. If it is not so conceived, it is, so far, arbitrarily conceived and must remain for us unintelligible, not alone in the sense that it leaves much unexplained in detail, as any general view must, but in the further and objectionable sense that one (apparently basal) character of experience is left standing outside as a negative instance. On this point, then, the case of the personalist against the absolutist is essentially sound.[66]

64. Once the notion of a transcendent God is denied, all that is left is a "universe," or system of thought and being, which must interpret itself. The ideal world cannot be presupposed by the sense world, since the two are defined in terms of each other and are thus correlative.

65. Gustavus Watts Cunningham (1881–1968) served in various capacities and institutions, focusing his attention on Hegelian and idealistic philosophy. The book to which Van Til refers was published in 1933 and, along with other works of his, was critical of the idealism of Bradley and Bosanquet.

66. G. Watts Cunningham, *The Idealistic Argument in Recent British and American Philosophy* (New York: Century, 1933), 536.

The Absolute was "to grow logically out of what is 'within our own experience.'" This was very definitely, says Cunningham, the claim of Bradley and Bosanquet themselves. If the Absolute is to stand, "it must serve as a principle of explanation of experience— that is, it must grow out of experience as a necessary implication of it. So much the absolutist himself admits, at least verbally. But his procedure seems to belie his profession; for he is apparently willing to truncate experience in order to fit it into the conception of the Absolute. Herein lies the basis of justification for the accusation frequently advanced against him to the effect that he does not, as he professes, derive the conception of the Absolute from an analysis and interpretation of experience, but, rather, forcibly bends experience at those points where it does not readily accommodate itself to the nuances of the conception of the Absolute as more or less arbitrarily defined."[67]

Now we can readily understand, says Cunningham, how it was that the Absolutists fell into the temptation of believing in an Absolute into whom we as human beings are "somehow" to be transmuted. This Absolute must "somehow" explain what we cannot explain. Any "general view" of reality must allow for the "negative instance." There is a novelty to life that refuses to be fitted into our logical schematism. This fact we must all admit. But this fact presents us with a clear-cut alternative. We can be consistent with our own basic starting point, or we can be inconsistent. If we are consistent, the God or Absolute in whom we believe must be a "necessary impli-cation" of our experience. He must be intelligible to us as we must be intelligible to him. There must be a clear-cut logical or rational relation between him and us. On the other hand, if we are incon-sistent, we define our Absolute independently of our experience. In that case, he will have a non-rational relation to us; he will be "somehow" related to us and we "somehow" related to him. God is not then intelligible to us and we are not intelligible to him.

The whole point may be stated differently by saying that we must either make God surround that which is irrational to us, or we must make that which is irrational to us surround God as well as ourselves. God either includes the "negative instance" or the

67. Ibid., 534–35.

"negative instance" includes God. God either controls the devil, or the devil, in some measure at least, controls God. Reality is either such that there is novelty for us, but no novelty for God, or such that there is novelty for God as well as for us.

The Absolute idealists, says Cunningham, have chosen the inconsistent position. If they had been consistent with their own theory of judgment they should have thought of an Absolute who is intelligible to us. And an Absolute who is not intelligible to us must, since he is by definition absolute and we are by definition something less than absolute, "sublate" or "transmute" us. Such an Absolute explains us by explaining us away.

That the criticism thus offered against absolutism is to the point may be seen from the fact that the absolutist is himself quite willing to have his Absolute tested by the ordinary tests of logical procedure. The Absolute is offered very definitely as a help to the logical understanding of experience. This point needs to be emphasized "since some of the critics of absolutism have at times written as if they supposed the absolutist to assume that his conception of the Absolute were somehow logically privileged and not subject to the ordinary rules of logical procedure. It is clear that the absolutist assumes nothing of the sort, at least it should be clear to any one who has taken the trouble to become acquainted with his argument. He is perfectly willing to subject the conception to the ordinary tests of intelligibility; and, in the main, he is in agreement with the preceding statement of what those tests concretely are. What he contends is that his conception is required by any adequate analysis of experience, and he is willing to have his conception tried by such analysis."[68] But now the difficulty is that Bradley and Bosanquet will have to give up their thinking of the absolute as not intelligible to us.

As for Bosanquet, we may say that in his best moments he forgot his acosmic longings. Frequently he defines the Absolute as the "Whole." Paraphrasing his thought we may say that the Absolute "is all that is." Accordingly, "a basal characteristic of the Absolute is 'negativity.'"[69] When first we look at experience, contradiction seems to characterize it. But this contradiction is emended until it

68. Ibid., 523.
69. Ibid., 141.

becomes frictionless in the form of negativity. Quoting from Bosanquet, we observe that friction "is the same characteristic which has been described as the fact that experience is always beyond itself—the character, indeed, which we have described from the beginning as that of the universal, or, in other words, the tendency of every datum to transcend itself as a fragment and complete itself as a whole."[70] This contradiction turns into negativity and negativity "is really affirmation—affirmation of differences, with contradiction removed." "When we say, then, that negativity is a characteristic of the Absolute, what is to be understood is that, in the Absolute, contradiction has entirely disappeared, while the spirit of difference survives in its highest form. The Absolute negates conflict and confusion, it affirms system and significant oppositions, and, to put the matter paradoxically, its negation and its affirmation are one and the same."[71]

All this indicates that we as human beings are, according to Bosanquet, not to be entirely "transmuted" beyond recognition after all. The contradiction of our finitude will at least abide as a permanent "difference" within the Absolute. This much we know, since it follows from our theory of judgment. To this extent the Absolute is not unintelligible to us; we have trimmed him down to some extent to the needs of our intelligibility. And to this extent we are also pushing the remnants of the irrational beyond God as well as beyond ourselves.

There is encouragement for us in all of this, to think that we as human beings make a real contribution to the life of the Absolute. We have spoken of the Absolute as "Beyond." But by this thinking of the Absolute as beyond we have never meant what the Christian theology means when it thinks of God as self-sufficient. On the contrary, "The perfection of the Absolute, however, must not be conceived as excluding the process through which these finite systems are completed. For its own self-completion the Absolute presupposes the temporal order, the hazards and hardships of finite selfhood; apart from this order and the content it furnishes the Absolute would be nothing at all. Its very perfection is dependent upon the temporal instruments through which that perfection

---

70. Ibid., 142, quoting from B. Bosanquet, *The Principle of Individuality and Value* (London: Macmillan, 1912), 231.

71. Cunningham, *The Idealistic Argument*, 142.

is achieved; its negativity belongs as much to them as to itself."[72] Thus Bosanquet speaks of the Absolute as "simply the high-water mark of fluctuations in experience, of which, in general, we are daily and normally aware."[73]

It appears that the Absolute of Bosanquet is, when his argument is most consistent with itself, first demoted from a "Beyond" to the "Whole," and then from the "Whole" to the "Universal" within human experience. Reality for Bosanquet seems to be like a string of beads. God is the string, the universal, while temporal plurality furnishes the beads. Without either, you do not have a string of beads.[74]

In his book *The Meeting of Extremes in Contemporary Philosophy*, Bosanquet divides philosophies into two classes. On the one hand, there is the class of the "progressists." They demand that there shall be "absolute and ultimate progression in the real." On the other hand there is the class which we may call the "perfectionists." For them the temporal series is only "an adumbration" of a "deeper totality which in its perfection knows no change." The former wish to put "the Absolute in time," while the latter wish to put "time in the Absolute."[75] Now the question is, whether these "extremes" are really as far apart as Bosanquet would have them appear.

Cunningham thinks they are not. If the Absolute must really depend for its content on the time-series, as Bosanquet says that it must, it follows that wholly new content may appear for the Absolute.[76] Thus the "negative instance" is really beyond God, as well as beyond man. Reality answers to the demand of our logical theory that the analytic and the synthetic aspects of judgment must be equally basic.[77] We are consistent with our basic theory of judg-

---

72. Ibid., 142–43.

73. Ibid., 140.

74. Note the correlativity of the Absolute with experience. Van Til's argument here, and above, is that Absolute idealism has not had a coherent view of its most basic concept.

75. Cunningham, *The Idealistic Argument*, 416.

76. As in theology, so also in philosophy, if the Absolute is thought to depend on time, then it cannot "absorb" time such that its progress is controlled. The "negative instance," that is, that which the Absolute cannot absorb or integrate, is beyond both God and man because both God and man are wholly time-conditioned.

77. See Rupert Clendon Lodge, "Bosanquet and the Future of Logic," *Philosophical Review* 32 (1923): 592–93.

ment and give up the notion that God is not himself surrounded by the irrational.

As a compromise between the alternative "time in the Absolute" or "the Absolute in time," Cunningham suggests a third possibility, namely, "the Absolute *through* time," and adds: "If the conciliatory position here suggested is accepted, of course the non-temporal character of the Absolute is forthwith surrendered, and a qualification of its character of all-inclusiveness is called for."[78] This, Cunningham holds, would really be in accord with the idealistic theory of judgment and with the scientific method. On the one hand, we must *posit a unity in experience* or we could ask no question about it. On the other hand, there must be the *wholly new,* or our questions would be answered in advance of the asking. Bradley was right in speaking of this twofold nature of reality as being ultimately mysterious. "This two-fold nature of Reality, by which it slides away from itself into our distinction, so as there to become a predicate—while all the time it retains in itself, as an ultimate subject, every duality which we loosen from and relate to it—is, if you please, inexplicable."[79] But Bradley and Bosanquet did not always bring out clearly that God and man together form reality, which reality has a novelty as well as a permanent aspect. They sometimes made it appear that the Absolute was wholly beyond time, and therefore beyond the difficulties that meet those who are in some sense subject to the limitations of time. But now we see clearly that God or the Absolute himself is faced with novelty; he has now no advantages over us.

The upshot of this brief examination of the idealist position is, that it has not accomplished what it set out to do. *Bare fact still stares us in the face.*[80] Hume has not been answered. Bare possibility and probability are still thought of as the most ultimate concepts of philosophy. The future must be to us the womb of chance out of which anything may come; rationality itself is nothing but a correlative to the irrational. And no Christian apologetic can be based upon the destruction of rationality itself.

---

78. Cunningham, *The Idealistic Argument*, 422.
79. Bradley, *Principles of Logic*, 2:629.
80. If the Absolute is "faced with novelty," then "bare fact still stares us in the face" because any fact, as novel, is what it is independent of the Absolute; it is wholly new and thus completely uninterpreted. It is a brute fact.

JAMES ORR'S APOLOGETICS[81]

It is this last point, we most humbly believe, that Orr and others who have based their hopes for a Christian apologetic upon the idealist argument have not fully recognized. There is throughout Orr's book, *The Christian View of God and the World*, the usual appeal to brute fact. We shall not take the time to show this in detail. A few remarks may suffice.

In the second chapter of his book Orr reasons, e.g., from the course of history. He traces a downward movement away from Christ which finally leads into pessimism and an upward movement toward theism. He speaks of the "logic of history" asserting itself. But can there be any logic in history unless there be logic, back of history? In other words, we cannot by the logic of history, as an entity conceived of as intelligible in itself to both Christians and non-Christians before they begin their argument, prove the existence of logic back of history. The logic of history conceived by itself, and as intelligible to the believer and non-believer alike, is nothing but a universal that is based upon brute facts. It, therefore, has no greater validity than the principle of analogy employed by Butler, which principle could not stand the criticism of Hume.

The third chapter of Orr's book is perhaps the most important for our present interest. The notes on the appendix to the chapter are informative. They show that Orr has given a valuable criticism of T. H. Green's argument for the existence of God. That is, he is not unaware of the dangerous tendency in idealism. He tells us that idealism tends either to make all things equal with God or to reduce God to a mere intellectual principle. This, in effect, is the criticism of idealism that we have made in our foregoing discussion. Then Orr goes on to agree with the criticism of absolute idealism made by Pringle-Pattison as spoken of above. We should therefore expect that Orr would go on from there to a careful distinction between Christianity and idealism in their modes of reasoning. Orr is not unmindful of the shortcomings of many arguments for the existence of God. He says we should not forget the saying of

---

81. It is perhaps best to see Orr as a kind of transitional figure from standard theistic proofs to a more transcendental approach to apologetics. As Van Til states above, there are areas of agreement between him and Orr; as we will see, there remain areas of compromise in Orr as well.

Jacobi that a God capable of proof would be no God at all.[82] Such a God would have something higher than himself. His own existence would have to be proved. Thus we land in an infinite regression. Orr seems to see, therefore, that the common or popular use of the theistic proofs, which starts from an already known universe to God, is invalid. But he says Jacobi's statement does not apply to a higher mode of reasoning: "It does not apply to that higher kind of proof which may be said to consist in the mind being guided back to the clear recognition of its own ultimate presuppositions. Proof in Theism certainly does not consist in deducing God's existence as a lower from a higher; but rather in showing that God's existence is itself the last postulate of reason—the ultimate basis on which all other knowledge, all other belief rests."[83]

But does Orr live up to this high standard? We believe that he does not. At various points he after all reasons from brute fact. This appears in this chapter as well as throughout the book most strikingly in his constant effort to find a basis of common agreement between those who confessedly reason on the basis of brute fact and those who hold to Christianity.

As an illustration of this seeking similarities between the Christian and the non-Christian view we may mention the fact that Orr thinks we as Christians can be in agreement with Herbert Spencer[84] on the question of mystery. He identifies the church's doctrine of the incomprehensibility of God with Spencer's doctrine of the unknowable, in the respect that both admit mystery.[85] But how can this be allowed from a Christian point of view? For the Christian, God is back of all mystery; for Spencer mystery surrounds God as well as man. No greater contrast is conceivable. For Spencer the knowledge that we human beings have is based ultimately upon observation of brute facts. God is not brought into the picture as the presupposition of the possibility of man's knowledge of facts. On the other hand, Orr argues, and argues rightly, that the very

---

82. Friedrich Heinrich Jacobi (1743–1819) was a critic of idealism, rationalism, and Hume. This quote comes from *Über die Lehre des Spinoza in Briefen an den Herrn Moses Mendelssohn* ("on the system of Spinoza in letters to Moses Mendelssohn"), published in 1789.

83. James Orr, *The Christian View of God and the World* (New York: Anson D. F. Randolph, 1893), 114.

84. Herbert Spencer (1820–1903) was a social Darwinist and a utilitarian. He is typically categorized as a political philosopher and sociologist.

85. Orr, *The Christian View of God and the World*, 103.

possibility of human knowledge presupposes God. But he neutralizes the force of this argument when he allows that a man who forgets all about such a presupposition has none the less the same knowledge about facts as a man who maintains it. He thus virtually allows that facts can after all be known truly without the presupposition of God.

Accordingly, Orr often speaks as though reason and the facts of nature as interpreted by reason present to us a known phenomenal realm independent of God. Before proceeding to a discussion of the theistic proofs Orr says: "The doctrine of God's existence must be shown to be in accord with reason, and to be in harmony with and corroborated by the facts of science and of the religious history of mankind."[86, 87]

Finally, at the conclusion of the chapter, Orr expresses a similar sentiment when he says: "It is not one line of evidence only which establishes the theistic position, but the concurrent force of many, starting from different and independent, standpoints. And the voice of reason is confirmed by the soul's direct experiences in religion. At the very least these considerations show—even if the force of demonstration is denied them—that the Christian view of God is not unreasonable: that it is in accordance with the highest suggestions of reason applied to the facts of existence; that there is no bar in rational thought or in science to its full acceptance. And this is all that at present we need ask."[88]

All this indicates that Orr is halting between two opinions. He has done good service in showing that brute fact is unintelligible, that we need to have God as the presupposition of our knowledge of the facts. On the other hand, he seeks to prove the existence of God from the facts as brute facts without the existence of God. Orr has not distinguished clearly between idealistic thought and Christian thought on this matter. It is only if we take seriously the argument as Orr himself has suggested it, only if we take the "Author of nature" or the presupposition of God seriously, that we can get away from brute facts. Then only can we talk about "facts" at all.

---

86. Ibid., 105.

87. This statement, it should be clear, is in direct opposition to other statements that Orr makes and to the position for which Van Til is arguing throughout.

88. Orr, *The Christian View of God and the World*, 133.

CHAPTER 4

CHRISTIANITY AND ITS FACTUAL DEFENSE

From the discussion in the preceding chapters we conclude that if we seek to defend the Christian religion by an "appeal to the facts of experience" in accord with the current scientific method, we shall have to adulterate Christianity beyond recognition. The Christianity defended by Bishop Butler was not a full-fledged Christianity. It was a Christianity neatly trimmed down to the needs of a method that was based upon non-Christian assumptions. And what was true of Butler is largely true of English-American evidences and apologetics in general.

This situation places us before a dilemma. It seems that if we wish to be "scientific" in our methodology we cannot defend a full Christianity, while if we wish to defend a full-fledged Christianity we cannot be "scientific." If this dilemma be a true dilemma we cannot but make the choice for a full-fledged Christianity.

If at this point our opponents smile and intimate that Christianity is, therefore, according to our own notion of it, simply a matter of irrational choice, we need not worry too greatly. For if the dilemma mentioned above be a true dilemma, it follows that our opponents as well as ourselves have chosen a position. We have chosen to follow full-fledged Christianity at all costs, while they have chosen to follow the "scientific method" at all costs.

Yet there is even so a basic difference between the two choices that are made. The choice we have made, we claim, is based upon the fact that we have first been chosen of God, while the choice our opponents have made, they claim, is made entirely by themselves.[1]

Still further we have become aware of the fact that we are chosen of God only after accepting the truth of Christianity from the Bible. Thus the Bible appears at the outset to us as the absolute authority by which we seek to interpret life.

From the point of view of our opponents, our position is by this time hopeless. How can there be any rational arguments with those who have substituted the position of authority for that of reason? So, for instance, Morris Cohen and Ernest Nagel, in their book, *An Introduction to Logic and Scientific Method*, divide the various methods of interpreting life as follows: First there is the method of tenacity. That means that we simply hold on to our beliefs that we have been taught in our childhood, because we do not have the mental energy to look into new hypotheses. Then there is the method of authority. Of course, they say, there is a legitimate appeal to authority. When we wish to know what diet or exercise will relieve certain distressing physical symptoms we ask the doctor. But this authority is only relatively final. We always reserve the right to modify the findings of the expert. But there is, he says, a second and objectionable kind of authority. Such an authority "invests some sources with infallibility and finality and invokes some external force to give sanction to their decisions."[2] He adds: "The aim of this method, unanimity and stability of belief, cannot be achieved so long as authorities differ. Buddhists do not accept the authorities of the Christians, just as the latter reject the authority of Mahomet and the Koran."[3] Thirdly, there is the method of intuition. But what people once believed on intuition, as they thought, has since been proved to be mistaken in many cases. There remains then the method of science of reflective inquiry. It alone is free from caprice and willfulness. The other methods, so far from leading us to certainty, lead us into an irrational interpretation of

---

1. This point, mentioned only in passing here, is of ultimate significance. The fact of the matter is that those who choose Christianity do so because God has first chosen them. Thus, the Christian's choice is preceded by God's and is not the Christian's alone or his first. In this way, again, Van Til's position presupposes the truths of Reformed theology.

2. Morris R. Cohen and Ernest Nagel, *An Introduction to Logic and Scientific Method* (New York: Harcourt, Brace and Company, 1934), 194.

3. Ibid.

life. On the other hand, the method of reflective inquiry, "which takes advantage of the objective connections in the world around us, should be found reasonable not because of its appeal to the idiosyncrasies of a selected few individuals, but because it can be tested repeatedly and by all men."[4]

This modern statement of the requirements of scientific methodology, so far from turning us back, can only establish us in our determination not to hide anything of our belief that Christianity is, for better or for worse, a religion of authority. In fact, it alone is a religion of authority. The other "religions of authority" teach a relative authority, an authority that is, after all, subject to the final judgment of man. We cannot develop this point here.[5] Suffice to intimate that we do not wish to hide the fact that in the last analysis we make every thought captive to the obedience of the revelation of God as it has come to us in the Scriptures of the Old and New Testaments.

It should be interjected at this point that when we say that we do not hide the fact that we submit to absolute authority, this does not imply that we must always and in every instance bring in the discussion of authority at the outset of every argument with those we seek to win for Christianity. This may frequently be omitted, if only we ourselves do not fall into the temptation of thinking that we can stand on neutral ground with those who hold to a non-Christian position.

What it implies, to say that Christianity is the religion of authority, may be learned if we now turn to a consideration of the teaching of Scripture on some of the points at issue between Christians and non-Christians.

THEISM

Fundamental to all the differences between Christians and non-Christians is the conception of God that both parties entertain.[6] If we search the Scriptures to see what sort of God it holds

---

4. Ibid., 195.

5. For a development of this point with respect to Islam, see K. Scott Oliphint, *Covenantal Apologetics: Principles and Practice in Defense of Our Faith* (Wheaton, IL: Crossway, 2013), chap. 7.

6. This point is central, and it shows again the dependence of Van Til's approach on Reformed theology. Thus, for example, when Paul confronts the "theists" at Athens, he begins with an argument on God's character and identity (see Acts 17:22–31).

before us, it does not take long to see that as the Bible itself comes to us with authority, so the God that speaks from it is a sovereign God. The God of the Bible existed as the self-sufficient Being before the world was. We are told that he exists as the Triune God. That is, there are three persons in the ontological Trinity, which are equally ultimate in the Godhead. God needed nothing beside himself in order to be conscious of himself. His affirmation of himself was internally complete.

Accordingly, when God did freely create something beside himself, this something, the universe, could never become a correlative to himself.[7] Least of all could man, who was one of the creatures of God, develop principles of interpretation or a method of reflective inquiry that could interpret life correctly without the presupposition of God. Every fact and every law in the created universe is brought into existence by God's creation. Every fact and every law in the created universe continues to exist by virtue of the providence of God. Every fact and every law in the created universe accomplishes what it does accomplish by virtue of the plan or purpose of God. God foreordains whatsoever comes to pass, through his Son Jesus Christ.

The full implication of these matters will appear when we contrast this position with the current conception of the scientific method. For the moment we wish to state the Christian principles of interpretation broadly. If we take the Scripture doctrines of God, of creation, of providence, and of the plan of God, we observe that we have a Christian philosophy of fact and a Christian methodology that is squarely opposed to the current philosophy of fact and the current scientific methodology. Scripture teaches that every fact in the universe exists and operates by virtue of the plan of God. There are *no brute facts* for God. As to his own being, fact and interpretation are co-extensive.[8] There are no hidden unexplored possibilities in God. And as to the universe, God's interpretation

---

7. That is, as Paul makes clear at Athens (Acts 17:24–25), the fact that God really relates to creation does not imply that he needs creation in order to be who he is.

8. That is, God's creation of every fact includes his interpretation of those facts. God exhaustively knows all that he creates, but what he creates is not identical with that knowledge; rather, it presupposes it. Creation, then, is an *interpretation* of the original knowledge that God has. Every fact *speaks* of his existence (Ps. 19:1–2).

logically precedes the denotation and the connotation of all facts of which it consists.

In contrast to this, the current philosophy of fact and of method takes for granted the ultimacy of brute facts. This point was involved even in the idealist conception of logic as we have traced it in the previous chapter. If any God is discovered by the current scientific method, it is invariably a God who, as the internally complete self-conscious being, is set over against a universe in which there are irrational facts, and the two are then made correlative to one another. It is taken for granted by the current scientific method that there is a realm that is truly known to man, even though God be not taken into the picture. Or even if it be admitted that we perhaps need a God for the interpretation of life, we need him only as a help to ourselves. We might compare this point of view to the attitude taken by science when a new planet appears upon the horizon. When a new planet is discovered, scientists can explain the movement of the heavenly bodies *somewhat better* than they could before. This new planet is only one force among many that influence the behavior of the heavenly bodies. And the new planet not only influences other planets, but is itself influenced in turn by the other planets which are on a par with itself as to their originality of existence.

CHRISTIANITY

Before developing these matters further, we may observe that the second aspect of biblical teaching concerns the question of sin and redemption. Here again it is the sovereign God who meets us. When man fell into sin, God, the triune God, graciously provided redemption for his people. He was sovereign in that he needed not to have given redemption to any, and he is sovereign in that he does not give it to all. This work of redemption on the part of God reveals itself in this world in supernatural form. Miracle is at the heart of Christianity. The incarnation of the second person of the Trinity, the death and the resurrection of Jesus, are but the central cycle of the larger circle of redemptive works that have proceeded from it.

As to the purpose of redemption, it was both restorative and supplementive. The miracle of redemption graciously dropped into the center of history by God, the creator of history, spreads its influence till it reaches the very circumference of the universe. There is no fact not affected for good or for evil by the redemptive work of Christ. And this includes the acceptance or non-acceptance of redemption. "He that is not for me is against me."

The consequence of this position is that here too we meet with the same basic alternative between Christian and non-Christian methodology. As Christians we hold it to be impossible to interpret any fact without a basic falsification unless it be regarded in its relation to God the Creator and to Christ the Redeemer.[9] On the other hand, the current methodology takes for granted that at best redemption is one among several independent facts that must be taken into consideration when we interpret facts. *For us there can be no true interpretation of facts without miracle*; for our opponents, miracle is at best a somewhat unruly fact.

Thus Christian theism stands before us as a unit.[10] It offers to men the conception of God the Creator and Redeemer as the ultimate category of interpretation of every fact of the world. It claims that no fact is intelligible unless seen in relation to central creating-redeeming activity of God as Creator and Redeemer.

That this implies a reversal of the method employed by Butler and the others whom we have discussed in the previous chapters is apparent. We do not offer Christianity to men apologetically, admitting that their interpretation of life is right as far as it goes. In particular, we do not accept the "appeal to facts" as a common meeting place between believers and unbelievers.[11] Christianity does not thus need to take shelter under the roof of "known facts." It rather offers itself as a roof to facts if they would be known. Christianity does not need to take shelter under the roof of a scientific method independent of itself. It rather offers itself as a roof to methods that would be scientific.

---

9. *True* knowledge of any fact, therefore, must include its relation to God as Creator, and to Christ, whose work is universal in its scope.

10. Since Christian theism is a unit, it is illegitimate to seek to prove a generic theism to which could be added the truths of Christianity. Christianity is not supplementary to theism but constitutive of it.

11. In this way, apologetics is not *direct*, in that it seeks common facts to which we can appeal, but *indirect*, in that it seeks to show those very facts to be ultimately unintelligible without presupposing the truth of Christian theism.

THE SCIENTIFIC IDEAL

We turn now to a discussion of the general difference between a truly Christian and the current scientific method by contrasting them on certain definite points. The first point to note is that of the scientific ideal. By the scientific ideal we mean the goal which science has set for itself. This goal of science is that of *complete comprehension*. Science, as we are told, must work with this ideal before it. We quote the words of Cohen on this point: "A completed rational system having nothing outside of it nor any possible alternative to it, is both presupposed and beyond the actual attainment of any one moment. It coincides in part with the Bradleyan Absolute, but it is an ideal limit rather than an actual experience. Unrealized possibilities are within it precisely to the extent that it contains endless time."[12, 13]

This statement of Cohen's presents fairly well the common notion of the scientific ideal. If we seek to evaluate this ideal from the Christian point of view, we note that it wipes out the basic distinction between the Creator and the creature. In this it is based upon the suppositions of all non-Christian philosophy. Speaking more particularly, there are two objections to this scientific ideal. As it does not make a difference between God and man, it does not allow that God has "already reached" that scientific ideal. Or rather, it does not allow that all facts exist by virtue of their previous interpretation by God. In the second place, the scientific ideal does not realize that it is illegitimate for a creature to set before itself the notion of comprehending all existence. To do so is to set before itself the being of God as penetrable to the mind of man, inasmuch as he is part of "existence." This would be to deny the incomprehensibility of God. For man to set before himself the ideal of absolute knowledge is to set God aside as the one who has created the universe and its laws. It would be to absolutize the law of non-contradiction and set it above God.

---

12. Morris R. Cohen, *Reason and Nature: An Essay on the Meaning of Scientific Method* (New York: Harcourt, Brace, and Company, 1931), 158.

13. Note how Van Til incorporates the "scientific ideal" via Cohen with the Absolute idealism critiqued above. The "ideal" of science must be the possible comprehension of all facts; otherwise, there would be facts fundamentally incomprehensible and thus irrational. But if irrationality is admitted, then science cannot proceed in its supposition of rational inquiry.

It may be profitable to *develop* this criticism of the absolute ideal of science more fully by indicating what is meant by the fact that it is in modern times called a limiting concept. The absolute ideal is said to be a limit toward which man must strive. This notion of a limiting concept has had its first modern expression in the philosophy of Immanuel Kant. Kant used this idea of a limiting, or regulative, concept in contrast to the notion of a constitutive concept. He said that we cannot actually by the employment of the categories of the understanding prove the existence of God. Yet we cannot do without the notion of God entirely. We need the notion of God as a correlative to the phenomenal universe. Human thought is itself constitutive. For that reason God's thought cannot be constitutive. Yet human thought is not comprehensive. For that reason it needs the notion of God as an ideal, as a limit toward which man must strive.[14]

It is difficult to think of a greater contrast than that between this Kantian limiting concept and the notion of God as the constitutive creator and interpreter of the facts of the universe. The former thinks of man as self-determinative and God-determinative. The latter interprets reality in terms of God. The former interprets reality in terms of man.

The idea of the modern limiting concept involves the notion of pure contingency.[15] The conception of brute fact underlies this ideal. There may always be new facts that may show our interpretations of previously "known" facts to have been mistaken. This fact that science does not look for objective certainty is the counterpart of the fact that it strives for complete comprehension. In the quotation given above, Cohen spoke of "unrealized possibilities" within the very Absolute that he says we need as an ideal. It is on account of these "unrealized possibilities" that the scientific ideal is said to be a limiting concept. The similarity between this position and that of the idealist logicians appears clearly if we recall that idealists are insistent on the need of an

---

14. For a discussion of Van Til's Christian application of the notion of a "limiting concept," see the introduction in Van Til, *Common Grace and the Gospel*, ed. K. Scott Oliphint (Phillipsburg, NJ: P&R Publishing, 2015).

15. That is, in the modern notion of a limiting concept, God, or the noumenal, is in no way constitutive of the facts. The facts are simply "there," to be interpreted by man. Thus, they are pure contingencies and wholly uninterpreted unless and until interpreted by man.

absolute but are equally insistent on the need of novelty for the absolute.

Cohen himself expresses the idea that science presupposes contingency. By contingency he does not mean merely contingency for us as human beings. He means contingency for God as well as for man. "To hold seriously to the popular dictum that everything is connected with everything else would make the scientific search for determinate connection meaningless."[16] Again he adds: "This uneliminable character of contingency is but the logical expression of the metaphysical fact of individuality. There is no universe without a plurality of elements, of atoms, of moments of time, etc. It is a blind hostility to pluralism, a preference for a lazy monism wherein all distinctions and differences are swallowed up, that leads to blatant panlogism from which all contingency is banished.[17] But the latter attempt defeats itself. In the end the universe of existence has the particular character which it has and not some other; and contingency is not removed by being funded in the conception of the whole universe or made into the essential characteristic of reason itself."[18]

It is apparent from this passage that the Christian notion of God as the ultimate interpretative category of experience is thus set aside. As Christians we hold that there would be no explanation of any fact unless all facts were already interpreted by God. Cohen would call this a blind panlogism, that has denied one aspect of reality, namely, its contingency, and has therefore made interpretation of fact impossible.[19]

INDETERMINATENESS

The same point may be expressed again by saying that for us as Christians the triune God of Scripture is the *completely self-determinate experience* on which we depend for the determinate character of our

---

16. Cohen, *Reason and Nature*, 151.

17. Panlogism is a Hegelian doctrine, summarizing Hegel's notion that "the real is the rational and the rational is the real." Reality is thought to be a rational system of logical categories.

18. Cohen, *Reason and Nature*, 152.

19. The non-Christian view has no way to think about *both* the reality of God's ordaining whatsoever comes to pass *and* the reality of contingency. Thus, in any non-Christian system, instead of contingency being defined in terms of God's all-controlling sovereignty, it is always thought to be ultimate and to be the negation of any kind of determining power.

experience. On the other hand, for Cohen God is indeterminate in order that our experience may be determinate. As Christians we think of God as having a complete plan for the universe. All things happen in relation to that plan. There is indeterminacy *for us*, but there is no indeterminacy for God. In contrast with this, Cohen expresses himself in these words:

> The total universe is by definition never actually complete in any moment of time and the principle of causality means that something occupying a given position in time and space can be determined only by something else also occupying a definite position in space and enduring over a definite time-interval. This is not to deny the determinateness of the physical universe in its distributive sense, i.e. in the sense that each thing in it is determinate. But the absolute collective whole is—at least from the point of view of scientific method—undetermined by anything outside of it; nor can the absolutely total universe be said to have any definite character such that from it we can infer that some particular entity has one rather than another determinate trait. Attempts to characterize the universe as a whole, as one (not many), continuous (not discontinuous), conscious or purposive, and the like, all involve a stretching of the ordinary use of words to include their opposites, and from this only confusion rather than determination can result.
>
> We may put this in a different form by saying that scientific determinism is concerned with the definite character of things rather than with their brute existence. Rational scientific investigation is not concerned with the mystery of creation whereby existence may have come into being out of the void.[20]

A little later, Cohen adds,

> A metaphysic of scientific method is, then, concerned with the nature of a world in which the result of scientific investigation is always subject to contingency and error, but also to the possibility of self-correction according to an invariable ideal.[21]

20. Cohen, *Reason and Nature*, 152–53.
21. Ibid., 155.

From this interpretation of the metaphysics of the scientific method by Cohen, it appears again what is meant by saying that the scientific ideal is a limiting concept, and also what is meant by saying that all knowledge is only probable knowledge. For Christianity, God's thought is constitutive. By God's thoughts the facts of the universe come into existence. We are, in contrast to Cohen, deeply concerned about the origin of facts. There is no contingency for God, and therefore no probability for God. There is contingency for us and therefore probability for us. But the probable character of our knowledge presupposes the certainty and comprehensiveness of God's knowledge. We may be uncertain as to whether a particular statement of physical law be correct. But this simply indicates that the knowledge of human beings can never be comprehensive. It never implies a basic scepticism. Then too there are certain facts of which we have absolutely certain, even though not comprehensive, interpretations. We are certain of God's existence. We are certain that the universe was created by God. We are certain that man fell into sin by eating of the fruit of the forbidden tree. We are certain that Christ died and rose again and sits at the right hand of the Father, and that He will come again to judge the quick and the dead. Our uncertainty about such matters is not based on an ultimate irrationalism. In this, exactly, is it distinguished from the uncertainty of modern scientific methodology. Scientific methodology as we know it in the literature of the day and as it has been developed out of the history of philosophy and science, presupposes an ultimate Chance back of the universe. It could not do otherwise, inasmuch as it thinks that it deals with brute or uninterpreted facts. "Science" thinks it deals with a stream of time out of which the absolutely novel proceeds constantly. "Eternity may thus also be viewed," says Cohen, "as the limit or ordering principle of a series of expanding vistas."[22] For that reason God can never be thought of as the final or ultimate cause of anything. Cohen says that since reality is in the last analysis indeterminate at the edges, it has no meaning to say that reality as a whole or anything beyond reality as a whole is the cause of any particular thing in this universe. He holds that there may be rational connections between various phenomena in the

22. Ibid., 156.

universe, but that it is unintelligible to speak of God as creating or being the cause of anything in this world.

BARE POSSIBILITY

The current scientific method presupposes the notion of bare possibility.[23] Christianity, on the other hand, presupposes the absolute actuality of God. This difference implies a life and death struggle. The question is simply upon what presupposition does life have significance, or, otherwise stated, upon which presupposition is intelligent predication possible? On which presupposition can there be any knowledge of facts? Only by thus challenging the modern "scientific method" can Christianity be defended. This ought to be plain from the fact just mentioned, that according to the scientific method God can in no sense be said to be the cause of the world or of any specific thing in the world. It is fatal to try to prove the existence of God by the "scientific method" and by the "appeal to facts" if, as Cohen asserts, the scientific method itself is based upon a presupposition which excludes God. That the "scientific method" is not neutral ought to be apparent from what Cohen says about it. Scientific method does, to be sure, begin with the facts, but it begins with *brute facts*.[24] It insists that facts are and must remain brute facts for God and man alike.

If there should remain any doubt that the scientific method as commonly understood is exclusive of Christianity, we may continue our discussion of it a bit further.

THE NON-EXISTENCE OF ANY FACT

What we have said thus far about the scientific method as described by Cohen, would seem to indicate at first blush that, according to it, any sort of fact might be thought of as existing. This is frequently expressed by saying that we can intelligently think of

23. That is to say, in scientific method, based on chance, anything is possible. Thus, knowledge of facts can be only approximate, not certain, since contingency is embedded in any fact.

24. Thus, the "facts" that science includes require a notion of brute facts and thus are not understood in the same way as the Christian would understand them. They cannot, therefore, be "common ground."

the non-existence of any fact. In the *Dialogues on Natural Religion* by Hume, even Cleanthes, the defender of Christianity, took this to be the foundation of all sound reasoning. If this be applied to God as well as to man, it signifies that God is not a necessary being. Now it is perfectly true that the existence of a necessary being cannot be proved if one, with Cleanthes, begins with brute fact. But this exactly shows the fatal character of beginning with brute facts. God as the absolutely necessary self-identifying being must be presupposed as the possibility of intelligent predication of "contingent facts." The "scientific method" begins by assuming that all facts, God as well as other facts, are contingent facts.

THE THEORETICAL RELEVANCY OF ANY HYPOTHESIS

For the consistent application of the "scientific method" it is necessary to hold that any sort of fact can exist. Corresponding to this claim that any sort of fact may be held to exist, is the notion that theoretically any sort of hypothesis is, to begin with, legitimate and relevant. It is not supposed that *practically* any hypotheses may legitimately be offered. It is not claimed that in practice any theory is as good as any other. It is taken for granted that we may discover a certain tendency in nature. In practice we must limit ourselves in the offering of such hypotheses as are consistent with that tendency. Nevertheless it remains true that, to begin with, any hypothesis is virtually asserted to be as relevant as any other.

Over against this contention that theoretically any hypothesis is as relevant as any other, we place the Christian position which says that no hypotheses which exclude the necessary self-existence of the triune God of Scripture can be relevant to any group of facts. There is only one absolutely true explanation of every fact and of every group of facts in the universe. God has this absolutely true explanation of every fact. Accordingly, the various hypotheses that are to be relevant to the explanation of phenomena must be consistent with this fundamental presupposition. *God's self-existence is the presupposition of the relevancy of any hypothesis.* If one should seek to explain the claim of the disciples of Jesus that their Master's body was raised from the tomb by offering the hypothesis of hallucination, we reply that the hypothesis is irrelevant. Our further study of the factual evidence in the matter is no more than a corroboration of our assertion of the irrelevancy of such an hypothesis. If one offers the hypothesis of biological evolution as the explanation of man's appearance on the earth, we reply that the hypothesis is irrelevant. Our further study of the factual material is no more than a corroboration of our assertion of the irrelevancy of this hypothesis.[25]

THE TEST OF RELEVANCY

To allow the theoretical relevancy of any sort of hypothesis is to imply that the relevancy of hypotheses must be tested by an *appeal to brute facts*. That Cohen thinks of the appeal to brute facts as the way in which the relevancy of hypotheses must be determined, may be learned from the following words:

In thus emphasizing the rôle of reason in scientific method we do not minimize the appeal to experiment and observation, but make the latter more significant. The appeal to experience is thus involved throughout: first as the matrix in which inquiry arises (as that which suggests questions), and then as that on which all theories must be tested. We start always with general assumptions and with contingent or empirical data. By no amount of reasoning can we altogether eliminate all contingency from our world. Moreover, pure speculation alone will not enable us to get a determinate picture of the existing world. We must eliminate some of the conflicting possibilities, and this can be brought about only by experiment and observation. The fact that two or more hypotheses are logically possible means that none of them involves self-contradiction. They cannot therefore be eliminated by logic or pure mathematics alone. Experiment or observation of crucial cases is needed for such elimination. When an hypothesis is first suggested we try to see whether it will explain the known facts. But we generally need new situa-

---

25. In other words, we must begin our study and evaluation of any and all facts with the truth of Christian theism. When we begin with that truth, certain hypotheses, such as the theory of biological evolution, are automatically ruled out as illegitimate.

tions to determine whether its explanatory power is superior to that of other hypotheses.[26]

It is important to see the exact point at issue here. The Christian position is certainly not opposed to experimentation and observation. As Christians we may make various hypotheses in explanation of certain phenomena. But these various hypotheses will always be in accord with the presupposition of God as the ultimate explanation of all things. Our hypotheses will always be *subordinate* to the notion of God as the complete interpreter of all facts, and if we make our hypotheses about facts subordinate to this God, it follows that there are no brute facts to which we can appeal in corroboration of our hypotheses. *We appeal to facts, but never to brute facts.* We appeal to *God-interpreted* facts.[27] This is simply another way of saying that we try to discover whether our hypothesis is *really* in accord with God's interpretation of facts. The ultimate test for the relevancy of our hypotheses is therefore their correspondence with God's interpretation of facts. *True human interpretation is implication into God's interpretation.*[28]

In contrast to this, the ordinary scientific method seeks to determine the relevancy of hypotheses by an appeal to brute facts. An ultimate chance is assumed as the matrix of facts. Then the chance collocation of facts is taken as the rational tendency among these brute facts. And the relevancy of an hypothesis is determined by its correspondence to this "rational tendency" in things. Thus the circle is complete.[29] We start with brute fact and we end with brute fact. We presuppose chance as God, and therefore conclude that the God of Christianity *cannot* exist.

CHALLENGING THE "SCIENTIFIC METHOD"

It is impossible to overemphasize the importance for Christians of seeing the difference between their position and the current

26. Cohen, *Reason and Nature*, 82.
27. The contrary to brute fact is not interpreted fact, as is sometimes thought, but *God-*interpreted fact, i.e., created fact.
28. This is why Van Til refers to his method, at times, as the method of implication.
29. Non-Christian methodologies conclude where they begin, i.e., with brute fact.

scientific method on the three points that we have considered. A Christian cannot allow the legitimacy of the ideal of complete comprehension. That this ideal is made, a limiting rather than a constitutive concept does not improve matters, but, if possible, makes them worse. It clearly implies that God as creative and constitutive of reality and of true human interpretation is, from the outset, excluded. It implies the elevation of chance to the place of God. Secondly, Christians cannot consistently allow the theoretical relevancy of every sort of hypothesis. This too implies an elevation of chance to the place of God. In the third place, Christians cannot allow the appeal to brute facts as a test of the relevancy of hypotheses. Once more this implies the elevation of chance to the position of God.

There is, accordingly, but one thing that Christians can do. They must challenge the legitimacy of the scientific methodology as based upon an assumed metaphysic of chance.[30] The traditional method of the defense of Christianity has not done this. It has toyed with the idea of neutrality. Accordingly, it was and is willing to allow the legitimacy of the current scientific ideal, the legitimacy of the notion that theoretically any hypothesis is relevant to any group of facts, and the notion that an appeal to brute facts is the test of the relevancy of any hypothesis. This attitude has been fatal. It has made possible the proof of nothing but a finite God, and of a Christianity that is cut after a naturalistic or semi-naturalistic pattern.

Sometimes men seem to have sensed something of this issue. So, for instance, the argument for miracles and their possibility has sometimes been taken out of the domain of physical experiment and placed exclusively in the domain of history. It is assumed that modern physical theory is correct in its method. But it is argued that by physical experiment no known law can be discovered which should make for the *a priori* impossibility of miracle. The reason for this is that scientific experiment in physics must always end in a margin of error. With the most refined instruments we cannot escape this margin of error. Accordingly, an experimenter, after he has taken a large number of experiments, must take what he

30. It is the *basis* of the method, rather than its function, that Van Til says must be challenged. We should not countenance a scientific method that thinks it can begin without God or without due recognition that this is God's universe.

thinks is the *average* result of his experiments. This involves a choice on his part. The scientist can never be wholly passive in scientific experiment. It is unavoidable that he should exercise his choice at some point of the process. Thus an element of uncertainty comes into the picture. The average any scientist has hit upon may not be representative of any particular fact. It follows that one cannot be certain that the resurrection of Christ or the raising of Lazarus has not taken place. We may therefore safely turn to history to see if the testimony for such miracles is reasonably sufficient. And if we find that it is, we may believe in the occurrence of miracles.

Is this sort of reasoning in defense of the miraculous valid and useful? We cannot think so. Suppose that we did go to history and discovered from history that the evidence for the truth of the story that an axe head floated upon the water is sufficient.[31] It is difficult to see how modern physical theory, which accepts experiment as the test of relevancy of an hypothesis, could allow for the possibility of such a fact. If a million experiments were taken with axes thrown into the water, such axe heads would sink each time. There would be no margin of error allowing for the entrance of subjective interpretation. All "known facts" would flatly contradict the notion of the floating axe. Accordingly the "hypothesis" that God made the axe head of the Old Testament story to float would have to be discarded.

But even if we could for a moment forget the consideration just advanced; suppose we did somehow find room to allow for the floating axe head as something that has happened. In that case the floating axe head would still be nothing but a brute fact for which we have so far found no explanation. It would simply be a *strange event.*[32] It would not be true that by a miraculous power of God the axe head was made to float. Thus it has profited us nothing to seek escape from the field of physics into that of history. If we allow the legitimacy of the current scientific method anywhere, we are at the mercy of our opponents.[33]

---

31. Cf. 2 Kings 6:1–7.
32. And, in a world governed by chance, strange events can happen.
33. Once we accept the assumptions of the current scientific method, in other words, on what basis could we interpret a floating axe head as God's work, with God's interpretation of it?

THE PRACTICAL EXCLUSION OF THE CHRISTIAN "HYPOTHESIS"

That the wolf of scientific method intends to feed on the lamb of Christianity can be learned from a consistent application of that method to the concept of miracle. We have already indicated that for the follower of the "scientific method" miracles can be thought of as nothing but strange events. To this we should now add that the Christian concept of miracle is sometimes definitely and clearly rejected simply by the application of the scientific method. We quote from William Adams Brown[34] to prove this point. Speaking of the intellectual difficulties involved in the acceptance of miracle, he says:

> Let us take the intellectual difficulty first. To establish the occurrence of a miracle, whether in the thirteenth century, or in the sixteenth century, or in the seventeenth, it was necessary to show that the event in question was incapable of being explained by natural law. This, though difficult, would not be impossible provided one knew just what was meant by "nature" and what events were explicable by natural law. But today we are no longer sure that we know where to place the exact boundaries of natural law. Natural law is only our name for certain recurrent sequences in the order of the occurrence of phenomena. Nature is not an independent power over against God which acts as a cause among causes. Nature is that part of the totality of things which admits of classification according to principles which embody the results of an analysis of past experience. To prove that an event is a miracle in the sense in which Aquinas or Calvin believed in miracle, it would be necessary not merely to show that it had not yet been possible to assign it its place in the observed sequence, but that it never would be possible to do so in the future, which manifestly cannot be done.

34. William Adams Brown (1865–1938) was, for most of his professional career, a professor at Union Theological Seminary. As a student of Adolph von Harnack, as will be clear from this quotation, Brown was instrumental in the promotion and development of theological liberalism.

Many modern opponents of miracle are content to rest their case at this point. They do not deny the possibility of miracles, but only the possibility of proving that any particular event is a miracle. Take any of the miracles of the past, the virgin birth, the raising of Lazarus, the resurrection of Jesus Christ. Suppose that you can prove that these events happened just as they are claimed to have happened. What have you accomplished? You have shown that our previous view of the limits of the possible needs to be enlarged; that our former generalizations were too narrow and need revision; that problems cluster about the origin of life and its renewal of which we had hitherto been unaware. But the one thing which you have not shown, which indeed you cannot show, is that a miracle has happened; for that is to confess that these problems are inherently insoluble, which cannot be determined until all possible tests have been made.

What, moreover, shall we say of these events, formerly deemed miracles in the technical sense, which today many scientists believe can be brought under law? For example, the miracles of healing or of demonic possession? We find analogous phenomena at the present day which seem to belong in the same category, such as the healings of Christian Science, or the exorcism of Christian missionaries in China. Must we, therefore, admit that the religious significance of the Biblical stories has been impaired and the evidential value of the events they record has been impaired and the evidential value of the events they record has been disproved? Such a conclusion would inevitably follow if the older methods of proof were correct. But modern defenders of miracle are not willing to admit that this is the case. The religious significance of the Biblical miracles, they tell us, is not impaired by any progress which we may have made toward a scientific understanding of their antecedents, for the very simple reason that the quality which gives them their significance for religion lies in a region to which the methods of science cannot penetrate.[35]

35. William Adams Brown, *God at Work: A Study of the Supernatural* (New York: Charles Scribner's Sons, 1933), 169–71.

NEUTRALITY—NEGATION

When reading such a passage we may well ask what has become of the boasted neutrality of the scientific method. But we knew it was not neutral. We are not surprised to find the negation of everything specifically Christian grow naturally out of a consistent application of the "scientific method." If we adopt the "scientific method" we must allow that it is quite possible that at some future date all the miracles recorded in the Bible, not excluding the resurrection of Christ, may be explained by natural laws. We should admit the ideal of complete comprehension of all facts under one principle of explanation that is open to the mind of man. There can then be no God whose mind is essentially higher than human minds. Such a God would have a plan of his own that he would carry out. This plan of God would not be open for inspection to human visitors. For that reason it cannot be tolerated by the "scientific method."

If we should ask what sort of explanation it would be that science would give of miracles, we may listen to Bernhard Bavink, in his book, *Science and God.*[36] Bavink discusses the question of miracles in the following words: "It is a complete error to attempt now to uphold belief in miracle, in the ordinary sense of the word, by basing it upon the purely statistical character of natural laws."[37]

What does Bavink mean when he says we cannot defend miracle by appealing to the purely statistical character of laws? He means that all facts are brute facts, and that therefore we cannot predict anything with certainty about any fact. We must therefore use the method of sampling. We must take samples out of the mass of facts about us. These samples are to be representative of the nature of the mass of facts we are seeking to interpret. But we must assume these samples to be representative. We take for granted that other uninvestigated facts will be like the sample we have been able to study. We can never be sure that this will be the case in any individual instance. There may be some very strange instances. So there may conceivably be some physical phenomena that do not fit into what we think of as the law of nature. On this point Bavink says:

36. Bernhard Bavink (1879–1947) was a German socialist who studied science and mathematics. Toward the end of his life, he was appointed to two separate positions in natural philosophy.
37. Bernhard Bavink, *Science and God* (New York: Reynal & Hitchcock, 1934), 131.

Let us take the example we have cited from Perrin of the tile. When this falls off a roof, there is a possibility every $10^{10^{10}}$ years that chance unevenness in the distribution of molecular pressure may give it a considerable impulse sideways, and thus, for example, divert it from the head of a passer-by which it would otherwise have struck, if its fall had taken place according to the normal (that is to say average) law of falling bodies. But if the argument is put forward in theological quarters that the possibility of a miracle is thus proved the result would only be to damage theology's own case. For in the first place as we have seen, the probability is so small that it may be regarded as practically identical with impossibility. If one such tile had fallen every second since the beginning of the history of humanity, no noticeable fraction of the time would have passed which, according to Perrin, would be necessary for the case to occur. And secondly, even if such an immeasurably small possibility should actually once be realised, there would again be a second, almost equally great, improbability that it should happen just at the very moment when the passer-by, who was to be 'providentially' protected, was under that particular roof.

Similar considerations apply, for example, to the walking of Peter on the water, which is naturally also imaginable as the result of unequal molecular pressure, but even less probable, and other miracles. Hence the theological world cannot be too strongly warned against attempting to make capital in this way out of the new discoveries.[38]

A little further Bavink adds, "The new physics now hands this whole cosmos over to pure chance, with its statistical laws. This might seem to be fundamentally less in keeping with our belief in an omnipotent, and above all an eternally wise God, than the old point of view."[39] This warning of Bavink should surely be taken to heart by orthodox defenders of Christianity. If we appeal to the margin of error and to the statistical character of natural laws in order to point out that science itself can allow for miracle, we jump for safety from the burning ship of determinism into the sea

38. Ibid., 131–32.
39. Ibid., 134.

of indeterminism. Death will pursue us in either case. A scientific method that is based upon a metaphysic of chance must seek to destroy the Christian position which is based upon the metaphysic of God as the self-attesting self-conscious being with a comprehensive plan for all reality.

THE CHRISTIAN "HYPOTHESIS" SAID TO BE IRRELEVANT

We have now seen that the "scientific ideal" is a forest fire that stops for nothing. Neutrality is, to be sure, spoken of and even lauded. But it is not put into practice. The same holds true for the question of the relevancy of hypothesis. Cohen claims that theoretically any hypothesis is relevant. But of course in practice we must exclude some hypotheses. Which kind of hypotheses does Cohen think we ought to exclude? The answer is plain. Such hypotheses must be excluded as would involve the truth of Christianity.[40] Speaking of Rationalism, Naturalism, and Supernaturalism, Cohen says:

It is frequently asserted that the principle of scientific method cannot rule out in advance the possibility of any fact, no matter how strange or miraculous. This is true to the extent that science as a method of extending our knowledge must not let accepted views prevent us from discovering new facts that may seem to contradict our previous views. Actually, however, certain types of explanation cannot be admitted within the body of scientific knowledge. Any attempt, for instance, to explain physical phenomenon as directly due to providence or disembodied spirits, is incompatible with the principle of rational determinism. For the nature of these entities is not sufficiently determinate to enable us to deduce definite experimental consequences from them. The Will of Providence, for example, will explain everything whether it happens one way or another. Hence, no experiment can possibly overthrow it. An hypothesis, however, which we cannot possibly refute cannot possibly be experimentally verified.

---

40. This is an important point. Any claim to neutrality and to an open-minded and open-ended investigation, if consistent, will inevitably rule out the possibility of Christianity.

In thus ruling out ghostly, magical, or other supernatural influences, it would seem that scientific method impoverishes our view of the world. It is well, however, to remember that a world where no possibility is excluded is a world of chaos, about which no definite assertion can be made. Any world containing some order necessarily involves the elimination of certain abstract or ungrounded possibilities such as fill the minds of the insane.[41]

It appears that the philosophy of chance on which Cohen himself builds the whole idea of scientific method cannot allow the concept of God as an absolutely rational being. We do not wonder that it cannot. To allow the concept of God would be to destroy the "scientific method." It was claimed that theoretically any hypothesis is permissible. The "hypothesis" of God is, however, excluded at the outset. And what are the bases for excluding the idea of God? It is expressed very pointedly when Cohen says that the idea of providence for instance "will explain everything whether it happens one way or another." Is this true? As Christians we hold that the doctrine of God's plan or providence does indeed explain everything. But we also hold that it is because of this very providence that things happen just as they do and not otherwise. In other words, we hold that the charge here made against Christianity must be returned to those who make it. It is only if we start with a philosophy of chance that things may happen any way at all. There is then no rationality at all.

APPEAL TO BRUTE FACTS AS THE TEST OF THE RELEVANCE OF HYPOTHESES

It is a cause for rejoicing that matters are put thus plainly by Cohen. Christians ought to be able to see from his statements, as well as from those of Brown and Bavink given above, that they cannot defend the teachings of Christianity by the use of the "scientific method." The final test applied by Cohen when he is sorting his hypotheses as to their relevancy is the appeal to brute facts as they are supposed to be known by man apart from God. By this method

41. Cohen, *Reason and Nature*, 158–59.

of appeal to brute facts, it is found that the hypothesis of God as it appears in the doctrine of providence cannot even be considered relevant. Speaking of this matter of appeal to fact in order to test the relevancy of hypotheses Cohen and Nagel say: "The hypothesis that the universe is shrinking in such a fashion that all lengths contract in the same ratio is empirically meaningless if it can have no consequences which are verifiable. In the same way the hypothesis that belief in a Providence is a stronger force making for righteous living than concern for one's fellow man can have no verifiable consequences unless we can assign an experimental process for measuring the relative strength of the 'forces' involved."[42]

We shall not pursue this question further. There will be occasion to point out more fully when, e.g., we discuss the method of the psychology of religion schools how this principle is applied. If one realizes that such experiences as regeneration and faith as well as external miracles such as the resurrection of Christ are, as far as science is concerned, simply awaiting the day of their explanation by natural law, be it statistical law, one ought to give up, once for all, the hope of establishing the truth of Christianity by the "scientific method." The procedure of the current scientific method is well illustrated by the sample Edwin G. Conklin[43] gives of it in his article in the book, *Has Science Discovered God?*, edited by Edward H. Cotton. First Conklin tells us there can be no real conflict between science and religion. They ought to be good friends, for they operate in different spheres. "What lies back of evolution no one knows."[44] That is the idea of neutrality. It sounds very good. It would seem then that theoretically any hypothesis might be deemed relevant. Yet it soon appears that the Christian hypothesis is not considered to be relevant. Conklin says: "No longer is it possible to think that man was created perfect in body, mind or morals, or that in physical form he is the image of God. No longer is it possible to think of God as 'the Good Man' or the Devil as 'the Bad Man.' "[45] Thus the Christian "hypothesis" is excluded as irrelevant. It is not long

---

42. Cohen and Nagel, *An Introduction to Logic and Scientific Method*, 207.

43. Edwin G. Conklin (1863–1952) was a professor of zoology at Northwestern University, the University of Pennsylvania, and Princeton University.

44. Edwin G. Conklin, "A Biologist's Religion," in *Has Science Discovered God? A Symposium of Modern Scientific Opinion*, ed. Edward H. Cotton (New York: Thomas Y. Crowell, 1931), 86.

45. Ibid., 79–80.

before Conklin positively asserts that the non-Christian concept of Chance must be accepted. "Undoubtedly chance has played a large part in the evolution of worlds and of organisms, but I cannot believe that it has played the only part."[46] To begin with, Conklin tells us that no one knows. Secondly, in effect, he tells us as Christians, "But you are wrong." Thirdly he adds, in effect, "I as an evolutionist and believer in chance am right." No one knows, but you are wrong and I am right; this is typical of the current scientific method.

We do not wish to suggest that there is intentional fraud in this matter. It only points to the actual exigency of scientific methodology. It cannot proceed differently. Nor does our criticism imply that we are not very appreciative of the great accomplishments of scientists who are not Christians. We readily allow that non-Christian science has done a great work and brought to light much truth.[47] But this truth which science has discovered is in spite of and not because of its fundamental assumption of a chance universe. Non-Christian science has worked with the borrowed capital of Christian theism, and for that reason alone has been able to bring to light much truth.[48]

To illustrate our attitude to modern science and its methodology we call to mind the story of Solomon and the Phoenicians.[49] Solomon wished to build a temple unto the Covenant God. Did he ask those who were not of the covenant and did not know the God of the covenant to make a blueprint for him? No, he got his blueprint from God. The timbers were to be laid in accordance with this blueprint. The timbers had to be fitted into the place made for them by this blueprint. Perhaps it took some of the builders a good while before they found the proper place for each timber. Perhaps they had various hypotheses as to just where this or that particular timber would fit. But they never doubted the ultimacy of

---

46. Ibid., 88.

47. This point should not be overlooked. Non-Christian scientists can make great progress, but it is in spite of their assumptions, not because of them, and it is further testimony that this is God's world, not a world of chance, which allows for any progress at all.

48. The idea of "borrowed capital" is crucial in Van Til's approach. Non-Christians, including scientists, must assume that the world is, in some sense, knowable and predictable in order to live and work. But such assumptions are foreign to non-Christian thought. So non-Christians must borrow from Christianity (albeit unwittingly) in order to make sense of their theories and hypotheses.

49. Cf. 1 Kings 5ff.

the blueprint itself. They offered no hypotheses that they did not think to be in accord with the blueprint. They did not appeal to brute timbers in order to test the relevancy of the blueprint. They knew the facts would somehow have to fit in with the blueprint.

But did this attitude of the builders of Solomon's temple imply that there was nothing useful to do for those who were not of the covenant? Not at all. The Phoenicians were employed as laborers to cut the timber. These Phoenicians were even recognized as being far more skillful than the covenant people in fashioning and trimming the timbers. They might even build temples of their own with the timber they cut. Such temples might resemble the appearance of Solomon's temple. Yet they would be nothing but temples reared to idols. Therefore these temples would sooner or later fall to the ground. Solomon knew this very well. He used the Phoenicians as his servants, not as his architects.

Something similar to this should be our attitude to science. We gladly recognize the detail work of many scientists as being highly valuable. We gladly recognize the fact that "science" has brought to light many details. But we cannot use modern scientists and their method as the architects of our structure of Christian interpretation. We deny the legitimacy of the ideal of science; we deny its principle with respect to the relevancy of hypotheses; and we deny the legitimacy of its appeal to brute facts. We challenge its whole procedure. Instead we offer the God and the Christ of the Bible as the concrete universal in relation to which all facts have meaning. We maintain that there can be no facts but Christian-theistic facts. We then go to the "facts," the phenomena of experience, and find again and again that if we seek to interpret any "fact" on a non-Christian hypothesis it turns out to be a brute fact, and brute facts are unintelligible.

CHAPTER 5

THEOLOGICAL EVIDENCES—GOD

We turn now to a brief consideration of some of the doctrines of Christianity in order to see what modern science does with them. Basic to all Christian teaching is its doctrine of God. What is the attitude of modern science with respect to God?

To this question we can give a fairly definite answer. Not as though all scientists agree on the matter in the form of their statements. Some disavow any belief in God. Others profess agnosticism. Still others, and they are perhaps in the majority today, claim to have discovered God by the pathway of science. But these three types of answers given by modern scientists agree on one point. Practically without exception modern scientists agree in denying the biblical notion of God. If they do believe in a god, they believe in a god who is but an extension of the universe or a principle within the universe.

PRE-KANTIAN SCIENCE

There can be no doubt that the growth of science accounts for a great difference between ancient and modern man. Ancient man thought of himself as at one with the universe. For him the macrocosmos and the microcosmos were scarcely distinguishable. Modern man, on the other hand, stands sharply over against nature.

This has made the question of epistemology all important for him. It brought the question of brute fact sharply to the foreground. Are some facts entirely beyond the reach of the mind of man? The earliest form of modern science asked this question and gave a definite answer in the negative. Mathematics was the first of the modern sciences to reach far out into the realm of space. There was, as someone has said, "faith in the harmony of the infinite universe and trust in mathematics as the key to its mysteries." Descartes proposed to begin his study of the universe with a few clear and distinct ideas. He wished simply to deduce all the consequences that these ideas contained. "Inspired by a vision, wherein the Angel of Truth appeared and spoke encouragingly to him, he created a new combination of algebra and geometry which is now called analytic geometry, but which he called 'universal mathematic'; and armed with this formidable weapon, he worked out a complete system of Nature in which everything from stars and stones to living animals and living human bodies is reduced to a combination of material particles moving according to mathematical laws in a universal homogeneous medium or ether."[1]

It was by this scientific method of Descartes that Spinoza[2] constructed his theology. He dealt with God more *geometrico*.[3] Spinoza was certain that he could prove the existence of God. He has been called the God-intoxicated man. For Spinoza the mind of man is but an aspect of the mind of God. There is really only one universal mind of which man's mind is a part. This universal mind rules all reality. Brute facts do not exist. The universal mind causes all facts to be just what they are.

We need spend no time to indicate that this Spinozistic conception of God is radically opposed to the Christian conception of God.

1. Walter Marshall Horton, *Theism and the Scientific Spirit* (New York: Harper & Brothers, 1933), 9.
2. Benedict de Spinoza (1632–1677) is typically counted, with Descartes and Leibniz, as one of the three primary representatives of rationalism in the history of philosophy. In his monumental work, *Ethics*, Spinoza denies the transcendence of God and argues that God is identical with nature. Thus, God and nature are identified, which is pantheism (*pan* = all, *theism* = God; all is God).
3. "*Geometrico*" refers to Spinoza's attempt to deal with reality "*more geometrico*," or in a geometric manner, which would include axioms, theorems, and so on. One of Spinoza's works was entitled *Renati Descartes Principiorum Philosophiae: More Geometrico Demonstratae* (1663), i.e., "Renee Descartes' Principles of Philosophy: Demonstrated in a Geometrical Manner."

Spinoza virtually identifies human and divine thought. Christianity begins with the notion of the sufficiency of God's thought and the createdness of man's thought. Spinoza's philosophy gives us the first modern illustration of the sort of god modern science will accept. It is an exclusively immanentistic god.

But Spinoza had done away with brute fact too summarily. If one does not begin with the biblical creation idea then there is such a thing as brute fact, and brute fact will not down. The empiricists were not slow to point out the fact that Spinoza had done violence to brute fact. Leibniz hoped to be able to meet this criticism of the empiricists and carry through the ideal of the mathematical explanation of all reality. By means of higher mathematics he hoped to bridge the gap between phenomena that observation seems to show us are utterly discrete. The qualitative differences between individual phenomena were reduced to functional differences in a mathematical series. Thus Leibniz hoped to make all phenomena penetrable to the mind of man. The qualitative differences of the various monads consisted merely in the degree of clarity with which they reflected the whole cosmos.[4] The "petites perceptions" of the material monads, said Leibniz, lead by imperceptible but logically traceable degrees up to the clear "apperceptions" of the spiritual monads. There is a strict logical continuity between them.

It seemed that a perfect method of science had been reached. It was on the basis of the mathematical method that Laplace[5] claimed to be able to predict all future events. Man, he thought, could penetrate to the very circumference of reality with the searchlight of mathematical method. What would become of Christianity in this scheme? The answer is at hand. Just as Spinoza denies the transcendence of God, Leibniz denies the uniqueness of Christianity. He discusses the relation between nature and grace. The "realm of nature" means for him nothing but the realm of that which is below reason but still governed by reason. God fits into the picture as the one who orders all things by Reason. God is but an aspect of universal Reason. The sovereign God of the Bible is reduced to the notion of universal Reason. The doctrines of redemption are woven into a naturalistic pattern.

---

4. For Leibniz, monads were the most basic units of existence.
5. Pierre-Simon Laplace (1749–1827) was a French mathematician and astronomer.

A POSTERIORI SCIENCE

This first manifestation of modern science was strictly *a priori* in its method.[6] We turn now to the *a posteriori* form of pre-Kantian science. Is not a true scientific method always inductive in nature? Perhaps the method of Leibniz and the early mathematicians was not truly scientific after all. Perhaps its sweeping denial of Christian theism was due to its false *a priori* character.

"In the eighteenth century, when the center of scientific activity and leadership passed from continental Europe to the British Isles, and applied mechanics replaced pure mathematics as the prevailing interest, the scientific spirit became more inductive and empirical."[7] Isaac Newton's great ambition was to deal with facts as they are. He worked upon the basis of the experiments of Galileo with the swinging lamp in the Cathedral of Pisa. He formulated his laws of motion on the basis of observation.

Locke's philosophy was largely an application of the scientific principles of Newton. Butler's *Analogy* was in turn largely an application to theology of the philosophical principles of Locke. In our first section we have noted the sad results of Butler's method. Nothing but a finite God could be proved by the "inductive method" of Butler. The uniqueness of Christianity had to be toned down to the requirements of a naturalist pattern. In short, the results of the *a posteriori* method no less than the results of the *a priori* method of pre-Kantian science were subversive of Christianity. In the latter it appears very clearly that the ideal of modern science is complete comprehension of all knowledge. In the former this does not appear so clearly, but is none the less true. Empiricism began with what it thought of as a "known realm" of facts. The "unknown" was thought of as simply in analogy with the "known." The known realm was thought of as known by man as such. For man to know the world it was not thought necessary that God should first create and therefore know it. The facts were assumed to be brute facts instead of God-interpreted facts. Thus man as autonomous was thought of as fully equipped to interpret at least one area of brute

6. In other words, science was conceived of as needing a rationalistic starting point if it was to progress, as is seen, for example, in Leibniz's monadology.

7. Horton, *Theism and the Scientific Spirit*, 45.

facts. And knowing one area of brute fact, he simply needed to extend the borders of his knowledge into the "unknown," by the same method by which he had learned about what he already knew. Even if God should seek to reveal himself to man, he would have to reveal only such matters as would be in continuity with what man already knew. God could never come to man as a sovereign God. Christianity could never come to man with unconditional grace.

POST-KANTIAN SCIENCE

We must go on to a consideration of post-Kantian science. In what does it differ from pre-Kantian science? There is no basic difference. Post-Kantian science has shown an even greater respect for brute fact than pre-Kantian science did. This appears primarily in the fact that the scientific ideal was reduced by Kant from an absolute ideal to that of a limiting concept.[8] For Kant the space-times coordinates formed the principle of individuation. In this he opposed Leibnizian rationalism. Leibniz thought of complete description as the principle of individuation. Every individual could be set into its logical niche. For Kant logic had no such comprehensive sweep. It was balked by a buzzing-blooming confusion of temporal facts.[9] This factual realm could never be wholly reduced to logical relations. The categories of the understanding can, according to Kant, at most show us aspects of truth. What a fact in itself is we can never fully know. We can do no more than make approximations to the knowledge of facts.

The far-reaching significance of this position of Kant requires careful attention. It still means that facts are not created but are *just there* somehow. The mind of man can never by its utmost efforts get back of this just-there-ness of facts. If the mind of man attempts to get back of the brute facts, argues Kant, it winds itself into a knot of hopeless antinomies. Here we hit upon the source of Kant's

---

8. Kant introduced the "dimensionalism" of the phenomenal, which included science, and the noumenal (as the limiting concept of the phenomenal), which was the realm not of science, but of faith. Thus, there is no "all-encompassing" absolute ideal, only the phenomenal facts.

9. The facts of the world, otherwise chaotic (i.e., "buzzing-blooming confusion"), are in need of the organizing categories of the mind in order to be understood. Even so, the "thing-in-itself" (i.e., the fact itself) can never be grasped.

criticism of the "theistic proofs."[10] Kant's criticism of these proofs cannot be met unless we lay bare the spectre of brute fact. This spectre can be banished only if we take the Christian conception of God as the Creator of the space-time world as the presupposition of all knowledge. A true science will have to build itself upon this Christian foundation. Unless one builds upon this foundation, complete scepticism stares us in the face.

Post-Kantian science has not faced this fact. It has simply reduced the ideal of complete comprehension for human knowledge from an absolute to a limiting concept. It has taken for granted with Kant that it is up to the human mind as such, itself a brute fact, to arrange these brute facts into universals or laws as best it can. It has taken for granted that in this procedure it is on the way to truth, forgetting that the whole structure of "truth" is then built upon brute facts. Thus modern science has virtually assumed that the addition of zeros will produce something more than zero.

The apparent success of modern science should not blind us to the fact that the whole structure is built upon sand. The success of modern science, we believe, is due to the fact that it really works with borrowed capital. If there really were brute facts, there would be no science. There can be no brute facts. All facts are, as a matter of fact, created and controlled by God. So too the mind of man is created by God. There are real universals in the world because of the creation of God. Even the mind of sinful man can see something of this in spite of his sin. Hence, though built upon a metaphysic which is basically false, the science of the non-Christian may reveal much of truth. When the prodigal son left home he was generous with his "substance." But it was really his father's substance that he expended.

With this background we can now turn to nineteenth century science. Naturally, one thinks at once of Lamarck, Darwin and De Vries. But we shall not enter upon the evolution question here with any fulness. We merely wish to point out one important matter. It was once more the assumption of the just-there-ness of facts

10. Kant's criticism of the theistic proofs forms section three of his *Critique of Pure Reason*. Kant begins by critiquing the ontological argument (Kant coined the term) and argues that once this proof is shown to be inadequate, the rest, depending as they do on existence, will likewise fall.

that underlay the efforts of Lamarck,[11] Darwin, and De Vries.[12] Darwin thought that species derived from one another by small gradual variations. De Vries thought that there were great jumps in nature. There was a difference between Lamarck and Darwin on the question whether or not the change from one species to another is effected primarily by environment or from within. For our purposes these differences fade into significance when we think of the non-Christian assumption that all three took for granted.

NEUTRALITY

That nineteenth century science took for granted the just-there-ness of facts appears most clearly from the philosophy of Herbert Spencer. Spencer's agnosticism is really no more than Kant's philosophy restated with the help of biological terminology.

It is this agnosticism that underlies the notion of scientific neutrality. Scientists speak a great deal of approaching the facts with an open mind. The story has been told over and over again how up to Darwin's time men had simply believed on authority that there is a God and that he has created man in his own image. Then Darwin looked at the facts dispassionately and found that man has come from the lower animals.

In reality this story is based upon a myth. Darwin took for granted the just-there-ness of facts. He took for granted that the mind of man can deal with brute facts. Thus at the outset he excluded the Christian conception of God. What holds for Darwin holds for other scientists. It is commonly taken for granted that the scientist who begins simply with the "facts" is neutral. Yet he cannot but take the facts either as created or as non-created. If he takes them as non-created he has already at the outset excluded the notion of God's interpretation of the facts. Thus he has virtually assumed his own mind to be the ultimate interpreter of the facts. In short, he has come to his task of interpreting facts with a non-Christian philosophy of facts.

11. Jean Baptiste Lamarck (1744–1829), a French naturalistic scientist, was one of the first to propose a theory of evolution.

12. Hugo Marie de Vries (1843–1935) was a Dutch botanist who was impressed with Darwin but who proposed that evolution occurred more through large-scale mutations than through Darwinian gradualism.

At this point we should distinguish between what has been called impure and what has been called pure agnosticism. Romanes makes this distinction in his book, *Thoughts on Religion*.[13] He says that the agnosticism of Spencer was an impure agnosticism. He himself once held to this impure agnosticism. When a young man, he says, he was enamored of the ideal of science as then understood. It was the ideal that man must know reality comprehensively. And he thought that this ideal could actually be realized. Accordingly he felt that there was no need for the concept of God. He even thought that the idea of God was scientifically illegitimate. But when he grew older he realized that science deals with the abstract aspects of reality only. Since that time he professed a pure instead of an impure agnosticism. This pure agnosticism he speaks of as an "attitude of reasoned ignorance touching everything that lies beyond the sphere of sense-perception—a professed inability to found valid belief on any other basis."[14] Romanes holds that pure agnosticism may be distinguished from impure in that the latter welcomes evidence of all sorts while the former does not. He says: "Pure agnostics ought to investigate the religious consciousness of Christians as a phenomenon which may possibly be what Christians themselves believe it to be, i.e. of Divine origin."[15] Thus, according to Romanes, pure agnosticism is really trying to be neutral. This appears still further, according to Romanes, from the fact that pure agnosticism is not intellectualistic. Impure agnosticism, he says, would not listen to anything but the abstract arguments of the intellect. The pure agnosticism, however, concludes that: "Reason is not the only attribute of man, nor is it the only faculty which he habitually employs for the ascertainment of truth. Moral and spiritual faculties are of no less importance in their respective spheres even of everyday life; faith, trust, taste, &c., are as needful in ascertaining truth as to character, beauty, &c., as is reason. Indeed we may take it that reason is concerned in ascertaining truth only where *causation* is concerned; the appropriate organs

13. George John Romanes (1848–1894) was a Canadian-born, English evolutionary biologist and physiologist and was one of the younger friends of Darwin.

14. George John Romanes, *Thoughts on Religion*, ed. Charles Gore (Chicago: The Open Court Pub. Co., 1896), 113.

15. Ibid., 108.

of its ascertainment where anything else is concerned belong to the moral and spiritual region."[16]

What shall we say of this "pure agnosticism" of Romanes? Does it really furnish a basis for a neutral attitude? Can Christianity get a fair hearing at the bar of the pure agnostic? Our answer is that there can be no such thing as pure agnosticism. The pure agnosticism of Romanes, no less than the impure agnosticism of Spencer, maintains that man can have knowledge of an area of brute fact. From this area God is excluded. Moreover, Romanes himself adds that whatever we may believe about the realm that is beyond scientific control, it must be in analogy with that which is known by science. He expresses his conviction on this matter in the following words: "The further we are removed from possible experience—i.e. the more remote from experience the sphere contemplated—the less value attaches to antecedent presumptions. *Maximum* remoteness from possible experience is reached in the sphere of the final mystery of things with which religion has to do; so that here all presumption has faded away into a vanishing point, and pure agnosticism is our only rational attitude."[17] In this manner the principle of continuity between the known and the unknown is maintained. If we are to believe in God at all, such belief must be the result of our ignorance. When we see that we cannot reach our ideal of comprehensive knowledge we allow that God may exist. He may then take care of such facts as we cannot ourselves control.[18] Such a God is no more than a finite God. Thus pure agnosticism no less than impure agnosticism has chosen at the outset against the Christian doctrine of God.

AGNOSTICISM IN RECENT SCIENCE

What difference then is there between a scientist who denies God outright and the one who says he does not know whether God exists? The difference, such as it is, can be only emotional; logically the two positions amount to the same thing.

16. Ibid., 118.
17. Ibid., 115–16.
18. Note how similar this view is to the standard method of theistic proofs. We prove what we can by reason alone, then we supplement what reason cannot ascertain by an appeal to revelation.

Is the claim to neutrality and pure agnosticism still made today? Indeed, it is very frequently made. We call attention to a few instances of it. In the book, *Has Science Discovered God?*, edited by Edward H. Cotton, a number of scientists give their views of God. Nearly all of them inform us that, of course, they are altogether neutral on the question of God's existence when they begin their investigations. So Kirtley F. Mather,[19] a geologist, says, "Knowledge and mystery have always had a habit of appearing hand in hand, and today we are beginning to suspect that the mind of man is incapable of grappling with the ultimate reality in any truly scientific way. There may be in the cosmos that which can actually be termed the Absolute; but all we know is the relative."[20] Here, as in the case of Kant, Spencer, Romanes, etc., God is brought in to take care of the remnants of the brute facts that we cannot altogether catch in the net of our understanding. Surely, to call such a God absolute is to use words without meaning.

Certain remarks of Robert A. Millikan,[21] the great American physicist, amount to the same thing. He says: "The assumption that our feeble, finite minds understand completely the basis of the physical universe is the sort of blunder that has been made over and over and over again throughout all periods of the world's history, and in all domains of thought. It is the essence of dogmatism—assertiveness without knowledge. This is supposed to have been the especial prerogative of religion; and there have been many religious dogmatists; but not a few of them, alas, among scientists. Every one will recognize Mr. Bryan, for example, as a pure dogmatist; but not every scientist will recognize that Ernst Haeckel was an even purer one."[22] The only point Millikan is willing to concede is that science does not know everything. He does maintain that science can know much without God.

---

19. Kirtley F. Mather (1888–1978) was a faculty member at Harvard University. He was involved in helping Clarence Darrow against William Jennings Bryan at the Scopes trial.

20. Kirtley F. Mather, "Sermons from Stones," in *Has Science Discovered God? A Symposium of Modern Scientific Opinion*, ed. Edward H. Cotton (New York: Thomas Y. Crowell, 1931), 4.

21. Robert A. Millikan (1868–1953) was a Nobel Prize winner and was known for his work in molecular physics.

22. Robert A. Millikan, "Christianity and Science," in *Has Science Discovered God?* ed. Cotton, 34.

Heber D. Curtis,[23] an astronomer, speaks of his agnosticism in the following words: "As we look back over the discarded scientific theories of the past, once regarded as inspired and now only of historical interest, we are more and more forced to the conclusion that in the final analysis any scientific theory is simply a belief."[24] Accordingly he says that many scientists, especially among the elder of them, "have learned to smile a little."[25] Einstein says, "Strange is our situation here upon earth. Each of us comes for a short visit, not knowing why, yet sometimes seeming to divine a purpose."[26] Julian S. Huxley adds, "The first, and in a way, most important ingredient of any religion congruous with science must be a reverent agnosticism concerning ultimates, and, indeed, concerning many things that are not ultimates."[27]

It is clearly apparent what scientific agnosticism implies. It implies not only a recognition of the fact that science has not yet covered the whole of reality with its interpretation. It implies definitely the rejection of the idea of an interpretation given by God to man. At least it implies full liberty to subject any statement of the Bible about man or the universe to the independent judgment of man. Thus the so-called attitude of neutrality is seen to involve the negation of the Christian conception of the Bible. Sir James Jeans[28] expresses this idea repeatedly in his book *The Mysterious Universe*. He tells us that some millions of years ago certain stars wandered blindly through space. The sun threw certain fragments into space. Then he adds, "In course of time, we know not how, when, or why, one of these cooling fragments gave birth to life."[29] Thus in the same breath we have an assertion of agnosticism, a denial of Christianity, and the assurance that Chance rules the

---

23. Heber D. Curtis (1872–1942) was an American astronomer known for his interest in solar eclipses.

24. Heber D. Curtis, "Modern Physical Science: Its Relation to Religion," in *Has Science Discovered God?* ed. Cotton, 59.

25. Ibid., 61.

26. Albert Einstein, "The Meeting Place of Science and Religion," in *Has Science Discovered God?* ed. Cotton, 93.

27. Julian S. Huxley, "Religion: Its Persistence and Human Character," in *Has Science Discovered God?* ed. Cotton, 106.

28. James Jeans (1877–1946) was a mathematician and astronomer. He was the first to propose that matter is continuously "created" throughout the entire universe.

29. James Jeans, *The Mysterious Universe* (New York: Macmillan, 1930), 3.

universe. This is typical. We shall look at a few denials of the existence of the God of the Scriptures.

OUTRIGHT DENIALS OF GOD

In the volume spoken of above we find several of the men who have avowed their agnosticism tell us that, of course, they cannot believe in the traditional notion of God. For it they substitute an idea of God that they think to be in accord with modern science.

If Kirtley F. Mather is asked whether he has discovered God he tells us that he has. "The emergence of personality in the evolutionary process is an event of transcendent importance, the full meaning of which is still unappreciated. It must have occurred, however, in response to personality-producing forces in the universe. It is to these particular portions of cosmic energy that I would apply the term God."[30] Elsewhere he says, "To explain humanity at its best, the evolutionist must ascribe to the universe those qualities which we do well to call divine."[31] Or again, "Thus in a scientific age the search for God leads to a new answer to the ancient question. The answer is theism. God is a power, immanent in the universe. He is involved in the hazard of his creation. He is striving mightily to produce a perfect display in the world of sense-perception, of his own true nature."[32] If we should complain that this is a theism without transcendence, Mather would answer, "Not all the resources of the universe are to-day in use, even as many now used were not in use a geological period ago. In other words, the theistic God is not only immanent; he is also transcendent."[33] Mather has reached this conception of God by the application of the scientific method. "In this New World the scientific method stands approved, vindicated by experience; unless it is applied to the problems of religion, the theologian can not expect to make any permanent gains in the midst of modern civilization."[34] This scientific principle has done away with all dualism, says Mather. It has taught us to apply the

---

30. Mather, "Sermons from Stones," 9.
31. Kirtley F. Mather, *Science in Search of God* (New York: Henry Holt and Company, 1928), 68.
32. Ibid., 69–70.
33. Ibid., 72.
34. Ibid., 28.

principle of continuity everywhere. "The dualistic philosophy which implied a conflict between rival administrators, God and Satan, or between spiritual ambitions and natural desires, was a product of the pre-scientific age."[35] "With monotonous regularity the world discovers that science is right, that theology is wrong."[36] Science cannot admit any authority above man. It cannot allow of a God who is transcendent in the sense that he has interpreted the facts and can reveal his interpretation of the facts to us. "Science has as its goal the complete description of the universe in which we live; religion seeks to find the most abundant life which man may possess in such a universe."[37] "The theologian must use the scientist's description of physical phenomena as an aid in discovering the higher values of life."[38]

Thus Mather finds that by the help of the scientific method he is bound to reject the biblical notion of God and substitute for it one that is but a principle within the cosmos.

As for Millikan, whose agnosticism we noted, we observe that he identifies God with nature outright. "The idea that God, or Nature, or the Universe, whatever term you prefer, is not a being of caprice and whim as had been the case in all the main body of thinking of the ancient world; but . . ."[39] For Millikan the old idea of God is something that we gradually outgrow if we listen to the voice of science. "If, as we pass from the seven-year-old to the thirty-year-old stage of our racial development, our conceptions of God become less childishly simple, more vague and indefinite, it is because we begin to realize that our finite minds have only just begun to touch the borders of the ocean of knowledge and understanding."[40]

Heber D. Curtis opposes the notion of a God concept that is fixed in the following words: "If you say that your belief in God is final and fixed, that your religious creed is inspired of him, and that no other belief is true, then I shall be offended and refuse to follow you because you are unscientific."[41]

As for Einstein, we have noted that he too says we do not know

35. Ibid., 19.
36. Ibid., 33.
37. Ibid., 43.
38. Ibid., 45.
39. Millikan, "Christianity and Science," 28.
40. Ibid., 39.
41. Curtis, "Modern Physical Science: Its Relation to Religion," 71.

why we are here in this world. Yet he is certain that the Christian idea of God is mistaken. He says: "I cannot imagine a God who rewards and punishes the objects of his creation, whose purposes are modeled after our own—a God, in short, who is but a reflection of human frailty."[42] His own God is identified with the abstract ideals of goodness, beauty, and truth.[43]

Julian Huxley, another "agnostic" is certain that the Christian notion of God is wrong. Speaking of the relation between religion and science, he says, "Where, then, does the solution lie? It would seem to lie in dismantling the theological edifice, which will no longer bear the weight of the universe as enlarged by recent science; and attempting to find new outlets for the religious spirit. God, in any but a purely philosophical, and one is almost tempted to say, a Pickwickian, sense, turns out to be a product of the human mind. As an independent or unitary being, active in the affairs of the universe, he does not exist."[44]

Sir J. Arthur Thomson[45] speaks of the process of the unification of science. But he does not wish to have men stress the "Lowest Common Denominator" in the universe. He would distinguish between the realm of things, the realm of organisms, and the realm of man. Then he adds, "Now along this line of thought we come upon the suggestion that God is to be thought of as the summation of all the powers of the Universe." Yet he does not wish to say that God is the "sum of all the energies" in the universe. " 'Energy' is a physical concept and measurable; God is a transcendental concept, of the Supreme Reality, and infinite."[46] Elsewhere Thomson speaks of God as "the constitutive principle of the Universe."[47] But he is careful to observe that even that can be no more than a suggestion since "no man by science can find out God."[48]

---

42. Einstein, "The Meeting Place of Science and Religion," 97.
43. Ibid., 94.
44. Huxley, "Religion: Its Persistence and Human Character," 105.
45. J. Arthur Thomson (1861–1933) was a Scottish naturalist and professor of natural history at the University of Aberdeen. He delivered the Gifford Lectures from 1914 to 1916, later published as the two-volume *The System of Animate Nature*.
46. J. Arthur Thomson, "How Science Changes Our Vision of God," in *Has Science Discovered God?* ed. Cotton, 174.
47. J. Arthur Thomson, *Science and Religion* (New York: Charles Scribner's Sons, 1925), 124.
48. Ibid., 100.

These examples may suffice. We can learn from them what science today means by God. Science begins with brute facts. It assumes the mind of man as the ultimate interpreter of these brute facts. The mind of man finds that it cannot actually give a comprehensive interpretation of the facts. There remains a realm of mystery. It is within this left-over area of science that God must be sought. Even so he is always essentially penetrable to the human mind. The realm of the mysterious as thought of by modern science is no more than the realm of the not-yet-explored. The ideal of complete comprehension is maintained as a legitimate ideal.

Broadly speaking, then, post-Kantian science is neither deductive nor inductive in the pre-Kantian sense. It does not claim to be able actually to see through the infinite. It does not expect to be able to see through all reality in any given length of time. It is not rationalistic in the Leibnizian sense. Nor is it intellectualistic. For the deductive and inductive ideal it has substituted the limiting concept. This seems to be more modest. It seems to allow for the recognition of another than the intellectualistic approach to reality. It seems to make room for a spiritual realm that is somehow beyond the physical and phenomenal realm. It seems, in short, to allow for *some sort of transcendence.* Kant thought he had made room for faith; modern science thinks the same. Neither of them did anything of the sort. That is, neither of them *allowed* room, let alone *made* room, for the orthodox Christian faith.[49]

RECENT SCIENCE IN ACCORD WITH RECENT PHILOSOPHY

We may point out briefly in this connection that the God of recent science is in accord with the God of recent philosophy. In order to do this we take note of what A. Seth Pringle-Pattison says in his book *The Idea of God in the Light of Recent Philosophy.*

In the first place recent philosophy agrees with recent science in that it holds to the idea of God as at most a limiting concept. This appears very pointedly from the emphasis placed upon the notion

---

49. This is a penetrating and important historical point. After Kant, science had a way to allow for the realm of faith as a limiting concept and thus was not beholden to either the rationalistic *a priori* or the empiricist *a posteriori*. Even so, the realm of faith no more pointed to the true God than did rationalism or empiricism.

that all human knowledge requires an experience foundation. Kant argued that there can be no rational cosmology, or psychology or theology.[50] All possible experience, he said, must be based upon the intuitions of sense.

Pringle-Pattison argues in a similar vein when he says: "Certainly, apart from our actual experience, God or the Absolute is a subject waiting for predicates, an empty form waiting to be filled."[51] But Pringle-Pattison does not wish to stop short with a Kantian position. He thinks we may hold that the phenomenal is an actual manifestation of the noumenal. He says: "But we need be at no loss for predicates: in the words of the Apostle, 'the invisible things of him from the creation of the world are clearly seen, *being understood by the things that are made,* even his eternal power and Godhead.' "[52] A little later he adds, "The nature of ultimate Reality is to be read, therefore, in its manifestation, and may be read there truly. We may be sure the revelation is not exhaustive, for all revelation must be *ad modum recipientis*; it must be proportionate to the capacity of the receiving mind."[53]

All this sounds very orthodox. It seems to accord with the idea of Paul in Romans that the universe is the handiwork of God. Even the incomprehensibility of God seems to be taught. The finite character of our minds is urged as the sufficient reason for our limited knowledge. In reality we have here a complete denial of the historic Christian doctrine of God. That this is indeed the case may be garnered from the fact that God as well as man is virtually said to be dependent upon the intuitions of sense for his knowledge of facts. For Pringle-Pattison, as for Kant, all possible experience, divine as well as human, is subject to limitations. All possible experience, both divine and human, must deal with brute facts. We quote: "The most exalted intelligence must read, as we do, in the volume of God's works, to learn His nature: his knowledge, like ours, is through the manifestation. Though it may be truer in the sense

50. This highlights the "limiting concept" of the noumenal. For Kant and Kantians, the noumenal consists of things-in-themselves, the soul and God. Thus, there can be no rational cosmology (things-in-themselves), psychology (the soul), or theology (God) because the things that compose the noumenal cannot be known.

51. A. Seth Pringle-Pattison, *The Idea of God in the Light of Recent Philosophy*, 2nd ed. (New York: Oxford University Press, 1920), 158.

52. Ibid.

53. Ibid., 175.

of being ampler and more adequate, and so correcting errors and solving difficulties incident to our more limited range of vision, this is but a difference of degree, not of qualitative distinction between absolute and relative, as if the one knowledge were true and the other vitiated by some inherent defect. Our knowledge is as true for us as the ampler knowledge for the higher being. Each is true as being an interpretation of the facts accessible at that particular stage. With new data comes new insight; but the new insight carries forward and incorporates the old—it does not abolish it."[54] Speaking of the Absolute he says, "Of the Absolute it has been finely said, 'its predicates are the worlds'. We learn its nature through the facts of the universe, especially so far as any system or scale of values is discernible in them. This is the immanent God on our knowledge of whom it has been the purpose of this first course of lectures to insist."[55] At an earlier point in the argument Pringle-Pattison says, "The qualities are the modes in which the substance exists and reveals itself; to know a thing through its qualities or phenomena—its modes of action—is to know the real thing in the only way in which God or man can know anything."[56] Criticizing the position of T. H. Green, he adds, "To think of the world as a permanent presentation, self-presented to an eternal percipient, does not meet the case, unless we confer upon the presentation just that degree of distinct and independent being which makes it a real object contemplated by the eternal percipient, and therefore capable of being similarly contemplated by other minds."[57]

All of this shows how deeply the idea of brute fact has become imbedded in modern philosophy as well as in science. The only God modern philosophy or science will accept is one who is a fellow philosopher or fellow scientist seeking to interpret brute fact as well as he may. Such a God is not qualitatively distinct from man. He is but an hypostatization of man. Even God's universals or laws cannot envelop the whole area of brute fact. He himself is surrounded by bare possibility and mystery. Together with us he may seek to penetrate into that mystery. Together with us he may set for himself the ideal of absolute comprehension in knowledge.

54. Ibid., 175–76.
55. Ibid., 174–75.
56. Ibid., 162.
57. Ibid., 197.

But together with us that ideal will always have to be for him a limiting concept. Brute fact will always be just ahead of him as well as just ahead of us.

RECENT SCIENCE IN ACCORD WITH RECENT RELIGION

As modern philosophy is in accord with modern science, so modern religion is in accord with both. Charles Hartshorne[58] has recently written a book entitled *Beyond Humanism*, in which this agreement between modern religion on the one hand, and modern science and philosophy on the other hand, appears. Hartshorne is very critical of the Humanists. They have not given heed to the higher things of life. But like Pringle-Pattison, Hartshorne rejects with scorn the idea of a God who is not essentially penetrable to the human mind. "The notion that God must be even higher than the maximal case of known variables is simply a set of words without meaning. For 'higher' is defined by these variables, or it is merely a veil for intellectual sabotage."[59] Accordingly Hartshorne does not differ from John Dewey as far as the latter's opposition to orthodox Christian theism is concerned.

> The idea of a God so perfect that he eternally realizes all possible values is fatal to religion, for it makes human choice of no significance whatever. Infinite value will exist no matter what we do. "Serving" such a God really means only serving oneself by securing his favor. But even this self-service cannot make any difference to the totality of values, since this totality is always an absolute maximum.
>
> In my opinion Dewey gives here an unanswerable objection to the theism of Augustine and Aquinas. However, I cannot regard this theism as having much to do with that of the Bible![60]

---

58. Charles Hartshorne (1897–2000) studied under both Husserl and Heidegger, but he was influenced most by C. S. Peirce. Hartshorne was a philosophical theist who held that God is always *becoming*. Thus, he is considered to be a process theologian.

59. Charles Hartshorne, *Beyond Humanism: Essays in the New Philosophy of Nature* (Lincoln: University of Nebraska Press, 1937), 122.

60. Ibid., 42.

For the God of Augustine and Aquinas Hartshorne substitutes one who will help us strive for the ideal as a limiting concept.

> The sum of the matter is that human life is in fact not merely finite, and yet, if humanists are right, is not genuinely super-finite. It is not merely finite, for each particular limit is provisional only, and progress a perpetual human obligation; yet without God the thought of the infinite ideal, by which alone this perpetual progress can be inspired, is intolerable, since its actualization is both desirable and impossible.[61]

For Hartshorne, as well as for Pringle-Pattison, God himself depends upon brute facts and gradually gathers his knowledge with respect to them. "We seek the truth about the actual world; and the ideal here is the whole truth about it. But how can such a truth-whole be conceived except in terms of a perfect mind and its omniscience? However, this omniscience is of the actual world, not of all possible worlds as though they were actualized."[62]

Similarly God's omnipotence is limited by brute facts. Hartshorne again agrees with Dewey in rejecting the notion of omnipotence as

> complete responsibility for all that happens. "All-powerful" is taken to mean possessing all the power there is, so that there can be no power not the power of God. If this is true, if power is not *divided* between God and other beings, then responsibility can certainly not be divided either. But the division of power, and hence of responsibility, is an analytic truth since, evil or no evil, power must be employed upon something, and that upon which it is employed must also possess some power, for the completely powerless or passive is nothing. Hence "all-powerful" can only mean possessing all *possible* power over all other things, that is, all the power there is except that which is inherent in those other things by their very existence.

61. Ibid., 49.
62. Ibid.

To maintain this conception of the omnipotence consistently we have to renounce the standard theological doctrine of the 'purely active' character of God; but naturalistic theism is in any case prevented by all its major principles from accepting that doctrine. Thus it is free from any motive for asserting the responsibility of God for evil merely on the ground that evil exists. Since God must be partly passive to the actions of the creatures, of whom men are an almost infinitesimal proportion, we cannot hold that he could coerce complete harmony or goodness in these actions.[63]

In these passages and throughout his book Hartshorne emphasizes his view that any true philosophy must begin and end with brute fact. It is by emphasizing this that he hopes to accomplish a complete reconciliation between science, philosophy, and religion. All three are to take brute fact for granted at the outset; all three ought to join with one another and with God in striving toward the complete understanding of the brute facts. All three, together with God, ought to realize that this ideal can, because of the bruteness of the facts, never be more than a limiting concept.

CURRENT DEFINITIONS OF GOD AND RELIGION

That Hartshorne is not alone in working on this program is evidenced from the notion of religion maintained by several modern philosophers. Religion is, generally speaking, thought of as the attempt to realize ideals that mankind has set for itself. Fulton J. Sheen in his book, *Religion without God*, has collected a number of definitions of God and of religion from recent philosophers. We give a few of them, as found in his book.[64]

Indeed the existence of a supreme being as a person external to ourselves and to the world, like a magnified human creature, is not affirmed by the religious consciousness, and if it were known to be a fact, would have no bearing on religion.[65]

63. Ibid., 53–54.
64. Fulton J. Sheen, *Religion without God* (New York: Longmans, Green, 1928), 44–47.
65. Bernard Bosanquet, *Value and Destiny of the Individual* (London: Macmillan, 1913), 254.

Religion is an emotion resting on a conviction of a harmony between ourselves and the universe at large.[66]

Religion is the force of faculty prompting to action in accordance with the highest ideals having reference to the future of the individual and race.[67]

The religious experience is best described as the experience of the ideal, the realization of the values which come in an exalted emotional moment that makes us one with our kind, at least with the best of our kind, who might include the whole of them.[68]

Religion is the projection in the roaring loom of time of a concentration or unified complex of psychical values.[69]

Whether God exists or not, is not important to the nature of religion.[70]

Religion is the projection and pursuit of ideal personal relations with the universe and man. . . . Because it is a process of projection and pursuit, religion is an ever moving process in the direction of complete personal adjustment and control in man's total environment.[71]

God is neither an entity nor an ideal, but always a relation of entity to ideal: Reality regarded from the standpoint of its favorableness or unfavorableness, to human life, and prescribing for the latter the propriety of a certain attitude.[72]

66. John McTaggart Ellis McTaggart, *Some Dogmas of Religion* (London: Edward Arnold, 1906), 3.

67. G. M. Irvine, *Churches, Religion, and Progress* (London: Watts, 1924), 13, 18.

68. Ellsworth Faris, "What Constitutes a Scientific Interpretation of Religion?" *Journal of Religion* 6 (1926): 241.

69. Joseph Alexander Leighton, *Man and the Cosmos: An Introduction to Metaphysics* (New York: D. Appleton, 1922), 545.

70. Sheen attributes this quote to Rudolf Eucken, *The Truth of Religion*, trans. W. Tudor Jones (New York: G. P. Putnam's Sons, 1911), 129.

71. Edwin E. Aubrey, "The Nature of Religion: A Study in Method of Definition," *Journal of Religion* 5 (1925): 189–91.

72. Ralph Barton Perry, *The Approach to Philosophy* (New York: Charles Scribner's Sons, 1905), 66.

Faith in God is synonymous with the brave hope that the universe is friendly to the ideals of man.[73]

This may suffice. It would not be difficult to garner similar utterances from other thinkers. There will be occasion to speak further of the matter when we discuss the psychology of religion literature. We merely observe here that recent science, recent philosophy, and recent theology agree with one another. They are basically opposed to the Christian position. The immanentistic finite God, the God penetrable to the human mind, the God who is an aspect of the cosmos, the God who is the unexplored realm of the mysterious, is the fruit and ripe result of the application of the modern scientific method. If the "scientific method" of today is a true scientific method, this conclusion is inevitable. But we have seen that the scientific method is based upon the philosophy of chance. This philosophy of chance, or of brute fact, destroys human predication. Upon its basis there is no connection between one fact and another fact. We shall have to bring the matter back to this fundamental point again and again. Christian theism alone can vanquish the spectre of brute fact.

73. A. Eustace Haydon in "The Definition of Religion: A Symposium," by Edgar Sheffield Brightman, Durant Drake, and A. Eustace Haydon, *Journal of Religion* 7 (1927): 128.

CHAPTER 6

CREATION AND PROVIDENCE

In the preceding chapter we dealt with modern science and what it says about God. We turn now to the questions of creation and providence. In the following chapter we take up the question of teleology. In this way we cover the field of theism as it is usually divided. The first chapter dealt with the question of being. That is the problem of the ontological argument. The present chapter deals with the question of causation. That is the problem of cosmology. The following chapter deals with the question of purpose. That is the question of teleology.

It is a well-known fact that Kant had essentially the same type of criticism to make on all three of the theistic proofs. In fact he led them all back to the ontological proof. His criticism was that the "proofs" imply an illegitimate jump from man's knowledge of the phenomenal world to reality beyond possible experience. Thought as such is an abstraction, says Kant. It is only in connection with the intuitions of sense-experience that it has meaning. Therefore it is impossible to extend thought to a realm beyond experience.

Applying this criticism to the concept of causality Kant finds that it is a category that is immanent in experience. The concept of causation is subordinate to that of explanation and explanation must be immanent within the universe. Explanation must be something that is within reach of the human mind.

Kant holds that if we seek to conclude from a series of causes that we observe in the phenomenal world to a cause of the world itself we contradict our own principle of explanation. It would mean that there is a God who is not penetrable to the human mind. He would be beyond our possible experience. In this manner we should involve ourselves in contradiction.[1] We should then have a God who was supposed to have caused or determined all things. That would destroy our freedom. That would destroy the contingency of temporal events. We would then be back to a position similar to that of Leibniz. We would also be doing violence to brute fact.

Just now we said that Kant thinks of the creation idea as bringing us back to a position similar to that of Leibniz. In reality Leibniz and Kant agree in holding to an exclusively immanentistic principle of interpretation.[2] Both would substitute *reason for causation* when the universe as a whole is up for discussion. Both would follow a principle of continuity that avoids any real transcendence. But Kant does not think reason can envelop the whole area of brute fact. More than that, he does not think reason can comprehensively interpret even one brute fact. Reason deals with universals. It must deal with universals. It seeks to bring individual brute facts into relation with one another. To do this it must subtract from the uniqueness of individuals.[3] When an individual is treated as a member of a class and we make general statements about the class we have subtracted from the uniqueness of that individual. I may put an individual into ever so many classes. Then I may add what I have said about each one of those classes. Still I will not have begun to exhaust the meaning of the individual.

Accordingly I must give up the notion of absolute truth. With all my categories I can but express aspects of the truth. Brute fact will never allow itself to be completely caught in the net of my

1. "Contradiction" refers to Kant's antinomies, in which it is impossible for reason to have a real concept of God or the noumenal, in that there can be no experience of such things. Thus, causality cannot apply to God.

2. An "immanentistic principle of interpretation" is one in which the facts of the world are understood with reference not to God but to the world itself or to things immanent in the world. In such an interpretation, there can be no transcendent reference point.

3. Since, in Kant's view, things-in-themselves are unknowable, knowledge is gained by the imposition of categories, or "universals," onto the experience of the facts of the world. But the facts themselves cannot be known. All that can be known are those universals as they attempt to bring together the experience of facts.

categories. There will always be more of brute fact for me to catch. When I apply the category of causality to the brute facts that meet me I do throw light on an aspect of the behavior of brute fact. But I can never apply the category of causality to the existence of brute fact itself. That would mean that I had explained the whole of brute fact. But when I claim to have explained the whole of brute fact I involve myself in contradiction and thus deny my own principle of explanation. If I am to continue to claim that I can explain anything at all I shall have to give up claiming to be able to explain everything, and give up the idea that everything is essentially explicable by the human mind.

Thus modern thought, as it is based upon Kant, is in no sense a return to Christian theism. It is rather a desperate effort to save the principle of exclusively immanentistic interpretation from bankruptcy. In the hands of the rationalists the principle had involved itself in complete self-contradiction. To avoid this contradiction and yet save the immanentistic character of interpretation, Kant emphasized more than ever the bruteness of brute facts. That seemed to release the strain between categories. Instead of each claiming to be supreme over the whole area of reality they could divide the territory. Or rather they could be thought of as each contributing a number to the program of intellectual interpretation. And even the whole program does not claim to represent the exclusive interest of the brute facts.

All this does not mean that Kant and modern philosophy after him have no patience with any sort of creation idea. On the contrary, Kant held the creation idea to be useful as a limiting concept. Human thought must seek to interpret brute facts as far as it can with the help of its own categories. Using the category of substance as functional, it must see how far it can explain reality with the help of it. Using the category of causality as functional, it must think back as far as it can and see how far it can explain reality with the help of it. Using the category of purpose as functional, it must look forward as far as it can and see how far it can explain reality with the help of this category. If thus used as limiting concepts, the application of these categories does no injustice to brute fact. And if thus used as a limiting concept the application of the categories to brute facts does no violence to the exclusively immanentistic character of the principle of explanation. The creation idea does not then lead to a really transcendent God.

It will now be apparent that modern thought and Christianity stand squarely opposed to one another on the creation concept. If anywhere, the contrast ought to be clear at this point. Brute fact is the issue. Modern thought assumes it. Assuming brute fact, it thereby reduces God to the level of man. He is at most a co-interpreter, with man, of brute fact. His thought is therefore not on a higher level than the thought of man. Man does not need to await the interpretation of fact by God before he gives his own final interpretation.

Over against this, Christianity holds that God is the creator of every fact. There are no brute facts. Thus God's thought is placed back of every fact. Thereby man's thought is made subject to God's thought in the interpretation of every fact. There is not a single fact that man can interpret rightly without reference to God as the creator of that fact. Man cannot truly apply the category of causality to facts without the presupposition of God. It is God who has "caused" all facts to stand in a certain relation to one another. Man must seek to discover that relation as far as he can.

As Christians we join the battle with modern thought at this point in a life and death struggle. We maintain that unless God has created the existence of the universe, there would be no possibility of scientific thought. Facts would then be utterly unrelated. No two of them could be brought into any sort of relation with one another. We could not even think of the categories of human thought as revealing aspects of reality without the presupposition of God.

This implies that God must really be taken as the presupposition of the possibility of human interpretation. If with Butler we first allow the nontheistic principle of exclusively immanentistic interpretation for an area of human life, we have no further argument against modern thought. For us to allow that we can interpret any one fact without God is to maintain the bruteness of that fact. It is also to reduce God's thought to the level of man's thought. It is to make of God a finite God. We can then at best prove the existence of a finite God. We can in that case never prove the existence of the Creator of heaven and of earth. He has been excluded from the outset.

RECENT PHILOSOPHY AND THE CREATION IDEA

Before turning to a consideration of recent science and its attitude to the creation idea, we note what post-Kantian philosophy has to say on the subject. Has there been any change from the attitude of Kant? The, answer is that, if possible, there is a still more vehement rejection of the biblical creation idea than in the case of Kant. The pragmatic types of philosophy naturally have no use for the creation idea. To them reality has simply sprung from bare possibility. It is only in the idealist types of philosophy that any place is found for a creation concept. But the idealist types no less than the pragmatist types reject the biblical notion of creation. In this they but follow ancient idealism. Like ancient idealism, modern idealism has no place for a real creation idea because it holds to the notion of an exclusively immanentistic principle of interpretation.

The more extreme of absolute idealists, such as Bradley and Bosanquet, are very outspoken in their opposition to the traditional creation idea. It is only among those who reacted against absolute idealism that we seem to find some appreciation of the idea of creation. But even they are careful to distinguish their creation concept from the traditional one. So for instance Pringle-Pattison, who led the personalist revolt against the absolutist idealists, says: "The first feature in the ordinary idea of creation to which I wish to draw attention is that creation is regarded as an event which took place at a definite date in the past, to which we can remount by a temporal and causal regress."[4] He is amazed to find that "so able a theologian as the late Professor Flint"[5] should think of "creation as an event." He then discusses Flint's argument for temporal creation. Flint, he says, examines the universe to see whether it gives evidence of being an event. "And," he says, "because such an examination reveals mutability stamped upon every particular fact in the universe, even its apparently most stable formations—so that each may be treated as an event dependent on a previous event, a phase in a universal process of transformation—we have

---

4. A. Seth Pringle-Pattison, *The Idea of God in the Light of Recent Philosophy*, 2nd ed. (New York: Oxford University Press, 1920), 299.
5. Robert Flint (1838–1910) was a Scottish theistic philosopher who spent most of his career at the University of Edinburgh.

the extraordinary conclusion drawn that the universe as a whole is an event or effect in the same sense. But surely such an argument is an example *in excelsis* of the fallacy of Composition."[6] Then he adds: "It is difficult to understand the importance attached by many theologians to a temporal origin of the physical universe, if we have abandoned the geocentric hypothesis and its corollaries."[7]

On this we may remark as follows. The criticism of Pringle-Pattison with respect to Flint is to the point. No defense of the creation idea can be made if we assume that the category of causality is already intelligible to some extent without it. The creation idea offers itself as the presupposition of the applicability of the causality concept. If the causality concept is thought to be applicable within reality without the presupposition of the creation idea we cannot reason on to the creation idea. But though Pringle-Pattison's criticism of Flint is to the point this does not prove that the creation idea is just a hobby of theologians. Without the creation idea as applied to the whole universe there would be no fruitful application of the causality concept within the universe.[8]

Pringle-Pattison continues to speak of the creation of the world by a "self involved Deity," and says: "But such a conception of creation belongs to the same circle of ideas as the waving of a magician's wand. It has no place either in serious thinking or in genuine religion. It was an old gibe of the Epicureans, familiar in Cicero's day, to ask what God did before He created the heavens and the earth, and how He came to choose just then to create them, after forbearing to do so for so many ages—a flippancy, no doubt, but a flippancy provoked in some measure by the shallow anthropomorphism of the doctrine assailed."[9] He says that Augustine did not really answer this question when he stated that time itself was created by God. "The world, on his theory, still had an absolute origin; and, even if it had never existed at all, the self-existent being of God would have been in no way affected. And this external and almost accidental relation between the two is inevitably implied in phrases which speak of divine existence 'before the world was'. But

6. The fallacy of composition is a logical fallacy in which one infers of the whole what is true of its parts.

7. Pringle-Pattison, *The Idea of God*, 299–300.

8. In other words, causality *presupposes* creation but does not, in and of itself, define it.

9. Pringle-Pattison, *The Idea of God*, 303.

this solitary, ante-mundane Figure is the residuum of a primitive and pictorial fashion of thinking, a magnified man, but rarified to bare mind, after the analogy of Aristotle's pure thinking upon thought, and left standing apart from the world he is invoked to explain."[10]

This passage affords an interesting illustration of the real reason why the creation notion is rejected. The creation notion involves the notion of the self-sufficient God. The existence of such a God would destroy the self-sufficiency of human explanation in life. It would destroy the assumed sufficiency of the exclusively immanentistic principle of explanation. "A God so conceived," says Pringle-Pattison, "is an Absolute in the old bad sense of a being existing by itself with no essential relations to anything else. But if God is the principle through which the world becomes intelligible, His relation to the world cannot be of the merely incidental character indicated. If the universe is to be understood through God, the nature of God must no less be expressed in thc universe and understood through it."[11]

In his book *The Idea of God*, C. A. Beckwith[12] expresses the same sentiment: "And even if the atoms themselves may be conceived of as having had a beginning of their present form, the energy out of which they arose must be affirmed to be eternal. . . . What we term cause has no other signification than uniform and concomitant variation among phenomena."[13] So also J. M. E. McTaggart[14] in his book, *Some Dogmas of Religion,* says that the notion of a changeless cause outrages reason.[15] C. F. D'Arcy[16] argues in similar fashion when he says, "It is quite possible to conceive a Deity who is not quite good, as we think of goodness, but to imagine such a being as the Sovereign Power of the Universe is to our minds absolutely

10. Ibid., 303–4.

11. Ibid., 304.

12. Clarence A. Beckwith (1849–1931) was a teacher at the United Church of Christ's Chicago Theological Seminary.

13. Clarence Augustine Beckwith, *The Idea of God: Historical, Critical, Constructive* (New York: Macmillan, 1922), 119.

14. John McTaggart (1866–1925) was a Hegelian idealist metaphysician thought by some to be the greatest metaphysician of the early twentieth century. For most of his life McTaggart was a fellow and lecturer in philosophy at Trinity College, Cambridge.

15. John McTaggart Ellis McTaggart, *Some Dogmas of Religion* (London: Edward Arnold, 1906), 196ff.

16. Charles Frederick D'Arcy (1859–1938) was a theologian and a bishop in the Church of Ireland.

intolerable."[17]Again we note the words of M. C. Carroll to the effect that: "Ultimate questions as to the value of *this* universe are obviously meaningless, since this universe as a whole is the final value and standard of values."[18]

James Ward[19] tells us that there is not one point on which philosophers are so well agreed as on the fact that God has not created the world.[20] He adds: "We cannot begin from God and construct the universe."[21] Or again: "If the categories of substance and cause are only valid *within* experience, they cannot be applied to experience as a whole. Whatever implications experience may involve, it surely cannot involve that of transcending itself. Such miscalled transcendence, if it have any validity, must really be immanence at bottom."[22] In his book *The Realm of Ends*, Ward reasons in a similar manner. He says: ". . . the solution of our problem . . . ultimately turns on the reality of individual existence."[23] Here is the heart of the matter. The creation idea would destroy not only the ultimacy of brute fact, but also the ultimacy of the human mind. A created mind cannot consistently act in an autonomous fashion. A non-created mind can.

Modern thought assumes that determinate experience itself springs from the void. It takes for granted that brute facts have somehow of themselves formed themselves in such order that the categories of cause and substance can be applied to them. Against this we maintain that there would be no determinate experience unless God exists and has created the world as absolutely self-determined Experience.

With the rejection of the creation idea goes the rejection of the transcendence of God. Says Ward: "In calling God transcendent we seek only to express that duality of subject and object which

17. Charles F. D'Arcy, "The Theory of a Limited Deity," *Proceedings of the Aristotelian Society*, n.s., 18 (1917–1918): 164.

18. Marion Crane Carroll, "The Nature of the Absolute in the Metaphysics of Bernard Bosanquet," *Philosophical Review* 30 (1921): 183.

19. James Ward (1843–1925) was an English psychologist and philosopher.

20. James Ward, *Naturalism and Agnosticism*, 2 vols. (New York: Macmillan, 1899), 2:120.

21. Ibid.

22. Ibid., 129.

23. James Ward, *The Realm of Ends, or Pluralism and Theism* (Cambridge: University Press, 1920), 282.

we take as fundamental to all spiritual being, not to suggest that his relation to the world must be thought under the category of external causation, like the interaction of object with object."[24]

This may suffice to intimate the hostility of recent philosophy to the creation idea of Scripture. It is with this background that we now ask whether recent science is in accord with recent philosophy on this point.

RECENT SCIENCE AND THE CREATION DOCTRINE

The first point we should be careful to note again is that the mere assumption of brute fact is in itself a denial of the creation doctrine. Moreover, it is a denial of the creation doctrine on *a priori* grounds.[25] We have found that post-Kantian science claims not to be *a priori* in its method. Even mathematicians like Sir James Jeans and Professor Eddington claim to test their mathematical speculations by experience. But when it comes to the very first step of scientific procedure, all non-Christian scientists are equally *a priori* in their methods.

Taking brute facts for granted, scientists must also take for granted the ultimacy of the human mind. If there are brute facts, God is not all-comprehensive in his interpretation. He is then finite. Therefore man is on a par with him. Man's thought is then not subordinate to God's thought.

We do not wonder that scientists who build upon these non-theistic assumptions will find no evidence for the creation doctrine in the universe. They may say they are perfectly open-minded on the question. They may profess agnosticism about origins. They may even affirm belief in creation. It all amounts to the same thing. They do *not* believe creation in the biblical sense of the term.

It is now quite generally admitted that the first generation of evolutionists were really philosophers as much as scientists. They taught cosmic evolution as being back of biological evolution. Herbert Spencer and John Fiske did much to popularize the notion of cosmic evolution. Recently scientists are said to be more careful.

24. Ibid., 447.
25. That is, the notion of brute fact assumes, without evidence or argument, that facts are initially uninterpreted.

They are specialists who do not readily go beyond their province. But listen to some of them.

James Jeans tells us about some of the new discoveries in astronomy and physical science. In the foreword to his book *The Mysterious Universe,* he says: "The question at issue is ultimately one for philosophic discussion, but before the philosophers have a right to speak, science ought first to be asked to tell all she can as to ascertained facts and provisional hypotheses." As a scientist he then tells us what he thinks in the first four chapters. Of the fifth chapter he says: "The last chapter stands on a different level. Every one may claim the right to draw his own conclusions from the facts presented by modern science."[26] We should therefore expect that in the first four chapters Jeans would carefully limit himself to scientifically controllable material. Nevertheless we have given to us a complete cosmogony at the outset. He says that "some two thousand million years ago" a certain star wandered about near the sun. The result was that the sun threw off planets into space. The earth is one of those planets. It gradually cooled. Then he speaks of the origin of life as follows: "In course of time, we know not how, when, or why, one of these cooling fragments gave birth to life. It started in simple organisms whose vital capacities consisted of little beyond reproduction and death. But from these humble beginnings emerged a stream of life which, advancing through ever greater and greater complexity, has culminated in beings whose lives are largely centred in their emotions and ambitions, their aesthetic appreciations, and the religions in which their highest hopes and noblest aspirations lie enshrined."[27]

A little later he adds: "Into such a universe we have stumbled, if not exactly by mistake, at least as the result of what may properly be described as an accident. The use of such a word need not imply any surprise that our earth exists, for accidents will happen, and if the universe goes on for long enough, every conceivable accident is likely to happen in time. It was, I think, Huxley who said that six monkeys, set to strum unintelligently on typewriters for millions of millions of years, would be bound in time to write all the books in the British Museum."[28] The concluding sentence of the book

26. James Jeans, *The Mysterious Universe* (New York: Macmillan, 1930), vii–viii.
27. Ibid., 2–3.
28. Ibid., 4.

of Jeans reads as follows: "So that our main contention can hardly be that science of to-day has a pronouncement to make, perhaps it ought rather to be that science should leave off making pronouncements: the river of knowledge has too often turned back on itself."[29] But it would seem that Jeans made a fairly comprehensive pronouncement at the outset. It is the announcement that the universe came by Chance. It is the announcement that the creation idea must at the outset be assumed to be wrong.

Yet we may observe that the last sentence of Jeans' book is in reality a pronouncement no less than the one given from the beginning. It is a pronouncement of agnosticism. Jeans argues that science in the nature of the case deals with universals only. It can merely give us "pointer readings" of the facts. Such agnosticism is natural if one begins with brute facts. In fact the agnosticism ought on this view to be more thorough than it is. Science cannot even give "pointer-readings" without the creation idea. If it does it is spite of, and not because of its method.

The second man we look at briefly is H. Levy.[30] In his book, *The Universe of Science*, he tells us: "There is no ultimate philosophy for an eminently practical venture like science."[31] That would seem to allow room for the possibility of creation. But Levy leaves no room for creation. He says that science proceeds by the process of isolation. It takes the brute facts and studies isolated aspects of them. "Science, like common sense, sets out in the first instance to search for systems that can be imagined as isolated from their setting in the universe without appreciably disturbing their structure and the process they present. Here is a child. Almost as soon as the term child has been applied to it we have effected the isolation, for, in thought at any rate, we have dismissed its history, its family relationships, its home, and its country. We have isolated it by classifying it in this case, by merging it tentatively with other objects under the general heading CHILD."[32] But if we should fear that in this method the individuality of the object investigated may be lost Levy says: "This method of isolation by detailed classification does

29. Ibid., 160.
30. Hyman Levy (1889–1975) was a Scottish philosopher, mathematician, political activist, and fellow of the Royal Society of Edinburgh.
31. H. Levy, *The Universe of Science* (London: Century, 1932), 79.
32. Ibid., 45.

not destroy individuality or uniqueness. It merely examines it by disclosing the *unique combination* of isolated systems that the object possesses."[33] We need not follow Levy any further in his analysis of the scientific method. Our main concern is to point out that back of his method lies the assumption of fact as brute fact. Back of his whole procedure also lies the assumption that revelation can have nothing to do with scientific investigation. Speaking of scientists and their hypotheses he says: "If, in the development of their theories, they make demands on the Universe so exorbitant that the experimenter cannot meet these claims, then repudiation must be his only alternative. For in the last resort he is the arbiter."[34] It is not so much then a direct denial of creation that we find in the book of Levy. He simply does not need the creation doctrine in the whole of his scientific procedure. And this is from the Christian point of view no better than a flat denial of creation.

This assumption that in the whole of scientific procedure we need not take the creation doctrine into consideration is common among scientists. So, for instance, C. D. Broad[35] has a very thorough work on science and its procedure entitled *Scientific Thought*. Among other things he brings science into relation with philosophy. Philosophy itself he says, consists of two parts. There is critical and there is speculative philosophy. In the past men have indulged in working out speculative schemes without due respect for the facts of science. But "One's Speculative Philosophy tends to be influenced to an altogether undue extent by the state of one's liver and the amount of one's bank-balance."[36] We must therefore listen first to what science has to say. Then we can turn to critical philosophy. It takes the notions of science and evaluates them. After that we can form such speculative philosophy as we can. Broad himself does not enter the field of speculative philosophy in this book. He limits himself he says, to critical philosophy. In fact, however, there is back of his critical philosophy and his scientific method the speculative

33. Ibid., 46.
34. Ibid., 65.
35. Charlie D. Broad (1887–1971) was an English philosopher who, for most of his professional life, was associated with Trinity College, Cambridge. Broad thought Butler's *Analogy* to be the best defense of theism in existence.
36. C. D. Broad, *Scientific Thought* (London: Kegan Paul, Trench, Trubner & Co., 1923), 21.

assumption that facts are just there. He has assumed that creation is not back of the facts.

What is true about Broad is also true about Sir Arthur Eddington[37] in his recent book, *New Pathways in Science*. He is willing to admit that science cannot give us a full interpretation of life. "Science is an attempt to read the cryptogram of experience; it sets in order the facts of sensory experience of human beings. Everyone will agree that this attempt has met with considerable success; but it does not start quite at the beginning of the Problem of Experience. The first question asked about scientific facts and theories, such as we have been discussing in this book is, 'Are they true'? I would emphasize that even more significant than the scientific conclusions themselves is the fact that this question so urgently arises about them."[38] This sounds very encouraging. It would seem that here a scientist is really going to ask about the origin of facts. At last we seem to have found a modern scientist who realizes that the nature of facts is one thing if they have been created and another if they have not been created. But we are disillusioned in the very next sentence after the one given. "The question 'Is it true?' changes the complexion of the world of experience—not because it is asked *about* the world, but because it is asked *in* the world. When we go right back to the beginning, the first thing we must recognize in the world of experience is something intent on truth—something to which it matters intensely that beliefs should be true."[39] Thus even when Eddington wants to ask about ultimate issues he definitely declines to ask the question about the origin of the universe. Even when he asks the question, "What is the ultimate truth about ourselves?"[40] Eddington leaves the creation idea out of the picture. When he does give us his own speculative philosophy it is similar to that of Jeans, as the following quotation shows:

It seems that normally matter collects in big masses with excessively high temperature, and the formation of small cool

37. Arthur S. Eddington (1882–1944) was a British astronomer, physicist, and mathematician of the early twentieth century. He was also a philosopher of science and a popularizer of science.

38. Arthur Eddington, *New Pathways in Science* (Cambridge: University Press, 1935), 310.

39. Ibid., 310–11.

40. Ibid., 311.

globes fit for habitation is a rare occurrence. Nature seems to have been intent on a vast evolution of fiery worlds, an epic of milliards of years. As for Man—it seems unfair to be always raking up against Nature her one little inadvertence. By a trifling hitch of machinery—not of any serious consequence in the development of the universe—some lumps of matter of the wrong size have occasionally been formed. These lack the purifying protection of intense heat or the equally efficacious absolute cold of space. Man is one of the gruesome results of this occasional failure of antiseptic precautions.[41]

We are not surprised that Eddington should come to such conclusions about man. He began with the assumption of a philosophy of chance; he would naturally end with a philosophy of chance.[42]

We cannot continue our discussion of this point. Modern science has at best proceeded along the lines just now indicated in the case of Eddington. William Cecil Dampier Dampier-Whetham[43] in his book *A History of Science* shows this very thoroughly. We give merely an instance of what he brings out throughout his book. Speaking of geology in the nineteenth century he says:

Nevertheless, attempts made to explain how the Earth reached its present state were still forced into conformity with Biblical cosmogonies involving cataclysmic origins by water or fire.

The first to contend systematically against these views was James Hutton (1726–1797), who published his *Theory of the Earth* in 1785. Once more a practical acquaintance with natural processes paved the way for scientific advance.[44]

The idea of Dampier-Whetham is that the creation notion was based upon speculation, while the evolution theory was based upon sober scientific investigation.

41. Ibid., 309–10.
42. This shows, again, that reasoning is always circular when it comes to ultimate assumptions.
43. William Cecil Dampier Dampier, who was born William Cecil Dampier Whetham and wrote as William Cecil Dampier Dampier-Whetham (1867–1952), was a British scientist, agriculturist, and historian of science.
44. William Cecil Dampier Dampier-Whetham, *A History of Science and Its Relations with Philosophy and Religion* (New York: Macmillan, 1931), 289.

From what has been said so far, some may infer that most scientists today deny that the universe had an origin at all. We are not greatly concerned about this point. Some scientists think the earth has had a beginning: others think it has had no beginning. Sir James Jeans is quoted by Dampier-Whetham as follows:

> Everything points with overwhelming force to a definite event, or series of events, of creation at some time or times, not infinitely remote. The universe cannot have originated by chance out of its present ingredients, and neither can it have been always the same as now. For in either of these events no atoms would be left save such as are incapable of dissolving into radiation; there would be neither sunlight nor starlight but only a cool glow of radiation uniformly diffused through space. This is, indeed, so far as present-day science can see, the final end towards which all creation moves, and at which it must at long last arrive.[45]

We have already quoted from Jeans' book *The Mysterious Universe* to show that for Jeans there is nothing but chance back of the universe. It does not help us then if modern scientists do hold to "creation" if they think of this creation as springing into being by chance out of the void.

The total picture we obtain from both modern science and modern philosophy is a complete rejection of the biblical notion of creation. It matters not whether this rejection comes in the form of an outright negation, in the form of agnosticism or in the form of substituting another meaning for the word creation. As orthodox Christians we have to face the fact that we are at this point, as along the whole line of thought, out of accord with modern thought. And it is at this point that the weakness of the method of defense of Christianity as advocated by Butler appears most clearly. It was based upon the assumption of brute facts and man's ability, apart from God, to explain at least some of them. If one grants this much one cannot present any argument against modern science on the question of creation. The assumption of brute fact is itself the most

---

45. J. H. Jeans, *Eos, or the Wider Aspects of Cosmogony* (London: Kegan Paul, Trench, Trubner & Co., 1928), 55, quoted in ibid., 483.

basic denial of the creation doctrine. And the assumption that man can of himself interpret brute facts is itself the denial of God as creator. We need therefore to challenge the very idea of brute fact. We need to challenge man's ability to interpret any fact unless that fact be created by God and unless man himself is created by God.

PROVIDENCE

What we have said in the first part of this chapter with respect to Kant and modern philosophy applies to the concept of providence as much as to the concept of creation. We can, for that reason, now be brief in our discussion of providence. Then, too, those who do not accept creation are not likely to accept providence. Accordingly we do not really expect to find any acceptance of the providence doctrine in modern science.

As Christians we believe that God has made the facts of this world and the laws of this world. He has made the facts and the laws for one another. Moreover, he continues to support both facts and laws. This support and guidance of both facts and laws we call providence. To this we must add a word about "special Providence." The Christian position holds that God has a sovereign control over the history of this universe. He may at any time add new factors to the course of its development. The notion of the catastrophic is inherent in the Christian philosophy of history. When we say this we are not thinking of redemption and its miracles. The idea of the catastrophic precedes the idea of redemption. The idea of the catastrophic comes to a specific form of expression in redemptive miracle. But we must not anticipate our discussion of teleology. We merely wish to intimate that in the discussion of providence we are really discussing one aspect of the whole question of the philosophy of history. The other aspect is discussed in the question of teleology.

For the moment then we wish to limit ourselves chiefly to a consideration of what is generally called natural law. Or, to be still more specific, we wish to speak of physical law. What does modern science think of physical law?

In general this question may be answered by saying that science takes for granted the ultimacy of law as it takes for granted the ultimacy of facts. This is involved in its rejection of the creation doctrine. And this makes a biblical notion of providence impossible. The basic difference between a Christian and a non-Christian concept of providence is found at this point. It is not merely a question of whether a person believes that God can suddenly intervene with a special supernatural act in nature. It is that, as noted above. But even before that we hit upon the question of the foundation of law itself.[46] It is not only on the question of special occurrences in nature that we differ with modern science; it is on the question of the basis of natural law itself that the rift appears. The Butler type of apologetics has failed to observe this basic point. As it has not questioned the legitimacy of the assumption of brute facts, so it has not at every point challenged the legitimacy of the assumption of self-contained, ultimate laws. It has granted that science can make a true explanation of brute facts with the help of impersonal laws. It is only when this process goes so far as to explain away the specific doctrines of Christianity that the Butler type of apologetics has demurred. Instead of this we should challenge the notion of brute law as we should challenge the notion of brute fact.

The question of an exclusively immanentistic explanation meets us very pointedly here. It is by the laws of physics that the physical phenomena are supposed to be explained. No physical fact is said to be explained unless it fits into the scheme of physical law. We have already spoken of this in our discussion of the method of evidences. The point we wish to emphasize here is that even if science were willing to admit the occurrence of the "special providence" in some sense, it would still give a completely anti-Christian explanation of physical phenomena. It would still assume that laws are self-sufficient in the sense that they are not created and sustained by God. God would be left out of the picture.

To make plain what we mean on this matter we may refer to some scientists to see what they say about providence. J. Arthur Thomson speaks of the matter in his book, *Science and Religion*, as follows:

> The religious concept refers to a Spiritual Order, which can only be spiritually discerned. It is the glimmering of an idea that behind all is the will of God. It is the idea of a Creation

---

46. In other words, how can a universe supposedly governed by chance countenance any notion of law-like regularity within it? If there are laws in nature, those laws require an explanatory foundation.

which was not an event over and done with unthinkable millions of years ago, but remains as an enduring Divine thought. But God's relation to His world must remain entirely beyond man's comprehension. The Divine Imagining is beyond man's imagination.

One way of thinking of it we may safely exclude. We must not think of something Divine that underpins the material universe and its psychical correlate. It seems inconceivable that the world should need any underpinning, else were there great imperfection in the creative institution of the Order of Nature. It is more conceivable that the "irreducibles," such as electrons and mind, which were the work of His hands, were quite able for the work that He gave them to do.[47]

Later he adds:

In objecting to the idea of underpinning, or the secondary subsidising of natural processes with grants from a spiritual Treasury, we are not departing from our belief in God, as "the constitutive principle of the Universe," "the source and home of all the order."[48]

It may appear difficult to understand why Thomson should be so sure that the idea of "underpinning" the universe may be safely excluded. Is it easy to conceive that the "irreducibles" of which he speaks are self-sufficient? He does, to be sure, say that these "irreducibles" have been created by God. But the God who has "created" them is himself, by definition, but an aspect of the universe. Thus the "irreducibles" are really taken as self-sufficient. We do not think it is conceivable that the "irreducibles" of the universe would be self-sufficient. At any rate Thomson himself must admit that he is in the realm of speculative philosophy here. He should have given a philosophical justification of his position.

The real reason why Thomson feels he must exclude the idea of providence is that it would be inimical to the notion of an ex-

47. J. Arthur Thomson, *Science and Religion* (New York: Charles Scribner's Sons, 1925), 56.
48. Ibid., 124.

clusively immanentistic principle of interpretation. It would mean that God might at any moment bring in the catastrophic. And even back of that it would mean that God's interpretation would have to be recognized in the investigation of every fact. And this is intolerable to modern science.

INDETERMINACY IN PHYSICS

At this juncture it may be questioned whether science is insistent upon a principle of continuity in its interpretation. Has not the conception of natural law changed in recent times? Has not a good deal been made of the fact that law is no longer thought of as absolute? Pre-Kantian science, we are told, whether of the rationalistic or the inductivist variety, thought of physical law as absolute. Then Kant came. He showed that law is a subjective contribution to the knowledge situation.[49] Its meaning was limited to possible experience. There is an area about which the mind cannot legislate. The reign of law is not universal. We can never subsume the whole of reality under the domain of law. Science deals with abstractions—Thomson speaks of this when he says of the scientific method: "It is not the only kind of knowledge; it is partial and abstract, for it deliberately restricts itself to verifiable factors that can be measured or registered, observed again and again, and even experimented with."[50] Jeans and Eddington make a good deal of the abstract character of science. C. E. M. Joad[51] in two recent books speaks of it again and again (*Guide to Modern Thought* and *Philosophical Aspects of Modern Science*). The point of this fact that science deals with abstractions is that it can, accordingly, never determine the individual completely. It can never explain the individual object without residue. It is therefore impossible to

---

49. In other words, for Kant, the categories of the mind are imposed on the facts in order to make sense of them. But this categorical imposition presupposes our experience and thus cannot obtain when there is no experience, or sense data.

50. J. Arthur Thomson, "How Science Changes Our Vision of God," in *Has Science Discovered God? A Symposium of Modern Scientific Opinion*, ed. Edward H. Cotton (New York: Thomas Y. Crowell, 1931), 165.

51. Cyril E. M. Joad (1891–1953) was an English philosopher and media personality. He was famous for his appearance on *The Brains Trust*, a popular BBC Radio wartime discussion program. He was also credited for popularizing philosophy in his day.

predict the future of any individual with absolute precision. When we deal with prediction about the behavior of individuals we can merely speak of likelihoods and probabilities. To the extent that our universals such as causation enlighten us about an aspect of individual things they can only tell us what the likely behavior of individual behavior will be.

To this argument from the abstract character of science we must add another. We are told by many scientists today that there is "free will" in the atom. In describing scientific theory, Joad says:

> The atom is not in a constant condition; it may absorb energy from without or radiate energy outwards. When it does the former, an electron jumps from an inner to an outer orbit; when the latter, from an outer to an inner. A peculiar property of these electronic jumps is that the jumping does not appear to pass over the intervening space between the orbit of departure and the orbit of arrival. It is simply observed to turn up in a new orbit, having last been observed in a different orbit: so far as the evidence takes us, one might be justified in saying that it goes out of existence in one place and comes into existence again at another. Another peculiar property of the jumps is that we do not know when they will occur or why. They seem, in fact, so far as our knowledge goes at present, to be uncaused.[52]

These two arguments, the one from the abstractness of science and the one from the "free will" in the atom amount virtually to the same thing as far as the question of law is concerned. Both arguments tell us that science cannot predict completely. Prediction itself is limited to aspects or aggregates of reality. The individual object cannot be completely explained. It is once more brute fact that appears more brute than ever. Accordingly laws have to be thought of as being no more than statistical averages. As statistical averages physical laws tell us what is *likely* to be true of a certain individual. The individual reveals an aspect of itself as a member of the class about which the law speaks. The individual may reveal several aspects of itself as it is a member of several classes. "Laws of behaviour are always generalized statements of what has occurred

52. C. E. M. Joad, *Guide to Modern Thought* (London: Faber & Faber, 1933), 80–81.

in the past. They can be nothing more. They are based on past evidence and have no *guaranteed* validity for the future. In this sense there is no determinism in science or anywhere."[53]

This conception of physical law as merely statistical average has in recent times been used in order to show that science is favorable to the notion of providence. But if we look at the matter carefully it appears that statistical law is no more favorable to the doctrine of providence than is absolute law. In the first place statistical law, as thought of by scientists, is no less deterministic than absolute law. The admissions that science deals with abstractions only, that there is "free will" in the atom, or that the laws of behavior are merely generalized statements about past experience do not imply that law, as far as it goes, is any the less deterministic than it was before. They only imply that law cannot go as far as men formerly thought it could go. They only imply that the behavior of a certain individual cannot be completely predicted.

It will be said at this point that recent science is basically indeterminist in its philosophy. Must not recent science be contrasted with the science of Leibniz and the other rationalists, on the point of determinism? Is there not a basic metaphysical irrationalism at the root of recent science? Granted this be true, and there is much truth in it, even so the principle of continuity is not given up by science. The ideal of complete comprehension is before the mind of the recent scientist no less than it was before the mind of Leibniz. Even if he grants that he can never in any given finite time expect to predict completely, he will not allow that his prediction, as far as it can, in the nature of the case, reach the individual, is not self-sufficient. For him the unique individual is a "not yet explored" something. His prediction may be based upon a philosophy of chance or indeterminism. In that case the scientist will assume that the laws are chance collocations of facts. But all this will for him have nothing to do with God's creation of or providence over facts.

THE "SUPERNATURAL"

Having clearly seen the basic difference between the modern concept of physical law and the doctrine of providence, we can

---

53. Levy, *The Universe of Science*, 140–41.

more readily understand that modern science cannot allow for the idea of the "supernatural." To allow for the idea of the supernatural is to allow for the idea of the sovereign transcendent God. On an indeterminist basis science can and does indeed allow for the strange and weird. The strange or the weird are for science nothing more than the individual that cannot be wholly explained, or the individual that is an exception to statistical law. We shall not here deal with the concept of the miraculous. That will come up under the question of redemption. The supernatural is inherent in the very bedrock of theism. Without recognizing it we have not recognized providence. A sovereign God cannot be subjected to experiment. He may do something that will not fit into our schemes. But science cannot accept that which is not open to experiment by would-be autonomous man.

Before concluding this chapter we may call particular attention to the fact that involved in the notions of creation and providence is the notion of revelation. If the universe is created by God and if it is maintained by God it is itself a revelation of God on a finite scale. But if God's providence is over this world he may at any moment introduce, as we have observed, new factors into its development. Similarly God may speak to man when he pleases in a supernatural fashion. We believe that he has done this in the Scriptures. In fact our doctrine of creation and our doctrine of providence come from the Scriptures. As sinners we could get them nowhere else. Calvin brings this out in his *Institutes* when he says that the sinner must be told by God not only that he is a sinner, but also that he is a creature. It is the characteristic of the sinner that he will not consider himself to be a creature of God. He feels this to be too humiliating for him. If he is a creature of God he must submit to God. But sin is the declaration of man's independence from God. Sinful man seeks to be autonomous. Thus the rejection of the Bible itself implies the rejection of creation and providence. On the other hand, those who accept creation or providence cannot logically reject the Bible. Sinful man is as much opposed to the one as to the other; saved man accepts the one as well as the other.

This does not mean that we hold creation or providence to be merely a matter of revelation in the sense that they are not rationally defensible. On the contrary, we hold that though we must, as sinners, get these doctrines from the Bible, they are indeed rationally defensible.[54] With them it is as with the rest of the Bible teaching; unless they be true there can be no interpretation of anything without them. The world of facts would be utterly discrete. There would be no laws at all. There would be none to interpret the facts and the laws. We need them because we need the self-sufficient God as the presupposition of our experience.

54. That is, presupposing the authority of the self-attesting Scriptures is rationally defensible in that, unless such authority is presupposed, one has no basis for understanding any facts or any laws.

CHAPTER 7

TELEOLOGY

The question of teleology must now engage our attention. In it we deal more specifically with the Christian philosophy of history. Christianity presupposes the self-sufficient God of the Scriptures. It is within the ontological Trinity that we find a self-sufficient purpose.[1] When God created the universe he created it for and unto himself. By his providence God sustains the universe in order to realize his ultimate purpose with it.

It follows from this that there is purpose *within* the universe because the triune God has a purpose *for* the universe. Every purpose within the universe must, in the last analysis, be referred to God. Without this reference to God, no purpose within the universe has meaning.

It follows also that every fact within the universe has a purpose, or function to fulfill. Even that which we think of as mechanical has a purpose. Mechanical laws are, from the ultimate point of view, completely teleological.[2]

It follows still further that the universe is *organically* teleological. This is true in a twofold sense. In the first place the "mechanical"

---

1. This is central to any teleology. The purpose of the universe both transcends the universe itself and is independent of it. Any other assumed purpose will remain immanentistic.

2. That is, even though "mechanical" laws seem to operate in a determined fashion, they still operate to the glory of God. Thus, that which is mechanical is teleological.

is subordinate to that which is self-consciously teleological. Man was created prophet, priest and king over the universe. This places a connection between the vicissitudes of man and the universe. In the second place the events of earlier history are preparatory to the events of later history. There is an *increasing* purpose through history. God is gradually reaching a climax with history. Every event leads up to that climax and contributes to it. That is the Christian notion of progress. The universe is successful; the Christian is an optimist; he alone can be an optimist. The universe is Christologically teleological.

If we think more particularly of man in this teleological scheme, we have the following. Man's thoughts and acts have meaning and fulfill a purpose, just because of God's purpose with all things. Man thinks analogically and acts analogically. He does whatever he does "to the glory of God." When he manipulates his immediate "impersonal" environment he is conscious of the ultimate environment which is personal. In all this he thinks God's thoughts after him and does God's works for him. Thus he is genuinely free. He is free because he is determinate.[3] He is finitely determinate because God is absolutely determinate.

Special mention should be made here of the fact that the question of evil or sin does not in an ultimate sense change the conception of teleology advanced. Evil did not come into the universe as a surprise to God. It is subject to his counsel. God accomplishes his ultimate purpose with the universe in spite of and even by means of sin and evil. Sin is a wilful transgression of the revealed will of God, but not a breaking of the counsel of God.

NON-THEISTIC TELEOLOGY IN PHILOSOPHY

In complete contrast with this Christian view of teleology is the non-Christian view. The non-Christian view denies the doctrines of creation and providence. It denies any reference to a transcendent, self-sufficient God. It is based upon a philosophy of chance. Bare possibility is taken as the most basic metaphysical category. Frequently all teleology is denied. But even if some sort of teleology

---

3. That is, man's freedom is what it is because of God's foreordination of that freedom.

is affirmed it is a teleology that is a chance collocation of brute facts. It is always an exclusively immanentistic teleology.

The modern form of this non-Christian immanentistic teleology is strikingly expressed by Kant. As noted above, he virtually reduced all the theistic proofs to the ontological one. According to Kant, speculative theology made an unjustifiable leap beyond the realm of possible experience. He said it took abstract thought and concluded to a Being that is beyond experimental proof. As against this he held to what he called the transcendental nature of thought. Thought, says Kant, is an abstraction, unless brought into connection with space time facts. Accordingly the categories of thought can never go beyond the phenomenal world. So then the category of purpose, like the categories of substance and causality, apply within our experience of the phenomenal world. Purpose cannot be spoken of in connection with the universe as a whole.[4]

As in the case of substance and causality, we may use the notion of purpose as a limiting concept. We may strive as best we can to bring life into unity with the notion of a "supreme" purpose. To be sure we shall never succeed in doing so completely. The mechanical cannot be completely subordinated to our purposes. And what is true of the mechanical is still more true of evil. Yet we must place before ourselves the goal of absolute perfection, both of ourselves and of the universe.

Idealist philosophy has followed Kant in his notion that teleology must be thought of immanentistically. It may seem sometimes as though idealist philosophy has returned to the notion of a transcendent purpose. It speaks much of God as the Absolute. It even speaks of God as the Beyond. It wants to interpret "the lower in terms of the higher." Yet, on the whole, idealism identifies the Absolute with the Whole. God then becomes the higher aspect of Reality as a whole. Thus purpose is reduced to an exclusively immanentistic category after all.

That idealism really teaches nothing but an immanent teleology may be seen from its notion of individuality. Bosanquet speaks of this at length in his book, *The Value and Destiny of the Individual.*[5]

---

4. This is the case, in Kant, because we can have no experience of "the universe as a whole." We experience only the data around us at any given time.

5. B. Bosanquet, *The Value and Destiny of the Individual* (London: Macmillan, 1913), 153ff.

He feels that if he is to believe in God as the Beyond he must reduce man to an adjective of God. He has no eye for the Christian theistic conception of analogical thought and action. He thinks univocally. If God does something or thinks something, man can ultimately have nothing to do with it. If man does something or thinks something God can ultimately have nothing to do with it. It is an either-or conception of thought. Christianity holds that God thinks and acts in an absolute sense and man thinks and acts after God on a created plane.

The personal idealism of such men as A. Seth Pringle-Pattison, although reacting against absolute idealism, still holds to an exclusively immanentistic teleology. Pringle-Pattison connects his discussion of the subject with that of Bosanquet.[6] Pringle-Pattison dislikes having the finite individual reduced to an adjective of the Absolute. He wants to maintain the "Imperviousness" of the finite individual. He had developed this criticism of Bosanquet and absolute idealism in his book, *Hegelianism and Personality*. He returns to a similar line of thought in his later book, *The Idea of God*. But this approach to the question is immanentistic no less than is the approach of Bosanquet. If man is, strictly speaking, impervious to God, it means that he thinks his thoughts independently of God. We have noted before that for Pringle-Pattison God no less than man is dependent upon brute facts. In the present connection Pringle-Pattison says:

> The modern scientific view thus tends to coincide with the ideal outlined by Kant at the close of the *Critique of Pure Reason*—"the systematic unity of nature", conceived as "complete teleological unity." This ideal, "essentially and indissolubly connected with the nature of our reason and prescribing the very law of its operation", impels us "to regard all order in the world *as if* it originated from the intention of a supreme reason". But, as he wisely adds, "the agency of a Supreme Being is not to be invoked by a species of *ignava ratio* to explain

6. See B. Bosanquet, *The Principle of Individuality and Value* (London: Macmillan, 1912), Lecture 4: "The Teleology of Finite Consciousness," and A. Seth Pringle-Pattison, *The Idea of God in the Light of Recent Philosophy*, 2nd ed. (New York: Oxford University Press, 1920), 323ff.

particular phenomena, instead of investigating their causes in the general mechanism of matter. This is to consider the labour of reason ended when we have merely dispensed with its employment, which is guided surely and safely only by the order of nature and the series of changes in the world—which are arranged according to immanent and general laws. . . ."[7]

To this Pringle-Pattison adds the following words.

The whole idea thus sketched constitutes an emphatic repudiation, on Kant's part, of what he had himself signalized as characteristic of the old argument—the view of purpose as external and contingent, super-induced upon the facts and manifested only in particular contrivances of nature.[8]

Or again:

And when we analyze our real meaning in the light of Kant's suggestion, we see clearly that, in attributing purposiveness to the universe or any lesser whole, what we are concerned about is the character of the reality in question and not the pre-existence of a plan of it in anybody's mind. A teleological view of the universe means the belief that reality is a significant whole.[9]

This view of Pringle-Pattison, based as it is upon Kant, sets forth clearly the modern view of teleology. The contrast between modern philosophy and Christianity is on this point, as elsewhere, complete and irreconcilable. There is one aspect of the problem, however, that calls for special consideration. What does modern philosophy do with sin and evil? Does it hold to a teleological universe even in the face of evil?

The answer of Idealist philosophy on this point is plain. There have been several major works dealing with this problem. Among

---

7. Pringle-Pattison, *The Idea of God*, 328–29.
8. Ibid., 329.
9. Ibid., 330.

them are the works of Josiah Royce[10] and Hastings Rashdall.[11] Following the example of Hegel these men have sought to knit evil into the pattern of a universe in such a way that there should be a balance in favor of the good. Evil is thought of as merely a stepping stone toward the good. Yet even here the absolute good is again nothing but a limiting concept. As all facts are taken to be ultimate so the fact of evil is also taken to be ultimate. Evil is another brute fact. It has nothing to do with the plan of God. It is just there somehow. God faces ultimate evil just as we face it. He cannot overcome it entirely any more than we can overcome it entirely. Good and evil are really equally ultimate aspects of the universe as a whole.

Idealism as well as Kant is opposed to Christianity in that it holds to an exclusively immanentistic conception of teleology. Other types of philosophy are certainly no less so. Some of these other philosophies are materialistic or mechanistic. As such they reject every sort of teleology. But even non-mechanist philosophies other than idealism hold to an exclusively immanentistic teleology. Pragmatism believes in teleology. It thinks that man must make nature subordinate to his wishes. But the universe which must be made subordinate to man is itself a product of chance. Thus there is not a particle of theistic teleology in pragmatism.

NON-THEISTIC TELEOLOGY IN SCIENCE

With this background we are prepared to inquire about modern science and its attitude to teleology. It has frequently been pointed out that the eighteenth century was unfavorable to teleology. There seemed to be teleology in the system of Spinoza but it was a rationalistic teleology. Such ideologies were largely deterministic and

10. Josiah Royce (1855–1916) was the leading American proponent of Absolute idealism. Royce, whom the pragmatist C. S. Peirce called "our American Plato," spoke of limited universes of discourse. Limitation is the product of negation, which allows for a hierarchy of relations. The "less good" (because it is limited) is lower than the "more good" (because it is lacking in the previous limitation). It is this limitation, Royce thought, that allows for order and for an understanding of such asymmetrical relationships. For Van Til's brief assessment of Royce, see Cornelius Van Til, "Recent American Philosophy," *Philosophia Reformata: Orgaan van de Vereniging voor Calvinistische Wijsbegeerte* 2 (1937): 1–24.

11. Hastings Rashdall (1858–1924) was an English philosopher, theologian, and historian. Along with G. E. Moore and others, he was known as a teleologist because of his views of utilitarianism.

therefore really no teleologies at all. Even those who, in opposition to Rationalism, held to the inductive method did not believe in a theistic teleology. The Newtonian universe was usually thought of as a machine. Newton himself, we are told, thought of it thus. As an orthodox Christian he believed in the God of the Bible, but as a scientist he thought of the world as a machine. God did now and then work in the world miraculously, but for the rest the universe seemed able to run its own course.[12] Thomas Paine thought of God as the "Almighty Lecturer." " 'The belief of a God,' he says, 'far from having anything of mystery in it, is of all beliefs the most easy.' " God is simply the maker of the world machine. Paine holds that this position is far superior to that of the materialists.[13]

In short, pre-Kantian science, whether rationalist or inductivist, thought of the laws of nature as absolute and self-existing. The deists before Locke were, generally speaking, inductivist, but both were equally insistent upon the self-sufficiency of the laws of the universe. If God had any purpose with the universe it was all expressed in the original act of creation. Even so they had no biblical view of creation.

In post-Kantian science, all this was gradually changed. Science caught up gradually with the Kantian notion of the limiting concept. Not as though the change was sudden. In fact the change was gradual. There is a good deal of materialism and mechanism in the nineteenth century. Nevertheless the concept of organism appears upon the scene. A. Seth Pringle-Pattison has, in the book already referred to, a chapter, "The Liberating Influence of Biology."[14] To be sure, Darwin himself held to chance variation as the origin of new species. But even so there was at least the fact of the emergence of life as of something new to be taken into consideration. Pringle-Pattison says:

> The great biological advance belongs to the century between us and Kant, and we should expect accordingly to find in the science and philosophy of to-day a more adequate interpretation of the

12. See Walter Marshall Horton, *Theism and the Scientific Spirit* (New York: Harper & Brothers, 1933), 45ff.

13. See ibid., 55–57, quoting from Thomas Paine, *The Theological Works of Thomas Paine* (Chicago: Belfords, Clarke & Co., Publishers, 1879), 49.

14. Pringle-Pattison, *The Idea of God*, 66.

characteristic attributes of life than is offered in the Kantian theory. On the whole, this expectation is not disappointed. The mechanistic tradition is still strong, among "the old guard" of physiologists, but among the more thoughtful biologists of a younger generation, a steadily increasing number of voices is heard pleading for "the autonomy of life". The last series of Gifford Lectures, delivered in this University by Professor Driesch, on the "Science and Philosophy of the Organism", sufficiently attests the prominence of this question at the present time.[15]

Two points should be noted here. In the first place the study of biology was in itself conducive to the thought of teleology. In the second place, among biologists there was a difference of opinion. The theory of De Vries that evolution is not mechanical but organic, pointed to a possible teleological interpretation of life as a whole. It is noteworthy that M. Bergson's[16] philosophy was very prominent toward the close of the nineteenth century. Speaking of Bergson, Pringle-Pattison says:

But undoubtedly the most striking feature of his thought is the extent to which it is determined by the biological way of looking at things. The intimate appreciation of living experience forms the basis of the whole *Weltanschauung* which he offers us. His philosophy connects itself, therefore, directly with the biological revolt against the reduction of reality to the interplay of physical constants.[17]

F. Heinemann[18] in his book *Neue Wege der Philosophie* traces the development of nineteenth century thought in a similar fashion. He speaks of three stages of development. First there is the *Geistphilosophie*.[19] It is represented by the monistic school of Hegel. It

15. Ibid., 69.
16. Henri-Louis Bergson (1859–1941) was a French philosopher who was influential especially in the first half of the twentieth century.
17. Pringle-Pattison, *The Idea of God*, 69.
18. Fritz Heinemann (1889–1970) was a German philosopher.
19. I.e., "philosophy of mind (or spirit)."

was largely rationalistic. We should not forget, however, that Hegel came after Kant and had learned of Kant to take the space-time coordinates as the principle of individuation. After the *Geistphilosophie*, says Heinemann, came the *Lebensphilosophie*.[20] In psychology Freud sought to get away from intellectualistic theories. Bergson's stress on intuition rather than on intellect as the source of knowledge is characteristic of this period. In history the school of Rickert[21] gained ascendency. History was henceforth to study the individual. The individual was no longer to be thought of as a mere illustration of an absolute law. He was to be studied in and for himself. In the third place we come upon the *Existenzphilosophie*.[22] It is but an extension of *Lebensphilosophie* in its reaction to *Geistphilosophie*.

With respect to this nineteenth century development we would remark that it indicates an ever increasing emphasis upon the self-sufficiency of exclusively immanentistic categories. Granted there is some sort of recognition of teleology, it is at most an immanentistic teleology. There is in the first place a great emphasis upon starting from experience as from something ultimate. The individual of Dilthey is an ultimate individual. It is *Das Einmalige*,[23] in the absolute sense of the term. It is brute fact from which he wishes to start. These individuals are no longer to be brought into the relational system of fixed qualities, but must be brought into a dynamical or functional "*Wirkungszusammenhang*," "*der als solcher zugleich wertgebend, zwecksetzend, kurz schaffend ist. Das ist der springende Punkt.*"[24, 25] Thus the universal of interpretation is to be sought without any reference to God. Dilthey's position implies the complete rejection of the ideal of absolute interpretation as an absolute ideal, and the substitution for it of the absolute ideal as a limiting concept. Heinemann says, in setting forth Dilthey's thought and the thought of the *Lebensphilosophie* in general: "*Es gibt*

20. I.e., "philosophy of life."

21. Heinrich J. Rickert (1863–1936) emphasized a difference between historical fact and scientific fact.

22. I.e., "existence philosophy" (Heinemann claims to have coined this term).

23. I.e., "the One."

24. Fritz Heinemann, *Neue Wege der Philosophie* (New Paths of Philosophy) (Leipzig: Quelle & Meyer, 1929), 201.

25. I.e., "causal relationship, which as such brings about the giving of worth and the establishing of purpose. That is the crucial point."

im Grunde keine letzten Antworten auf die Fragen des Lebens, sondern nur den Prozess des Fragens und Antwortens selbst."[26, 27] We shall speak of these matters more fully in a following chapter.

Summing up the development in the nineteenth century science we see no evidence of an approach to Christianity. The reaction of the *Lebensphilosophie* represented by such men as Dreisch, Bergson, Dilthey and Freud indicates a tendency away from idealism but does not indicate an approach to Christianity. This reaction merely indicates a deeper descent into the self-sufficiency of brute fact and man's interpretation of brute fact.

CHANGES IN TWENTIETH CENTURY SCIENCE

But now we turn to the twentieth century. Many Christian apologists have become very enthusiastic about the changes in recent science. They seem to see a real approach to Christianity in it. Nineteenth century science was still largely materialistic and mechanistic, but the twentieth century, we are told, has reintroduced the concept of teleology in a real way. We shall briefly analyze the foundation of this contention.

In the first place it is said that scientists now tend to think of the universe as spiritual while formerly they tended to think of it as material. And as we associate the spiritual with the personal and with the higher aspects of life, this change in viewpoint on the part of science is said to be favorable to Christianity.

Appeal is made particularly to such men as Sir James Jeans and Sir Arthur S. Eddington. Both of these men have given us extensive popular interpretations of their scientific findings. They have sought to estimate the religious significance of the present day conclusions of science. We shall look at Eddington's view first.

In 1929 Eddington published his book, *The Nature of the Physical World*. In this book Eddington contends that we cannot really know the physical universe, as common sense thinks it can. He gives an illustration as follows:

26. Heinemann, *Neue Wege der Philosophie*, 207.
27. I.e., "There are basically no final answers to the questions of life, only the process of asking and answering itself."

The word elephant calls up a certain association of mental impressions, but it is clear that mental impressions as such cannot be the subject handled in the physical problem. We have, for example, an impression of bulkiness. To this there is presumably some direct counterpart in the external world, but that counterpart must be of a nature beyond our apprehension, and science can make nothing of it. Bulkiness enters into exact science by yet another substitution; we replace it by a series of readings of a pair of calipers. Similarly the greyish black appearance in our mental impression is replaced in exact science by the readings of a photometer for various wavelengths of light. And so on until all the characteristics of the elephant are exhausted and it has become reduced to a schedule of measures. There is always the triple correspondence—

(a) a mental image, which is in our minds and not in the external world;

(b) some kind of counterpart in the external world, which is of inscrutable nature;

(c) a set of pointer readings, which exact science can study and connect with other pointer readings.

And so we have our schedule of pointer readings ready to make the descent. And if you still think that this substitution has taken away all reality from the problem, I am not sorry that you should have a foretaste of the difficulty in store for those who hold that exact science is all-sufficient for the description of the universe and that there is nothing in our experience which cannot be brought within its scope.[28]

It is upon the indirect nature of knowledge that Eddington lays a great deal of stress. He draws from it two main conclusions. One of these pertains to the unpredictability of events and the other to the right of mystical interpretation.

Speaking of "The New Epistemological Outlook," Eddington says:

Scientific investigation does not lead to knowledge of the intrinsic nature of things. "Whenever we state the properties

28. A. S. Eddington, *The Nature of the Physical World* (New York: Macmillan, 1929), 253–54.

of a body in terms of physical quantities we are imparting knowledge of the response of various metrical indicators to its presence and nothing more" (p. 257). But if a body is not acting according to strict causality, if there is an element of uncertainty as to the response of the indicators, we seem to have cut away the ground for this kind of knowledge. It is not predetermined what will be the reading of the weighing-machine if the body is placed on it, therefore the body has no definite mass; nor where it will be found an instance hence, therefore it has no definite velocity; nor where the rays now being reflected from it will converge in the microscope, therefore it has no definite position; and so on. It is no use answering that the body really has a definite mass, velocity, position, etc., which we are unaware of; that statement, if it means anything, refers to an intrinsic nature of things outside the scope of scientific knowledge. We cannot infer these properties with precision from anything that we can be aware of, because the breach of causality has broken the chain of inference. Thus our knowledge of the response of indicators to the presence of the body is non-existent; therefore we cannot assert knowledge of it at all. So what is the use of talking about it? The body which was to be the attraction of all these (as yet unsettled) pointer readings has become superfluous in the physical world. That is the dilemma into which the old epistemology leads us as soon as we begin to doubt strict causality.

In phenomena on a gross scale this difficulty can be got around. A body may have no definite position but yet have within close limits an extremely probable position. When the probabilities are large the substitution of probability for certainty makes little difference; it adds only a negligible haziness to the world. But though the practical change is unimportant there are fundamental theoretical consequences. All probabilities rest on a basis of *a priori* probability, and we cannot say whether probabilities are large or small without having assumed such a basis. In agreeing to accept those of our calculated probabilities which are very high as virtually equivalent to certainties on the old scheme, we are as it were making our adopted basis of *a priori* probability a constituent of the world-structure—adding to the world a kind of symbolic texture that cannot be expressed on the old scheme.

On the atomic scale of phenomena the probabilities are in general well balanced, and there are no "naps" for the scientific punter to put his shirt on. If a body is still defined as a bundle of pointer readings (or highly probable pointer readings) there are no "bodies" on the atomic scale. All that we can extract is a bundle of probabilities. That is in fact just how Schrödinger tries to picture the atom—as a wave centre of his probability entity.[29]

Here we have both items spoken of above. There is the substitution of statistical law for absolute law; i.e., the idea of real probability instead of probability merely based upon ignorance. Secondly there is the "symbolic texture that cannot be expressed on the old scheme."

What he means by this "symbolic texture" can perhaps best be learned from his little book, *Science and the Unseen World*, published in 1930. The title of this book, the contents of which was given as the Swarthmore Lecture for the Society of Friends, indicates that Eddington thinks he is able to justify the "Mystical outlook" on life. Inasmuch as science can give us no direct knowledge of the universe we must trust the intuitions of our own consciousness, he thinks. In this little book Eddington again emphasizes the indirectness and abstractness of scientific knowledge.

And if to-day you ask a physicist what he has finally made out æther or the electron to be, the answer will not be a description in terms of billiard balls or fly-wheels or anything concrete; he will point instead to a number of symbols and a set of mathematical equations which they satisfy. What do the symbols stand for? The mysterious reply is given that physics is indifferent to that; it has no means of probing beneath the symbolism. To understand the phenomena of the physical world it is necessary to know the equations which the symbols obey but not the nature of that which is being symbolised.[30]

29. Ibid., 303–5.
30. Arthur Stanley Eddington, *Science and the Unseen World* (New York: Macmillan, 1929), 30.

Now all this contains a challenge to materialism, says Eddington. Science no longer pretends to say that ultimate reality is material. How could it, since it claims to know nothing about ultimate reality?

Penetrating as deeply as we can by the methods of physical investigation into the nature of a human being we reach only symbolic description. Far from attempting to dogmatise as to the nature of the reality thus symbolised, physics most strongly insists that its methods do not penetrate behind the symbolism.[31]

This sounds very encouraging at first blush. Yet we have become somewhat wary of recent expressions of agnosticism on the part of science. They have sometimes had a sting in them. Do we find this to be the case with Eddington? Following the sentence just quoted, he continues:

Surely then that mental and spiritual nature of ourselves, known in our minds by an intimate contact transcending the methods of physics, supplies just that interpretation of the symbols which science is admittedly unable to give. It is just because we have a real and not merely a symbolic knowledge of our own nature that our nature seems so mysterious; we reject as inadequate that merely symbolic description which is good enough for dealing with tables and chairs and physical agencies that affect us only by remote communication.[32]

And what do we seem thus directly to know about ourselves? Negatively we know that we are free. Natural law cannot hem us in. "Natural law is not applicable to the unseen world behind the symbols, because it is unadapted to anything except symbols, and its perfection is a perfection of symbolic linkage. You cannot apply such a scheme to the parts of our personality which are not measurable by symbols any more than you can extract the square root of a sonnet."[33]

31. Ibid., 36.
32. Ibid., 36–37.
33. Ibid., 53.

Eddington goes on to describe the nature of the unseen world, without limiting his remarks to the self with respect to whom he says we have immediate knowledge. He says,

> When we assert that God is real, we are not restricted to a comparison with the reality of atoms and electrons. If God is as real as the shadow of the Great War on Armistice Day, need we seek further reason for making a place for God in our thoughts and lives? We shall not be concerned if the scientific explorer reports that he is perfectly satisfied he has got to the bottom of things without having come across either.[34]

Thus Eddington somehow feels that God may exist. With respect to matters of the Unseen World, reasoning fails us altogether, he holds. It is in our consciousness as such that we touch the unseen.

> Obviously we cannot trust every whim and fancy of the mind as though it were indisputable revelation; we can and must believe that we have an inner sense of values which guides us as to what is to be needed, otherwise we cannot start on our survey even of the physical world. Consciousness alone can determine the validity of its convictions.[35]

Of this position of Eddington, C. E. M. Joad made a criticism in his recent book *Philosophical Aspects of Modern Science*. He feels that Eddington has really done very little but set forth the position of subjective idealism. He says that Eddington needs the brute facts, which he says science cannot reach, as a criterion by which to measure the truth of his scientific pointer readings. "Thus the world of common experience is the datum from which the physicist starts and the criterion by which he determines the validity of the structure he raises. It is, therefore, presupposed as real and objective throughout."[36] To this criticism of Joad's, Eddington replies in his book *New Pathways in Science* in the following words:

34. Ibid., 67.
35. Ibid., 74.
36. C. E. M. Joad, *Philosophical Aspects of Modern Science* (London: George Allen & Unwin, 1932), 46.

The argument appears to be that unless a datum is presupposed to be objective no inference can be based on it. This is so astonishing a suggestion that I wonder whether it can possibly be Mr Joad's real opinion. The data furnished by individual experience are clearly subjective, and it is ultimately from these data that the scientific conception of the universe is derived—for what we term "collective experience" is a synthesis of individual experiences.[37]

Speaking of a similar criticism of Joad, Eddington continues as follows:

His difficulty rather suggests that a cyclic scheme of knowledge with which science has familiarised us is not yet appreciated in philosophy. I have formerly [the reference is to *The Nature of the Physical World*, p. 262] illustrated the nature of a cyclic scheme by a revised version of "The House that Jack Built" which instead of coming to an end repeats itself indefinitely—". . . that worried the cat, that killed the rat, that ate the malt, that lay in the house, that was built by the priest all shaven and shorn, that married . . .". Wherever we start in the cycle we presuppose something that we reach again by following round the cycle. The scheme of physics constitutes such a cycle; and equally we may contemplate a wider cycle embracing that which is beyond physics. Starting at the point of the cycle which corresponds to our individual perceptions, we reach other entities which are constructs from our perceptions.[38]

The argument with respect to idealism and realism faces us here in modern garb.[39] From the Christian point of view both the realist and the idealist are mistaken. Both begin with the assumption of brute fact. Both begin with the assumption of the self-sufficiency of the human mind. It is for this reason that the argument takes the form it does. Upon the presupposition of the existence of the

---

37. Arthur Eddington, *New Pathways in Science* (Cambridge: University Press, 1935), 294.
38. Ibid., 294–95.
39. That is, the debate between Eddington and Joad is between whether we simply know our ideas, which come to us by way of experience (which is a Kantian way of thinking), or whether we know the object itself (which is what realism wants to argue).

triune God of the Scriptures there could be no argument about idealism and realism. It is evidence of a false intellectualistic ideal for science to wish to have a comprehensive understanding of the facts of the universe. It is because man wants to be as God that he tries to understand facts comprehensively. Then when he finds that his universals are not comprehensive he concludes to agnosticism. He takes for granted that if he cannot catch the facts in his net completely, God is confronted with the same limitation. The result is that he thinks the facts of the phenomenal world are surrounded by an ultimate void. The Unseen World of Eddington is the void that surrounds both God and man. We have already noted that in spite of his agnosticism he does accept a philosophy of chance. And as to man, he is for Eddington simply a late-comer in the evolutionary history of the universe. Accordingly there can be no revelation of God to man. "Religious creeds are a great obstacle to any full sympathy between the outlook of the scientist and the outlook which religion is so often supposed to require." Or again:

> The scientific objection is not merely to particular creeds which assert in outworn phraseology beliefs which are either no longer held or no longer convey inspiration to life. The spirit of seeking which animates us refuses to regard any kind of creed as its goal.[40]

That there is in the general scientific view of Eddington no real approach to Christianity appears most clearly when we look more narrowly at his notion of teleology. It is nothing but the negative counterpart of a causality concept in the non-theistic sense of the word. Eddington simply denies the comprehensiveness of the concept of causality. And what cannot be comprehended by an immanentistic causality is assigned to teleology. But a Christian conception of teleology must first show that there is teleology back of causality. It must show that all human concepts of causality and teleology, as far as they pertain to phenomena, presuppose God's comprehensive purpose with the whole universe. If this is done there is no need of dividing the field between causality and teleology. We can then admit causality and at the same time teleology with respect to the same facts.

40. Eddington, *Science and the Unseen World*, 89.

When this is done we have refuted the position both of the realist and of the idealist. When Joad discusses the relation between causality and teleology he comes to conclusions that are remarkably similar to those of Eddington. We note briefly what Joad says about teleology in relation to causation. He thinks they cannot parcel out the area of life between them. Yet they have each of them certain limitations.

So far we have been content to apply and to illustrate the principles of Mechanism and Teleology, and to show how they ramify through every sphere of natural happening and human activity. There are, however, certain outstanding difficulties to which each of the principles whose ramifications we have been discussing are exposed.[41]

Mechanical causation, if treated as ultimate and universal, is exposed to the criticism that it obviously fails to account for some mental phenomena, notably those involved in moral, aesthetic and religious experience.[42]

To the doctrine of teleological causation it may be objected that it is prima facie inapplicable to the behavior of physical phenomena. It seems absurd to say of an egg which is placed in a saucepan of hot water that it is striving to achieve the condition of being hard-boiled, or of the assemblage of the scattered parts of a car in a Ford factory that each, as it is fitted into its appointed place, is seeking to fulfil the end of the complete or perfected car. Even when applied to living organisms, the notion of teleological causation seems to entail the pre-existence of the end which is aimed at, in order that it may be in a position to exert the influence which, it is said, inclines, if it does not compel, the developing process in the organism which seeks to realize the end.[43]

To this we need only reply that the end of all created things exists in the mind of God before the things exist. God is not the

41. C. E. M. Joad, *Guide to Philosophy* (London: V. Gollancz, 1936), 199.
42. Ibid., 200.
43. Ibid., 210.

Vis a Tergo[44] and the *Terminus ad Quem*[45] to which the finite facts are vaguely drawn. In that case the egg would have to jump into the frying pan of its own accord if it were to be teleological. But if self-consciously created man takes the phenomena of the created world and manipulates them to the glory of God, it is quite possible to say that the category of teleology applies to the frying of the egg. The man fries the egg so that he may be well nourished and thus enabled to live his life teleologically, that is, to the glory of God. If things are thought of as organically teleological, all the debates about the relative areas of causation and teleology fall away. Nor need there then be any difficulty about their overlapping. God created all things. His providence is over all things. He leads all things to their intended goal.[46] God's universal therefore precedes the facts and laws of the created universe. Before this background man can labor and do all things teleologically through Christ to the glory of God.

A few words must now be said about the position of James Jeans. It is in many respects similar to that of Eddington. Both draw idealist conclusions from the fact that scientific knowledge is "indirect" or abstract. Both claim that indeterminism has replaced determinism in physical theory. But there is a noteworthy difference between the two. The method of Jeans is as follows: He reasons that the counters of science have become gradually more and more general. And all of them are directly dependent upon the activity of the mind. The human mind must do its interpreting of the universe with the help of mathematical symbols. In fact the matter of interpretation is chiefly if not exclusively a matter of mathematical symbols. And this seems to set a barrier between the mind and the facts which the mind is supposed to know. Accordingly we find in Jeans the customary assertion of agnosticism:

> To speak in terms of Plato's well-known simile, we are still imprisoned in our cave, with our backs to the light, and can only watch the shadows on the wall. . . . The shadows which reality throws on to the walls of our cave might *à priori* have been of many kinds. They might conceivably have been perfectly meaningless to us, as meaningless as a cinematograph

44. I.e., "force from behind," or cause.
45. I.e., "end to which," or telos or end.
46. Thus, from him, through him, and to him are all things (Rom. 11:36).

film shewing the growth of microscopic tissues would be to a dog who had strayed into a lecture-room by mistake.[47]

We see here how Jeans takes for granted the existence of the brute facts of the universe. But what interests us now particularly is something else.

It is true, in a sense somewhat different from that intended by Galileo, that "Nature's great book is written in mathematical language." So true is it that no one except a mathematician need ever hope fully to understand those branches of science which try to unravel the fundamental nature of the universe—the theory of relativity, the theory of quanta and the wave-mechanics.[48]

This is an example *in excelsis* of the pride of sinful man. All honor is due to the accomplishments of the mathematician. To seek by an absolutized mathematics to lay down what God can or cannot do is indeed a gigantic and non-Christian thought. For Christian thought it is God's thought that determines the possibilities of the created universe. In that case man will not seek to construct a mathematics that will envelop God. In that case man will look to mathematical relationships within the created universe as one aspect of the way God has created things.

The fruitlessness of the approach of modern mathematics as illustrated by the contention of Jeans appears from the accidental way in which the mathematical construction of human thought is brought into contact with the facts. Jeans develops the analogy of the case to which reference has been made. He wonders how the shadows that we see on the wall fit on to actual facts. They seem somehow to fit the facts, but how it is that they do must remain an ultimate mystery. Then he adds: "To drop our metaphor, nature seems very conversant with the rules of pure mathematics, as our mathematicians have formulated them in their studies, out of their own inner consciousness and without drawing to any appreciable extent on their experience of the outer world."[49] It is no wonder

47. James Jeans, *The Mysterious Universe* (New York: Macmillan, 1930), 135–36.
48. Ibid., 135–36.
49. Ibid., 138.

that this accidental relationship is said to obtain between subject and object upon the basis of an assumed metaphysics of chance.

We are not greatly impressed therefore when Jeans tells us that he believes in God. For him God is nothing but a magnified mathematician, who is on the level with his colleagues on earth in that both face brute facts which may or may not fit into his mathematical scheme. The "Great Architect of the Universe" who "now begins to appear as a pure mathematician"[50] has nothing to do with the Christian conception of God. And this enables us also to estimate the conception of teleology entertained by Jeans. Speaking of teleology he says:

> To-day there is a widespread measure of agreement, which on the physical side of science approaches almost to unanimity, that the stream of knowledge is heading towards a non-mechanical reality; the universe begins to look more like a great thought than like a great machine. Mind no longer appears as an accidental intruder into the realm of matter; we are beginning to suspect that we ought rather to hail it as the creator and governor of the realm of matter—not of course our individual minds, but the mind in which the atoms out of which our individual minds have grown exist as thoughts.[51]

By the sound of words we have here the Christian doctrines of God, of creation, and of purpose. In reality we have none of these. At every point Jeans is diametrically opposed to the Christian view. His is again an exclusively immanentistic teleology. We need not discuss Jeans' views of indeterminacy as he sets them forth more fully in his book, *The New Background of Science.* Nor need we instance the realistic criticism given by Joad on the indeterminacy concept. It is invariably built upon the negation of the causality concept as all inclusive. Invariably, too, the causality concept whose comprehensiveness is denied is the non-Christian causality concept. But to deny the comprehensiveness of the non-Christian causality presupposes the recognition of its validity to a certain extent. In fact those who hold to indeterminacy in recent physics do not

50. Ibid., 144.
51. Ibid., 158.

deny the legitimacy of the non-Christian causality concept. Most of them, if not all of them, agree with the sentiment expressed in the words of Levy when he said with respect to prediction:

The subject-matter of such studies as have been successful has consisted mainly in things that can be circumscribed, roughly speaking, in space and time of moderate dimensions, the world that man experiences, and as a feature of that world we cannot deny the type of predictable and therefore deterministic activity science has exposed. The range of space and time over which this is valid is, of course, a matter for experiment, but in the attempt to extend the range there are a number of points that have to be carefully watched if we are not to fall into a fallacy that has spoilt much of the discussion on this matter. Whatever further may develop, *the form of determinism already separated out by science, stands.* That rests on inescapable evidence.[52]

We have limited our discussion of scientific teleology chiefly to the question of indeterminism in recent physical and mathematical theory. We might have instanced other fields. There is, for instance, a good deal of discussion in the field of psychology about teleology. McDougall's[53] teleological psychology is frequently mentioned by apologists who seek to find a similarity between Christianity and recent scientific thought. But it was chiefly on physics and mathematics that science relied for its notion of determinism. Dampier-Whetham says: "Philosophy has been wont to draw its strongest evidence for scientific determinism from physics, where it was thought that there was a closed circuit of mathematical necessity." Accordingly now that in physics indeterminism seems to have made its entry, the bulwark of determinism appears to be broken. But in all this there is little cause for rejoicing from the Christian point of view. The new indeterminism is nothing but a bit of chance sprinkled between the crevices of determinism. Or, we may say, the determinism of a previous generation is now thought of as ice-blocks afloat on an ocean of chance.

52. H. Levy, *The Universe of Science* (London: Century, 1932), 145.
53. The reference is to William McDougall (1871–1938), who taught at Oxford, Harvard, and Duke. He was a leading advocate of "hormic," or purposive, psychology, which argued that a central aspect of psychology was striving toward a goal.

PROBABILITY

The entire modern point of view is well summed up by Hans Reichenbach[54] in his book *Atom and Cosmos.* He first speaks of the nature of causality as follows: "Causality is a blind concatenation through causes; its symbol is the machine, which moves its piston only because a certain pressure of gas acts on it, not for the sake of any meaningful function."[55] This shows clearly that the causality concept is thought of as working independently of God. Reichenbach then continues to point out that since Galileo's time science built its structure upon the notion of causality. "The whole development of natural science in the following centuries is a single triumph of this great idea."[56] Then he adds:

> The French mathematician Laplace gave this determinism its classical formulation: if there were a perfect intelligence, its supreme spirit could comprise all happenings of the world in one formula, from which, by the insertion of definite numerical values for the variable, time, the state of the world at any desired future, or, for that matter, past time could be calculated.[57]

Then he shows that in recent times vitalistic ideas have triumphed over mechanistic ideas in the realm of biology.

> Nevertheless, such objections availed nothing against the causal concept, so long as the idea of causation triumphed in physics, the most exact of all natural sciences, for the consideration could not be neglected that physiological processes must ultimately be reducible to mechanical motions of atoms and molecules, and that, accordingly, all the imperfection of causal explanations which we observe can be only provisional, and non-existent for the spirit imagined by Laplace, which can

54. Hans Reichenbach (1891–1953) has been called the greatest twentieth-century empiricist. He sought to critique scientific method on the basis of a radically empirical epistemology.
55. Hans Reichenbach, *Atom and Cosmos: The World of Modern Physics* (New York: Macmillan, 1933), 268.
56. Ibid., 269.
57. Ibid., 269–70.

compute the motions of the milliards of atoms in advance, just as well as we do those of the planets.

It is only now, therefore, that we have to speak of a real crisis for the causal concept, when doubts as to the perfect determination of all natural happenings gains ground even in physics, and when, as we have shown, these doubts, precisely in the mechanics of the interior of the atom, have led to conscious renunciation of causal conceptions.[58]

Reichenbach then enters upon a discussion of the problem thus raised by the rejection of the comprehensiveness of the causality concept in the following fashion:

It was investigations of a philosophical direction which next looked into this question; and, specifically, they proceeded from an analysis of the probability concept. The central significance of this concept had never been recognised in earlier epistemological discussions. It had been regarded as more or less parallel to human imperfection; that is, the merely probable correctness of prophecies as to nature was regarded as a result of human ignorance, which one endowed with perfect powers of learning could avoid.[59]

Then he adds:

The symbolical idea of Laplace, which we have already mentioned, grew precisely out of such conceptions. It is found in a work of his on the philosophy of the theory of probability; and Laplace wished thereby to express the opinion that a superhuman intelligence would not need the laws of probability, but would foretell the result of a game of chance, just as astronomers foretell the courses of the planets. This conception is named the subjective theory of probability; it leads to determinism, the doctrine that all which happens in nature follows flawless principles, and that all uncertainty of prophecy is occasioned by human weakness only.

58. Ibid., 270–71.
59. Ibid., 272.

The philosophical critics of the probability concept, on the other hand, held that a subjective theory can never prove the objective validity for reality of assumptions concerning probability, as that reality is expressed in the frequency laws of statistics. It is, in fact, not at all clear why, for instance, each face of a die should be uppermost about a hundred times out of six hundred throws, if the equal probability of the faces corresponds only to human ignorance; we cannot imagine that nature should pay such close attention to man's incapacity. This argument against the subjective theory of probability is conclusive, and an objective theory was therefore set up, which attempts to present the validity of laws of probability as an objective fact in the occurrences of nature, just as the validity of causal laws signified such a fact. According to the objective theory, the regularity of statistical processes, such as those of aggregates of molecules, means a fundamental trend in natural events, the understanding of whose laws is quite as much the task of natural science as is the understanding of causal laws. From this point of view it seems senseless to see anything merely provisional in the use of statistical laws; even the Laplacian superman—as the French mathematician Cournot remarked in the 'forties of the last century—would not renounce the use of statistical laws, but, on summing up the computations concerning the separate casts of the die, would still discover that, on the average, all sides appear with equal frequency.

Starting from such a view of the probability concept, it was possible to take the next step, uniting the concept of probability to that of cause; for both concepts, as we have pointed out, present objective realities. In fact, the two are firmly chained together, and it can even be shown that the causal principle would be an empty, useless assumption, if the principle of probability was not also there. It is not at all true that we ever find strict laws in nature. For all that we observe, each time, is that a law has been approximately fulfilled; a hurled stone, a flowing electrical current, a deflected ray of light, when exactly measured, will never show the course prescribed by the mathematical formula, but there will always be little deviations, so-called errors of observation, which may be decreased by better experimental devices, but can never be fully eliminated.[60]

In this passage Reichenbach sums up the matter of indeterminacy fairly. It is difficult to see how one could expect any approach to Christianity from his view of science. As already pointed out, the only God such a view can allow for is one who, together with man, faces a universe of brute fact. When formerly we thought of the universe as run by absolute causal law, we could think of God as predicting all things. That was not because he had made or caused all things, but because he happened to be a more profound mathematician than we. Jeans thinks of God in that fashion. In him there is something of a rationalist. Yet he too holds to indeterminism. Hence he too must picture God as wondering how his thoughts fit on to reality. Together with Reichenbach he must think of God as using the probability method. But a God who as a clever mathematician watches a universe of chance to see what he can do in order to predict its behavior is hardly the God of Christianity.

This leads us to remark in conclusion that the Butler type of Evidences has no valid argument against this position. Butler's view is, as we have seen, based upon the notion of brute fact. It is also based upon the non-theistic notion of probability. But by a probability argument based upon brute fact one can get nothing but a god similar to the one of Reichenbach and Jeans. Hume once upon a time reduced such an argument for God to an absurdity. If used today, it would be reduced to absurdity again.[61]

The only way we can meet the position of modern science is by pointing out that the non-theistic probability notion, whether of the subjective or of the objective kind, reduces experience to nonsense. Such a notion is based upon a philosophy of chance. And a philosophy of chance is the opposite of a philosophy of rationality. There can be no causality and there can be no computation

60. Ibid., 273–75.
61. This has been Van Til's concern since the beginning of this syllabus. Given his apologetic, assuming brute facts as it does, Butler is in no position to challenge modern science or modern philosophy. Once one gives away the Christian foundation of God's sovereign creation and control of all facts, there is no way to get it back.

of statistical averages except upon the presupposition of God as Creator and Redeemer of the universe. The God of Christianity has a purpose with the universe; for that reason there is purpose within the universe. A true immanentistic teleology requires a transcendent teleology.[62]

62. In other words, if there is going to be true purpose in the universe, it must originate with the true purpose of God.

CHAPTER 8

ANTHROPOLOGICAL EVIDENCES—
GENERAL PSYCHOLOGY

I n the preceding chapter we remarked that the world is organically teleological. Man therefore stands at the center and head of the whole creation of God. He represents the universe with God and represents God with the universe.

As to his own being he was created as a covenant-personality. He was to interpret himself and the universe intellectually, as a prophet. He was to dedicate himself and the universe to God, as a priest. He was to rule over the universe, under God, as a king. God had made him in God's own image. Man was a self-conscious and morally perfect being. His body and soul are but two aspects of his being. The one would not be complete without the other.[1]

This man, thus created by God, rebelled against God. He became a sinner. "Sin is any want of conformity unto or transgression of the law of God."[2] As a sinner man is subject to the wrath of God and

---

1. There is so much rich theology packed into this paragraph that it is impossible to summarize it adequately. Notice, however, that man is to fulfill the threefold office of prophet, priest, and king. He can do that only through the quintessential prophet, priest, and king, Jesus Christ. Notice as well that man is a *unity* of body and soul. Both aspects of man's character were always meant to be intact. Sin has temporarily ruptured that integrity, but it has not destroyed it.

2. Westminster Shorter Catechism, Q & A 14.

is morally polluted. Only those who are in Christ are saved from sin. But even they are saved in principle only while in this world. They still sin against their wills. They are still subject to disease and death. After death their souls and bodies will be reunited so that the whole man may forever be with God. And when man is fully redeemed, the whole creation will also be fully redeemed. The lost are lost forever in self-conscious suffering, but as such do not disturb the renewed creation of God.

It is not necessary to set forth a detailed biblical anthropology. We presuppose it in order to note its reception by modern science. In the present and in the following chapter we deal chiefly with that aspect of man's personality which we usually speak of as the soul.[3] In this chapter we shall naturally come into conflict with modern psychology, while in the next chapter we shall come into conflict with modern psychology of religion. We wish first to see something of the trend of modern psychology as such. Then we turn more particularly to the psychology of religion.

In his article, *Die moderne Religionspsychologie,*[4] Karl Beth begins by saying that he who would understand the psychology of religion must first look at psychology in general and study its recent development. The reason for this is not far to seek. Those who work in the field of the psychology of religion have come to the study of religion with the stated intention of applying to it the methods and insights of modern psychology. They hoped in this way to obtain a new and more valuable interpretation of religion. And it is but natural that these men will seek to apply the latest and best methods and results of psychology in general to the subject matter of the psychology of religion. So, for instance, Ames[5] is a functional psychologist and it is this functional psychology by which he interprets religion. He says: "The point of view employed is that of functional psychology, which is necessarily genetic and social."[6] Accordingly we shall give a short survey of the trend of things as it appears in the several schools of psychology today.

3. The etymological meaning of the word *psychology* is "study of the soul (*psyche*)."

4. Karl Beth, "Die moderne Religionspsychologie," *Theologische Rundschau,* n.F., 4 (1932): 311–12.

5. Edward S. Ames (1870–1958) was a psychologist and sociologist who associated himself with John Dewey's Chicago school of pragmatism.

6. Edward Scribner Ames, *The Psychology of Religious Experience* (Boston: Houghton Mifflin, 1910), vii.

In order to understand the recent trend in psychology, we must note that the psychology of the earlier nineteenth century was, generally speaking, that of associationism.[7] This psychology had its origin, as far as modern thought is concerned, in the philosophy of Descartes. Descartes separated the mind from the body in dualistic fashion. He defined the mind primarily in intellectual terms. "*L'ame pense toujours*"[8] was the main principle of his psychology. "The essential nature of mind (for Descartes) is *thinking* substance, as which it can be completely identified." The emotional and volitional aspects of personality were largely discounted or only inconsistently recognized.

Upon this basic conception of Descartes the association psychologists built when they formulated the laws by which the mind was supposed to work. Those laws themselves they conceived of after the analogy of physical laws, as physics was conceived of by Descartes, that is, in mechanical fashion. There was thought to be a direct proportion between the stimulus and the response in the mind in a way similar to the proportion observed in physical momentum. The gradual refinements in psychology were all in the direction of finding more definite and more intricate relationships of proportion between stimulus and response. Psychometrics was developed. Fechner[9] brought in logarithms to show the relation between stimulus and response. In order to carry through this program of psychometrics it was necessary to reduce the mental phenomena to their most elemental constituents. By this *Elementaranalyse* the soul was reduced to something that could be handled much as a blockhouse can be built up from individual blocks. The same blocks can be placed in different relation to one another in order to obtain different kinds of houses.

The chief characteristics then, of this psychology as they are noted in the histories of psychology, are (a) its intellectualism, and (b) its atomism.

Nineteenth century psychology, based as it was upon a Cartesian

---

7. Associationism in psychology holds that the mind consists of elements such as sensations and ideas that it organizes by way of associations. This view has been traced back to Aristotle.

8. I.e., "The soul always thinks."

9. Gustav T. Fechner (1801–1887) was a student of E. H. Weber and developed what has come to be called Fechner's Law, which states that the magnitude of a subjective sensation increases proportionally to the logarithm of the intensity of the stimulus.

foundation, was not at all Christian. The mind of man was virtually thought of as being independent of God. The laws by which one mind was brought into fruitful relationship with other minds were abstract laws that were somehow found in the universe. Thus both the particular and the universal and their relationship to one another were thought of as independent of God. But there was at least this much resemblance between a truly Christian psychology and the Cartesian psychology that they both placed man far above the beast. To this it is sometimes added that both placed the intellect above the other aspects of the mind. This is not correct. Christian psychology does not place the intellect ahead of any other aspect of man's personality in the sense that one should be more truly human than another. Man is equally prophet, priest, and king. All that Reformed theology has meant by emphasizing the priority of the intellect is that it is only through intellectual interpretation that we can communicate with one another about the meaning of reality.[10]

With the advent of the twentieth century, psychology has made a new advance, and that an advance farther than ever away from Christian theism. When we say that this began with the turn of the century we do not mean that the tendency was not already operative, and to a certain extent prepared for, somewhat earlier. This further advance away from Christian theism occurred *when men wiped out the borderlines that separated man from the beast, and the beast from the inorganic world, thus reducing man to a focus of action and interaction in the sea of an ultimate irrationalism.* Let us note some of the stages by which this result was accomplished.

In the first place we must observe that as there was a general reaction to the *Geistphilosophie* on the part of the *Lebensphilosophie* in the latter part of the nineteenth century, so the new psychology reacted against the intellectualism of associational psychology. The sharp distinction that even Kant had made between sense, intelligence and reason gave way to a view in which the intellect lost its high place of authority.[11] This might have been done in

10. Van Til, against what he saw in Gordon Clark and others, affirmed the priority of the intellect *psychologically* but did not want to affirm it *logically*. By that he wanted to argue for the integrity of man such that there is no logical privileging of any of man's aspects, while also recognizing that we are, by nature, knowers.

11. James Mark Baldwin, *History of Psychology: A Sketch and an Interpretation*, 2 vols. (New York: G. P. Putnam's Sons, 1913), 2:27.

the interest of a Christian type of thought. Christianity has always sought to equalize all the aspects of man's personality. However, the dethroning of the intellect was not done in the interest of theism but in the interest of irrationalism. Psychology was but following the lead of Schopenhauer and Von Hartman in their ultimate metaphysical voluntarism when it searched in the non-rational for a deeper insight into the nature of the human soul.

In the second place the new psychology reacted against the separation of the soul from the body. This too might have been in the interest of Christian theism. Heinemann has quite misinterpreted the Christian conception of the relation of the soul to the body when he says: "The Christian Middle Ages understands the soul as vapor, breathed into the lifeless body by God, and thus as a created being of a higher origin, originating from an incorporeal place and returning to it as immortal."[12] The Christian position is not that the soul existed in an immaterial world before its union with the body. The Christian position is rather that both soul and body came into existence together. Moreover, as they came into existence together they will also be immortal together. True, there is a time when they are separate, that is from the time of death to the time of the resurrection, but this period of separation is to be followed by a permanent reunion. So then the Christian position has never been guilty of abstract separation of the soul and the body. Accordingly, in so far as the new psychology seeks to bring soul and body into close harmony with one another, we can only rejoice.

However, we should again observe that union of soul and body by modern psychology is in the interest of wiping out the distinction between them. Heinemann significantly says that the soul of modern psychology resembles the *Vitalseele*,[13] the simple life principle of the ancients.

The first step led directly to the second. The descent into the volitional and emotional was in the direction of a further descent into the corporeal. Heinemann says: "If man thus appears as deeply

---

12. Here and in footnote 14, for convenience, we have placed Van Til's German quotation in the footnote section and put the translation in the body of the text. "Das christliche Mittelalter kennt die Seele als Hauch, von Gott dem leblosen Körper eingehaucht, so als geschaffenes Wesen höheren Ursprungs, aus einer unkörperlichen Region stammend und als unsterblich in sie zurückkehrend." Fritz Heinemann, *Neue Wege der Philosophie* (New paths of philosophy) (Leipzig: Quelle & Meyer, 1929), 274.

13. I.e., "vital soul."

interwoven with the historical event, then the emphasis on the appetitive level is nothing but an embedding of the psychological into the physical, a biologizing of the soul, which is at the same time a dynamization of it. The psychological life is a power play which is understood here quite scientifically as an exchange of force. By this, the soul has become again what it always was: the vital soul."[14]

We see that the first step, that is the emphasis upon the emotional and the volitional, has not worked in the direction of finding a better balance between the intellectual and the other aspects of personality, but in the direction of doing away with the distinction of soul and body, which is basic to the theistic conception of man.

In the third place the new psychology reacted against the old in that it laid greater *emphasis upon child psychology*. The older psychology was almost exclusively an adult psychology. Children were treated as miniature adults. The new psychology tries to do fuller justice to the individuality of childhood than the old psychology could do. Jastrow[15] says: "What we may accept is the principle that the child is an authentic embodiment of the earliest, racially oldest, most persistent, truest to nature, depository of natural behavioristic psychology."[16]

This third step follows naturally upon the second. The intellectualism of the older psychology could do scant justice to the individual. All men were cut after the same abstract pattern of rationality that was somehow taken for granted on the basis of observation of a large number of "normal" adults. But the emphasis of the new psychology upon the emotional and the volitional naturally also meant an emphasis upon the *individuality* of each person. The emotional and the volitional life of man is notoriously unwilling to be cut according to one pattern. And this emphasis led to the idea that children too should be regarded as individuals at each stage of their existence. In other words the concept of the *variability* of

14. "Erscheint so der Mensch als tief verflochten in das historische Geschehen, so bedeutet die Betonung der Triebschicht nichts anderes als eine Einbettung des Seelischen ins Körperliche, eine Biologisierung der Seele, die zugleich eine Dynamisierung ist. Das seelische Leben ist ein Kräftespiel, das hier freilich recht naturwissenschaftlich als Energieumsatz verstanden wird. Damit ist die Seele wieder das geworden, was sie in der Antike war: Vitalseele." Heinemann, *Neue Wege der Philosophie*, 285.

15. Joseph Jastrow (1863–1944) was an American psychologist and one of the first scientists to study the evolution of language.

16. Joseph Jastrow, "The Reconstruction of Psychology," *Psychological Review* 34 (1927): 179.

personality was introduced into psychology. A child is thought of as an independent type of being instead of as a little adult. A child is, to the extent that it is a personality at all, thought of as a unique personality. In accordance with this enlargement of the field into relation with which the grown-up personality is set, it is as true to say that the adult must be interpreted in terms of the child as to say that the child must be interpreted in terms of the adult.

With respect to this third step we wish to observe again that it too might have been taken in the interest of Christian theism. Individuality is a concept that is embedded in the very foundations of Christian theism. As Christianity has done justice to the emotional and the volitional elements in human personality so it alone has done justice to the individuality of each person. Orthodox theology has constantly maintained that the image of God in mankind cannot be fully expressed until every individual man has contributed his unique personality. Associationism had inherited the abstract universalism of Platonic-Aristotelian philosophy, but had ignored Augustine and Calvin. So too Christianity has constantly done justice to childhood. The Old and the New Testament have in their educational principles made provision for the child as an emotional and volitional as well as intellectual being by insisting not only upon abstract intellectual presentation of truth but also upon surrounding the child with an atmosphere that will influence him at his emotional center.

But we must add that the third step of modern psychology has not actually been in the direction of Christian theism. The *variability* concept by virtue of which psychology seeks to do justice to childhood is based upon an ultimate *activism*. Modern psychology thinks of personality as being exclusively a self-accomplishment on the part of man. At this point it is directly opposed to Christianity which holds that personality is created by God. According to the Christian view, then, variability can mean only that human personality is not fully developed when created, but grows into the pattern set for it by God. The activity by which personality realizes itself is, to be sure, very genuine and significant but it is genuine and significant only because it acts against the background of the plan of God. The integration of personality, that is, the constant readjustment of the particular and the universal within itself, and the constant readjustment of the whole personality as an individual to the universal found in the universe beyond itself, takes place by a more ultimate and constant readjustment of the individual together with his surroundings to God who is the absolute particular and the absolute universal combined in one ultimate personality. The integration of personality according to the Christian view is an integration toward and by virtue of the triune God of Scripture as the only ultimate self-sufficient personality.

In contrast with this the modern concept of the integration of personality is an *integration into the void*. We can best appreciate this if we note that its *concept of purpose itself has been completely internalized*. In the same connection in which he brings out that according to Freudianism the soul has become a *Vitalseele*, Heinemann says that Freud has, willy-nilly, to recognize the *"Sinnhaftigkeit des psychovitalen Geschehens."*[17, 18] By that he means that the idea of purpose itself is something non-rational.

This leads us to note the fourth step of the descent into the irrational on the part of modern psychology, namely, its *emphasis upon the unconscious*, whether of the adult or of the child. The adult is not only to be interpreted in terms of the child, but the child and the adult are both to be interpreted in terms of subconscious drives. It was not enough to coordinate feeling and will with the intellect or even to insist upon the primacy of the feeling or of the will; modern psychology has made the whole of conscious life to a large extent subordinate to man's unconscious life. Modern psychology has, to a large extent, sought the explanation of the conscious life in the fields of the unconscious.

It is well known that the psycho-analytical schools of Freud, Adler and Jung have done much to seek to interpret our waking life by our dream life. We consciously purpose to do something, but the reason for our conscious purpose, they say, is an unconscious drive. We are not concerned with the fact that Freud sought to explain the whole of self-conscious life by the sex drive while Adler sought to explain it largely by the selfishness instinct. The differences within the psycho-analytical school do not concern us. It is enough to note that their explanation is an explanation of the rational or self-conscious by the irrational and subconsciousness.

17. Heinemann, *Neue Wege der Philosophie*, 285.
18. I.e., "the meaningfulness of the psychovital events."

We should also note in this connection that the psychology of McDougall in this respect resembles that of Freud and his followers. It is often quite mistakenly supposed that McDougall affords much comfort to those who believe the Christian position, since he at least holds to the concept of purpose while such schools as Behaviorism[19] cling to a mechanistic interpretation of all mental phenomena. Behaviorism, to be sure, is anti-teleological. But it is scarcely better to say that you do allow for the concept of purpose, and even insist upon its originality in the field of psychology, if you bury this concept of purpose in the lowest depths of irrationalism and therewith place it at the farthest possible remove from Christian theism. McDougall says that his concept of teleology has nothing in common with the concept of teleology as held to by the theologians, since the latter is externalistic while his own is exclusively immanentistic. He even goes so far as to say that purpose is not primarily to be related to any intellectual activity of man at all.

Even this fourth step of modern psychology has good elements in it. As Christians we believe that man was originally created with the love of God in his heart. That is, we believe that man was a priest as well as a prophet. More than that, we also believe that man was in part conscious and in part unconscious in his activity. We hold that man was created a *character*. In his unconscious as well as in his conscious activity man was directed toward God. Scripture is full of the idea of the subconscious. David prays that he may be forgiven for sin of which he is unaware. We say that we are conceived and born in sin, which does not merely refer to the agency of the parents, but means that we are sinners when we come into the world even though we are not self-conscious. We are worthy of eternal punishment because of our relation to Adam. The church has never limited personal responsibility to the self-conscious activity of man. The activism involved in the Arminian conception is not truly representative of the Christian position.

But this only brings out the antithesis between the truly Christian position and the non-Christian psychology of the day more sharply. It is sometimes asserted that modern psychology has corroborated the Calvinistic position rather than the Arminian, inasmuch as

19. Psychological behaviorism attempts to explain human behavior by way of external stimuli and responses. B. F. Skinner (1904–1990) was perhaps the best-known behaviorist.

both modern psychology and Calvinism emphasized the significance of the relationship of the individual to the subconscious and the historical while Arminianism does not. There is truth in this contention. In so far as modern psychology has shown that the individual's conscious life is dominated by drives that come up from his unconscious life, it has stood with Calvinism against Arminianism. On the other hand, it may be said that modern psychology is closer to Arminianism than Calvinism because of the *activism* that characterizes it. Arminianism has departed one step from the position of Christian theism inasmuch as it will not allow that man was created a character. Modern psychology has gone all the way in that direction and has said that man's character is exclusively his own accomplishment. Arminianism, inconsistently but happily, turns back to God after the first step in the direction of human autonomy inasmuch as it believes the creation doctrine; modern psychology has no such limitations and places man in a void.

It ought now to be clear that there are only two positions that are internally consistent on this point. If one begins to walk down the path of complete activism, one cannot stop until he has come to the place where modern psychology has come. If God has not created man, then man has somehow come upon the scene from the realms of chance and one's character has nothing to do with God. Of course it may still be said that one's character is not wholly one's own since each individual is surrounded by cosmic influences of all sorts. But, in any case, God has been put out of the picture altogether. Hence it is necessary, if the Christian conception is to be defended at all, that it be defended by rejecting modern activism in its entirety. God has created man with intellect, feeling and will. God created man soul and body. God created the first man as a full-grown person but has caused later generations to spring up by growth from childhood to maturity. God has related man's self-conscious to his subconscious life, his childhood to his maturity. Every activity of every aspect of the human personality, at any stage of its development, acts as a derivative personality before the background of the absolute personality of God. *Man is an analogical personality*. It is this consistently biblical and Christian theistic concept alone that can be defended against the activism of modern psychology. Arminianism, here as elsewhere, offers no sound defense of Christianity against modern man-centered thought.[20]

If put in this way the issue is taken out of the surface areas in which it is usually discussed. Many Christian apologists use all their ammunition by contending against modern psychology on the ground that it immerses man in the meshes of drives, etc., over which he has no control. It is said that Christianity insists on the responsibility of man and that it is this that we must seek to defend against modern psychology. Now it is true that Christianity holds man responsible. But *to argue in the blue for freedom* does not help to establish man's responsibility. It is true that in general modern psychology allows for no responsibility, but the most basic reason for this is not that it has immersed man's will in the midst of instincts and drives. The real reason why modern psychology has left no room for responsibility is found in the fact that it has taken the whole of the human personality in all its aspects, self-conscious and subconscious, and immersed it in an ultimate metaphysical void. Man cannot be responsible in and to the void. Hence the only way in which we can establish human responsibility is by showing the ultimate irrationalism of all non-theistic thought of which modern psychology is but a particular manifestation. In that way we place man self-consciously and subconsciously in every aspect of his person before the personality of God. Man is responsible in the whole of his personality, but only if he is the creature of God. Man *before the God of the Scriptures* is the only alternative to man *in the void.*

The fifth step of modern psychology in the direction of ultimate irrationalism is its study of abnormal psychology. Jastrow says: "Prominent in the reconstruction of psychology is the recognition of the abnormal and its significance as a clue to the understanding of behavior."[21]

The study of abnormal psychology is a good thing. It has undoubtedly thrown light not only on the behavior of the abnormal but also on the behavior of the normal. This is not in dispute. It is not the *fact* that men turned to the study of abnormal psychology

---

20. Van Til is linking Arminianism to this discussion of modern psychology because both hold that man creates his own character by way of his choices, his environment, or any number of personal factors. In both cases, God is not the creator and sovereign over all of man's choices.

21. Jastrow, "The Reconstruction of Psychology," 184–85.

that is important, but the *reason* why they did it. The reason was the assumption that the normal and the abnormal are both of them normal in the sense that they are both naturally to be expected in human life. Hence it is said that one can really get as much light on the normal behavior of man by studying his abnormal behavior as one can get on the abnormal behavior of man by studying his normal behavior. On this point we again quote Jastrow: "The abnormal, like the genetic, is a nature-made product, and thus authentic and directive; the abnormal is the normal magnified and distorted; the normal is the abnormal in miniature and under control."[22] To this he adds: "The accusation or the pleasantry as suggested by the reaction from this trend that psychology first lost its soul, and then its mind, carries the truth of historical vicissitude; but he who loses his soul shall find it."[23]

One need only to read a book like McDougall's *Outline of Abnormal Psychology* to see the extent to which the assumption expressed by Jastrow in the quotations given has influenced modern psychology. McDougall's psychology is typical in its anti-intellectualism. McDougal seeks the real place of purpose in the drives of man. Still further his psychology is typical in that it emphasizes the social. This emphasis upon the social is extended so far as to include the abnormal. Throughout McDougall's book on abnormal psychology it is taken for granted that new light can be shed upon the normal by the study of the abnormal because the abnormal is *natural* as well as is the normal.

It is at this point that modern psychology appears once more in its antitheistic and anti-Christian character. As Christians we rejoice that psychology has finally come to the study of the abnormal. The Christian position has preceded non-Christian scientists by centuries in the study of the abnormal. Non-Christian science has for ages taken for granted that somehow the abnormal is an inexplicable mystery quite out of harmony with the effort at a complete intellectual interpretation of life. Just as Plato's ideas of mud and hair and filth were there and remained there to disturb his attempted subordination of all experience under the category of the good or the one, so non-Christian thought assumes that evil is as ultimate

22. Ibid., 185.
23. Ibid.

as the good. It always has assumed this. The logical consequence of this position is that men should give up seeking any rational interpretation of life at all. But till recent times men have not been willing to accept the consequences of an ultimate irrationalism, nor yet now are they fully willing. Yet it is undeniable that the descent into the irrational has been rapid in modern thought. It could not be otherwise. If there is irrationalism somewhere in the universe, and if it is taken for granted that this irrationalism is as ultimate as rationality itself, it follows that irrationalism must be thought of as never to be overcome. One rotting apple in a bushel will spoil the whole bushel in time. One spot of ultimate irrationality will not only spoil rationality in the future but even now makes all talk about complete rationality meaningless.

With its conception of the triune God of Scripture as self-contained absolute rationality, Christianity teaches that man was created wholly rational. That is, though man was not created with the ability to grasp the whole of rationality comprehensively, yet his rationality was sound. Hence irrationality in the mind of man, that is insanity, must be the result of a deflection of man from the source of absolute rationality. Accordingly the Christian brings in his doctrine of sin when he discusses abnormal psychology. Not as though every insane person is a particularly great sinner. There are, to be sure, particular forms of sin that readily lead to insanity. Yet there are many insane persons who are not nearly so great sinners as others who are normal. We explain this on the ground that responsibility is corporate. Jesus said that the tower of Siloam fell upon those upon whom it fell not because they were greater sinners than others, but because of the sinfulness of the race.[24] All men have merited God's punishment. So all men have merited insanity, because of their departure from the only rational God. Eternal punishment is the abyss of irrationalism into which they will fall who do not return to the God of rationality.[25]

It appears from this that the assumption underlying the study of the psychology of the abnormal, as it is usually undertaken today,

---

24. Luke 13:1–5.

25. Note here how rationality is defined in terms of conformity to God and his character and word, and irrationality is defined in terms of a rejection of God and his word. This is fundamentally different from how any philosophy would define those terms.

is indicative of a further departure from Christian theism than was the case with earlier psychology.

The sixth step of modern psychology in the direction of the irrational is its study of the soul of "primitive man." To quote again from Jastrow: "Worthy of a separate enumeration is the recognition of the place of the primitive psyche in the interpretation of behavior-trends from the simplest to the most complex."[26] Freud and his school look upon the study of primitive phenomena as a "reservoir of psychic trends." And of the anthropologists like Tylor, Frazer, Levy-Bruhl and others, Jastrow says that "they have supplied a genealogy to an important chapter of modern psychology, portraying as an amazing reconstruction the procession of the intellectual shifts and increments in rationality."[27]

In the first five steps enumerated we dealt with an extension of the field in the direction of space only, but in this step we meet for the first time with an extension of the field in point of time. Hence it is really at this point for the first time that the full significance of the doctrine of evolution comes to view.

At this point, too, Christian thought has an explanation of its own to offer. It says that man was created perfect. That is, man was created as an adult with full rationality. This sets off the Christian position clearly and distinctly from all evolutionary views. There can have been no "increment of rationality" in the sense that the rational has slowly developed from the non-rational. On the other hand, Christianity does not claim that man did not develop in the sense that by the exercise of his increased rationality he increased his rational powers and his rational accomplishments. It is quite in accord with Scripture that man should at first live close to nature and should use implements taken immediately from nature such as those that are found by archaeology. God gave to man a program in accordance with which he should bring to light the forces of nature gradually. Man did not do this as well as he might have done it if he had not sinned. Through sin his growth was not only retarded but also made abnormal. Hence we see that man's progress in civilization has been very slow. If as Christians we use

26. Jastrow, "The Reconstruction of Psychology," 180.
27. Ibid., 181.

the term "primitive man" at all we should be clearly conscious of the fact that we do not mean by it the same sort of being that the modern psychologist means by it. It is not as though every one knows just what primitive man is and that all that remains to be done is to draw certain conclusions from his works. On the contrary the whole debate between Christianity and non-Christianity is involved in the question as to what the "primitive man" is. If Christianity is true the real primitive man was Adam who came upon the scene of history as a full-grown man. On the other hand, if the teaching of current evolution is true, primitive man is an independent growth, that is, a growth out of bare vacuity.

Modern psychology has adopted the evolutionary philosophy. With respect to this we may quote the words of Jastrow: "Modern psychology had a fortunate childhood because it came upon the scene when the struggle for existence of evolution had already been successfully waged by its historical sponsors."[28] Modern psychology is deeply imbedded in a non-theistic metaphysics which it has taken for granted uncritically. Yet the claim is made that it was at the time of the emergence of the modern outlook that doctrinaire methods were first done away. To quote from Jastrow: "If we return to the era of the emergence of the modern outlook, we readily recognize that the speculative and doctrinative type of introspection was doomed."[29]

Suffice it in this connection to have called attention to the fact that modern psychology has raised primitive man to a position next to that of modern man in so far as principles of explanation are concerned. Modern psychology assumes the non-Christian position with respect to the concept of this primitive man.

The final or seventh step of modern psychology in the direction of the irrational is the elevation of the animal as a principle of explanation for man. Without this last step the others would have no significance. If mankind has come from the God in whom Christianity believes, the adult man is the standard of interpretation of all rationality in mankind.[30] We may take this adult in the

28. Ibid., 171.
29. Ibid., 177.
30. By "the standard of interpretation of all rationality," Van Til does not mean to negate the Christian notion that God is our ultimate standard of interpretation. In this

various stages of his growth and note that each stage has its own peculiarities, but we cannot allow that the child, the abnormal person, primitive man, and finally the animal, can be put on the level with the adult as a source of explanation of life as a whole. On the other hand, if man is what non-Christian thought says he is, the normal adult stands on no higher level as a principle of interpretation of life as a whole than the child, the abnormal person, and the animal. In that case the animal even has a certain priority over the primitive man, the latter over the child, and the child over the man, on account of the fact that man was originated from and through them.

The recent schools of psychology have been more consistent than the association psychology in the application of the non-Christian concept of man. In former generations man sometimes sought to find interesting parallels of rationality among the animals. Some thought they had discovered religion in the animal world. Yet somehow they began from the normal adult man as a sort of standard. Recently, however, there has been a great emphasis upon animal psychology. The assumption is that the behavior of animals sheds direct light on the behavior of man. Just as non-Christian logic likes to speak of thought without asking whether it should perhaps make a distinction between human thought and divine thought, so modern psychology speaks about behavior without asking whether it should perhaps speak of human and of animal behavior in distinction from one another. Of course psychologists do speak of human behavior and of animal behavior, but it is taken for granted that if any laws can be discovered in the one field they can without any further criticism be transferred to the other field. The interesting debate between the behaviorists, the Gestalt psychologists and the hormic psychologists[31] brings this out. Watson the Behaviorist, Koffka the Gestalt psychologist, and McDougall the hormic psychologist are all of them interested in animal psychology. This in itself shows that the interest in animal

context, he is making the point that, all things being equal, adulthood is the *telos* of human existence; that is, it is the end to which all human existence is meant to move. Human existence in itself, therefore, from a Christian perspective, has a teleological *terminus* such that the measure, or standard, for human existence is found in its *completion*.

31. Hormic psychology, a term coined by William McDougall (1871–1938), focuses on the *goal* or *purpose* of man, given our innate *instincts*. *Hormic* is taken from the Greek *hormē*, which can be translated as "impulse."

psychology is characteristic of recent psychology as a whole. But more important than that they are all interested in the subject is the fact that they all take for granted that the animal behavior is directly illuminative for the understanding of human behavior.

Thus we have reached the end of the road beyond which no man can go. Let us sum up what we have found. We have not enumerated all the recent schools of psychology in order to enter into the debates that they have between themselves. We have rather sought to trace one general tendency that pervades them all. One can find a good survey of the recent schools of psychology in the two books, *Psychologies of 1925* and *Psychologies of 1930*. But in reading these books one is likely to be confused because one is tempted to listen carefully to the debate in which these schools are engaged. Woodworth's *Contemporary Schools of Psychology* will help us to get something of the trends that appear in those schools. Even so, Woodworth and others like Brett and Baldwin, who give histories and surveys of the schools of psychology, themselves take the modern theory for granted. They do not bring out what is important from the Christian point of view. They think of the main question as being something in which we are not directly interested. Accordingly, we have to survey the tendency of the modern schools of psychology with the distinct purpose in mind of ascertaining what their attitude to Christian theism is.

This attitude, we found in our survey, has been in the direction of irrationalism. The net result is that man now stands before us, if we allow modern psychology to draw the picture, as a *Feldwesen*.[32] That is, man is thought of as a focus of action and interaction of cosmic forces which have sprung into existence by chance. The field to which man is related and in terms of which he is to be explained is not only the whole world as it now is, but the whole world as it has somehow become in the millennia of the past. Ultimately then we must say that the field is the void. It is this concept that is substituted for the concept of Christianity.

Thus we have a complete contrast of the consistently Christian and the consistently non-Christian view of man as the two types of psychology involved in each of these two views picture them. We have found new corroboration of the interpretation of the problem

32. I.e., "field of existence."

of evidences as given in a previous chapter. Modern psychology as well as modern philosophy in general is seeking the absolute particular, or brute fact. From the adult as a standard to the child, from the child to the abnormal and from the abnormal to primitive man, and from primitive man to the animal, each of them thought of as independently contributing new light on the behavior of man, this is the story of recent psychology.

We may well ask the question how modern psychology is going to get back to any sort of universal and more particularly how the psychology of religion is going to get to the universal that it is seeking by applying the method and the materials of modern psychology in general.

CHAPTER 9

ANTHROPOLOGICAL EVIDENCES— THE PSYCHOLOGY OF RELIGION

I n the psychology of religion we meet with a particular form of modern general psychology. Yet we have a special interest in the psychology of religion. It deals directly with matters pertaining to Christianity.

THE RELIGIOUS CONSCIOUSNESS

The object of study in the psychology of religion literature is "the religious consciousness." Men hope to find in the study of the religious consciousness something that has never been found before. They hope to find out what religion really is. In the past men have spoken of religion as the science of God. Men have taken for granted that religion had an objective reference. Now religion may have an objective reference, but if it has we must discover this from a study of the religious consciousness itself.[1] John Baillie[2]

1. John Baillie, *The Interpretation of Religion* (Edinburgh: T. & T. Clark, 1929), 134ff.
2. John Baillie (1886–1960) was, along with his brother Donald, highly influential in the Church of Scotland. After a relatively short stint teaching in the United States and Canada, he returned to teach at New College, Edinburgh, while his brother was teaching at St. Andrews. Raised in the Free Church, where his father was a minister, Baillie spent most of his life working in ecumenical relations and was influential in the World Council of Churches.

assures us that in thus studying the religious consciousness the psychology of religion is but following the best methods of philosophy and science. "We are then doing no more than following the very oldest tradition in this matter if we define the business of theological science as *the interrogation of the religious consciousness with a view to discovering what religion really is.*"[3] Baillie is right in his claim. From the Greeks to the moderns, philosophy and psychology have assumed that the consciousness of man does not need the interpretation of God before it can begin its own interpretation.

Thus we meet at the outset with a complete rejection of the Christian position. Or rather, we meet at the outset with the assumption of the truth of the non-Christian position.

Naturally this rejection of the traditional position is done under cover of neutrality. So James Bissett Pratt[4] says that at the outset one is permitted to adopt any definition of religion that he pleases. It is merely a question as to whose definition will stand the test of scientific method. Discussing a definition of religion he says:

> Again let me admit, or rather insist, that this, like all other definitions of religion, is more or less arbitrary. Whoever wishes to do so has certainly a perfectly logical right to give a much narrower or a much broader definition of the term, provided he is willing to take the consequences. He may, if he chooses, even confine religion to belief in Jehovah, on condition that he will stick to his definition and consistently call irreligious all men who do not so believe. A narrow definition based upon a particular theological belief, however, has two patent disadvantages. In the first place, it necessarily leaves out a great number of people and a great number of phenomena which are by general consent recognized as religious. Thus if we hold that belief in a personal God is the criterion of religion we not only run counter to the general view which classes Buddhism in its original form (that great stumbling block to most definitions) among the religions, but we are forced to call irreligious many deeply spiritual souls nearer

3. Baillie, *The Interpretation of Religion,* 14.
4. James Bissett Pratt (1875–1944) was an influential philosopher of religion at Williams College and was president of the American Theological Society from 1934 to 1935.

home, who certainly have something more within them than can be included under philosophy or morality.[5]

THE METHOD OF THE PSYCHOLOGY OF RELIGION

In the passage quoted from Pratt it is taken for granted that we need not introduce the distinction between false and true when studying the religious consciousness. This at once excludes the claim of Christianity to being the only true religion. Yet it soon appears that the psychology of religion needs some sort of criterion by which to judge the various phenomena that offer themselves as being religious. If any general statements are to be made about religion, a criterion of judgment is indispensable. The psychology of religion, like modern science in general, is face to face with the problem of brute fact. What is to be done with all the various religious phenomena? Shall we simply enumerate them? If we do we have not really gained much. How do we know that when people speak of their religion they have really given expression to what is deepest in them? How do we know that religion can really find expression at all? Perhaps it is true that in all we say about religion we still have not caught the real thing. This is expressed in the saying: *Spricht die Seele, so spricht, ach, schon die Seele nicht mehr.*[6]

The struggle has been to find the most immediate and therefore the most genuine expression of religion. In the psychology of religion men wish to find the "native witness of religion." They wish to see religion as it acts when not encrusted in a theological system. On the other hand men seek to find universally valid conclusions about the phenomena of religion. But the nearer they seem to come to direct expression of the religious sentiment the narrower is the realm of its validity. If the soul does not really express itself when it expresses itself in words, the psychologist can turn to no other method than that of introspection. But if he turns to introspection

5. James Bissett Pratt, *The Religious Consciousness: A Psychological Study* (New York: Macmillan, 1920), 3–4.

6. I.e., "Alas, does the soul speak; yet it is no longer the soul." This statement has been attributed first to the German poet Friedrich Schiller (1759–1805) and then to Johann Wolfgang von Goethe (1749–1832).

alone his words will not be received by others. Thus there will be no science of the psychology of religion.

We note the similarity of this difficulty to that of science in general. The universals cannot fully express the particulars. The universals give but aspects of the particulars.[7] Brute fact cannot be categorized. It must remain ultimately mysterious. Very little of this difficulty appears in the manuals on the psychology of religion. They speak of the various methods of study used in the psychology of religion. They speak of introspection, of autobiography, and of the questionnaire. They express preferences for the one method or the other. They seek somehow to combine the three methods. But there is evidently in their procedure no well thought out conception of the relation of the universal to the particular.

One would think then that, at the outset at least, the Christian religion might be allowed to stand on a par with other religions. Yet such is not the case. Speaking of the danger of defining religion too narrowly, Thouless[8] says: "Such writers remind us of Mr Thwackum who when he mentioned religion meant the Christian religion; and not only the Christian religion, but the Protestant religion; and not only the Protestant religion, but the Church of England."[9] It is in a similar vein that Farmer[10] speaks when he says: "It is curious how folk insist on approaching religion from the theological end, which is almost as foolish as trying to approach a rose from the angle of the theory of relativity."[11] Thus Christianity is really excluded at the outset by the method followed.

Yet most of the writers on the psychology of religion hold that Christianity is somehow the best of the religions. Baillie speaks of this when discussing the psychology of religion.

7. That is, the universal "religion" is expressed only in its particulars, e.g., Buddhism. Each religion, therefore, is a "brute fact" unable to be interpreted in terms of any unifying notion or idea.

8. Robert H. Thouless (1894–1984) was a British psychologist whose work included parapsychology and psychokinesis. His most popular work was *Straight and Crooked Thinking*.

9. Robert H. Thouless, *An Introduction to the Psychology of Religion* (New York: Macmillan, 1923), 2.

10. Herbert H. Farmer (1892–1981), after a short pastorate, was professor of systematic theology and apologetics at Westminster College, Cambridge University, followed by an appointment as lecturer in philosophy of religion.

11. Herbert H. Farmer, *Experience of God: A Brief Enquiry into the Grounds of Christian Conviction* (London: Student Christian Movement Press, 1929), 31.

The science was at the beginning provided with its motto and device by Max Müller when he gave utterance to the now celebrated words, *"Wer eine Religion kennt, kennt keine"*—"He who knows but one religion knows none at all."[12] The intention of this saying is clearly to claim that a proper theoretical interpretation of religion has for the first time been rendered possible by our modern historical knowledge of the religion of other peoples and epochs.[13]

In criticism of this view, Baillie says he cannot do better than use the words of Harnack which seem to have been spoken in sly reference to Müller's dictum just quoted. Harnack said: *"Wer diese Religion kennt, kennt alle."*[14] But Harnack certainly did not mean that the Christian religion was to be taken as true and others to be taken as false. Baillie says of him: "And he was no doubt alive to the truth of the view which would find the typical structure of the religious consciousness present in *any* authentic example of it, and would at the same time find the whole truth of it nowhere else but in its best or Christian form."[15]

We see in this position of Baillie how he is struggling with the difficulty already mentioned. He wants to get at the absolutely particular. Still he must also find some standard by which to judge these absolute particulars.

Summing up what we have found thus far we may say: (a) the religious consciousness is assumed to be an ultimate entity, (b) this religious consciousness gives forth a witness and part of this witness *may* have to do with God, (c) there are authentic manifestations of the religious consciousness found everywhere, and (d) the religious consciousness must interpret itself.

In this way the psychology of religion hopes to get at the real *essence* of religion. It is evident that this approach to religion excludes Christianity at the outset. It is taken for granted that man, even sinful man, has the true principles of explanation within himself.[16]

---

12. This statement is attributed to the founder of comparative religions, Max Müller (1823–1900).
13. Baillie, *The Interpretation of Religion*, 120.
14. I.e., "Anyone who knows this religion, knows all."
15. Baillie, *The Interpretation of Religion*, 121.
16. The point Van Til is making is that a true evaluation of religion must begin not with ourselves but with Scripture.

It is not a matter of surprise then if we find that when the psychologists of religion deal with specifically Christian doctrines these doctrines are rejected. The whole of the supernatural must be rejected inasmuch as it must be the ideal of science to explain all phenomena by one principle. Pratt says: "Leaving aside hypotheses that involve the supernatural, he must seek—very likely in a plodding and prosaic fashion—to find out what can be done with the natural."[17] Here we meet again with the ideal of absolute comprehension as a limiting concept.[18] As to the measure of success that has attended the efforts of the scientist to explain religion by the exclusion of the supernatural, Pratt says: "And in our particular problem his methods have not as yet proved inadequate. The prophet and mystics have, indeed, been greatly influenced by the subconscious, but it is far from clear that there is anything mysterious about the ultimate source of this subconscious influence."[19] The only God that can be tolerated is therefore a God who is penetrable to the human mind.

Similarly the only assertion of prophets or apostles that can be accepted as true is that which can be verified by experience. On this point Pratt says: "Inasmuch as nothing can be communicated to other men or verified by them but that which is presented to common human experience, science is limited to describing the experience data of human beings and the relations between them."[20] It is plain that with such a standard the Christian conception of regeneration could never get a hearing. Nor can there come to us any objective revelation. Speaking of the prophet, Pratt says: "The prophet ponders long over the condition of his people, the will of God and the problem of his own duty. Then some day suddenly the sought-for solution rushes into his mind—he finds a message ready-made upon his tongue, and it is almost inevitable that he should preface it with the words: 'Thus hath Yahweh showed me!' "[21]

The whole situation may be well summed up in a story given by Bouquet[22] in his book *Religious Experience, Its Nature, Type and*

17. Pratt, *The Religious Consciousness*, 63.
18. That is, absolute comprehension is a "limiting concept" in that it is needed (whether or not it is attained) if one is to comprehend any particular religion.
19. Pratt, *The Religious Consciousness*, 63.
20. Ibid., 27.
21. Ibid., 65.
22. Alan C. Bouquet (1884–1976).

Validity. He compares various metaphysical views to see which are favorable and which are unfavorable to religion. He thinks naturalism is unfavorable to religion. He feels that we need something in the nature of transcendence to justify religion. Then in comparing the various views discussed, he says:

> The case has been well compared by an American psychologist to an account which might be given by a man who had seen the sun for the first time after having lived under abnormal conditions, and given to a company of blind men who had never seen it. The seer would describe quite frankly the bright round object of his vision: but the blind psychologist would say that he could account for the phenomenon by certain conditions prevailing within the eye, "Raised eyelids, stimulated retina, afferent impulse in the optic nerves, the stimulation of the visual centres in the occipital lobes." Both would be right. The explanation of the psychologist would be correct within its own limits and it could not prove the objective existence of the sun merely by the movements going on within the eye, for it might easily say that these movements produced the appearance of a luminous ball which was therefore a projection from inside the eye. And yet it would be generally admitted that the seer in question really did see the sun.[23]

From the Christian point of view we should say that practically all the psychologists of religion are like these blind men. They insist on explaining religion exclusively from the "inside." Christian believers, on the other hand, may be compared with the man who had been blind but who later saw the sun. He knew what it was to be blind and what it was to see. He could therefore understand his blind friends while they could not understand him. Christians having been born again, can understand those who have no experience of the new birth. But those who have not been born again cannot do justice to the unique experience of those who have. They must continue to explain that experience in the only categories that are open to them.

23. A. C. Bouquet, *Religious Experience: Its Nature, Types, and Validity* (Cambridge: W. Heffer & Sons, 1932), 56–57.

We do not agree with Bouquet, however, when he says that both the blind men and the seer were right from their different points of view. The blind men were entirely wrong. They had no understanding of what it means to see the sun at all. In contradiction to the words of the seer they sought to explain the phenomenon of seeing from the inside. They did, to be sure, observe the movement of the eyeballs, etc. But they gave an entirely mistaken interpretation of these phenomena. The blind men as well as the seer moved their eyeballs. The only point in question was whether the blind men or the seer was right about seeing the sun. Of course, we answer that the seer was wholly right and the blind men were wholly wrong.

THE ORIGIN OF RELIGION

So far we have spoken of the religious consciousness as the self-sufficient source of explanation and of the non-theistic method of study employed by the psychology of religion literature. To this we may add some remarks on the nature of religion as thus discovered. Something of this has already become apparent. In fact it is easy to predict what religion must be on the assumptions made. Yet it is useful to see in some detail what men have said about the matter.

In the first place we wish to examine more fully the manner in which the orthodox Christian view is rejected. It is rejected by the assumption of religion as a brute fact. We are told over and over again that we must make no metaphysical assumptions when we study the phenomena of the religions. We are told that the traditional position constantly makes such assumptions. It has, we are told, a whole scheme of metaphysics in the light of which it interprets the religious experience. In contrast to this we are to go to the facts and study them with unbiased mind. In the first place we must go to history to find out about the origin of religion. We find that man gradually evolved from the beast. Religion and morality have somehow sprung from the non-moral and the non-religious. Men evolved the religious attitude in response to their physical needs. They made gods for themselves in order to get rain and sunshine. They made gods for themselves because they lived in dread of the power of nature.

We need not enlarge upon this matter. It is too well known to need further elucidation. What does need elucidation is the fact that men can seriously offer such a presentation and still think they are not taking for granted a complete scheme of metaphysics and epistemology. What does need elucidation too is the fact that men will accuse Christianity of intellectualism in its conception of religion and then assume an intellectual interpretation of reality themselves.

To say that we can find the origin of religion by simple historical study is to assume the non-Christian position. It takes for granted that history is self-explanatory. It therefore at the outset excludes God as the creator of history. In this the psychology of religion is but following the lead of Kant. Kant, as noted above, held that every reference to a transcendent God is illegitimate. It would mean that God could think apart from brute facts.

It would be fatal to oppose this Kantian epistemology as it underlies the recent psychology of religion literature with the method of Butler and his school. We should then have to grant the legitimacy of starting with brute facts. We should then have to admit the competence of the mind of sinful man to judge of these brute facts. With these assumptions the picture given by the psychology of religion can be made to appear as possibly true. Is there not a great deal of evidence that early man did just the sort of thing that we are told he did? Does not the evidence indicate that man has made gods in his own image? Yet there is evidence for an original monotheism. But even so we cannot reach to the high position of the Bible account. That account speaks of an originally perfect man. Where is the factual historical evidence that such a man ever existed?

We cannot resort to possibilities and probabilities. The Bible requires absolute faith in its truthfulness. We cannot resort to a dualism between our faith and our rational interpretation of life. The Bible says that we are created as unified personalities. The only method of dealing with this whole problem is that spoken of repeatedly. We should allow men to work out a complete interpretation of life upon the basis of the principles they have assumed. They will then run into a blind alley. So in the present instance. Starting with brute fact the psychology of religion must end with brute fact. Starting with self-sufficiency it cannot find in history any criterion with which to judge between better or worse. Starting with the normalcy of the mind of sinful man, the abnormal is made an aspect of the normal. Truth cannot be distinguished from error. Light cannot be distinguished from darkness.[24]

When the bankruptcy of the non-Christian interpretation of the origin of religion thus appears we point out that the "facts" are in accord with the Christian position. We presuppose God. That gives meaning to history as a whole. God is the maker of all things. He created man in his own image. Man's consciousness could therefore function fruitfully when it sought to interpret life in accordance with God's interpretation of it. But man became a sinner. He sought within his own consciousness the principle by which to interpret life. Eve equated the words of God with the words of the devil. She put on a par the interpretation of history given by the maker of history, and the interpretation of history given by one who was himself immersed within history. This was, in effect, the reduction of God to the level of an historical being. Eve thought that both God and the devil were like scientists who placed before themselves the ideal of complete comprehension of the meaning of brute facts, as a limiting concept. Accordingly she thought that the interpretation of neither of them could be comprehensive and certainly true. She would have to make up her own mind at a venture. She took for granted that man must interpret the whole of history in exclusively immanentistic categories.[25]

It is but natural that after this evil beginning mankind made gods in its own image. God was after that pictured as being no more than a magnified man. Then too there would naturally be many gods. We expect evidence for early polytheism. To be sure, man could not quickly forget his original home. So we also expect evidence for early monotheism. All this has meaning only on the basis of the Christian philosophy of history.

---

24. While this line of reasoning should be obvious to any Christian, it is all too easy to miss it. Van Til's point is that any notion of psychology or of religion that begins with the presumed autonomy of the human mind, rather than with what God has said, is doomed to self-destruction; it cannot be sustained, because it begins in the wrong place.

25. In other words, once Eve was confronted with the words of Satan, she was deceived into thinking that the decision whether or not the tree was forbidden was up to her, not up to God. This was "immanentistic" thinking because the categories for what was true and what was false were thought to reside within her, rather than with what God had spoken.

THE NATURE OF RELIGION

Yet it is upon the assumption of the self-sufficiency of history that the psychology of religion proceeds. Upon such a basis we expect that men will be able to find no common definition of religion. Leuba[26] has collected some forty-eight definitions of religion in his book. They are similar to some of those we have given from the book of Sheen. Pratt remarks about these definitions as follows:

> Professor Leuba enumerates forty-eight definitions of religion from as many great men (and elsewhere, adds two of his own, apparently to fill out the even half-hundred). But the striking thing about these definitions is that, persuasive as many of them are, each learned doctor seems quite unpersuaded by any but his own. And when doctors disagree what are the rest of us going to do? Can we be justified in talking about religion at all?
>
> The truth is, I suppose, that "religion" is one of those general and popular terms which have been used for centuries to cover so vague and indefinite a collection of phenomena that no definition can be framed which will include all its uses and coincide with every one's meaning for it. Hence all definitions of religion are more or less arbitrary and should be taken rather as postulates than as axioms. In this sense I shall myself propose a tentative definition of religion, not at all as a final or complete statement, nor because I think it of any great importance, but because I intend to write a book about religion and it therefore seems only fair that I should tell the reader in advance not what the word means, but what I am going to mean by the word.[27]

From this passage of Pratt it appears what will happen to the notion of religion if the traditional position be given up. All human experience is then a matter of brute fact. One interpretation of it is practically as good as another. All definitions are allowed an equal

---

26. James H. Leuba (1867–1946) was an American psychologist of religion and a naturalist. He self-consciously sought to interpret religion naturalistically.
27. Pratt, *The Religious Consciousness*, 1–2.

standing. There is only one definition that must be excluded. That is the orthodox Christian one. The reason for this is plain. If the Christian conception of religion were allowed, it would disallow all the others. We preach the unknown religion as Paul preached the unknown God. We beg not for a place in the Parthenon; we demand the destruction of the Parthenon.

If we look at some of the definitions actually proposed, we find that they offer amid a great variety a basic similarity. They all "lose themselves in their round globe." Leuba has classified the definitions of religion as follows:

In the first place: "*Religion is the feeling* (or emotion) *or the attitude* (or behavior) *called forth by the mysterious or the sacred.*"

In the second place: "*Religion is the quest after the meaning of life,* or, from a somewhat different point of view, *it is the determination of what is most worth while.*"

In the third place: "*Religion is a belief in something human which has the power of making life what it should be.*"

In the fourth place: "*Religion is devotion to the welfare of humanity.*"

In the fifth place: "*Religion is an experience implying the existence of a spiritual world.*"[28]

Every one of these classes of definitions is based upon an assumed intra-cosmical principle of interpretation. What is the "mysterious" spoken of in the first class of definitions? From the Christian point of view it would be the incomprehensibility of God who has revealed himself according to the measure of man's ability to receive such revelation. In Leuba's statement it is taken to be something beyond what man can understand by himself. In reality all things are mysterious on this basis. There can be no distinction between sacred and secular on an assumed historical relativity. What is the "meaning of life" spoken of in the second class? It is taken for granted that the answer to this question must be found in history itself. And what can make life what it should be? Man must discover this for himself in the course of history. Yet he can never discover this because all of the brute facts of history are on a par with one another. What is for the welfare of humanity? One says one thing

---

28. James H. Leuba, *God or Man? A Study of the Value of God to Man* (New York: Henry Holt and Company, 1933), 14–16.

and another says the opposite. There is nothing but confusion on the subject. No final answer can be given. And what is the nature of that "spiritual world" of which the last class speaks? No one knows or ever can know. Brute facts can never be fully interpreted by the universals of science.

Yet it is frequently said that no man of intelligence can really hold to the orthodox view of religion today. Leuba tells us in no uncertain terms that we are obscurantists if we hold to the orthodox view. He traces the history of the idea of God. Some gods were invented and moralized, he says. Other gods were invented and depersonalized. The former was in the interest of the heart. The others were in the interest of the head. What did the Christian Church do with these gods? We give Leuba's words:

> The God of the Christian creeds unites these two incompatible features: he possesses the essential mental traits of a human person, and can, therefore, sympathize with man and minister to his happiness. He is also an infinite, impersonal Absolute and, as such, cannot be affected by man's behavior. The social, personal traits of God are due to man's desire for some one able and willing to protect, comfort, do justice, and otherwise gratify the needs of the heart; his impersonality is the outcome of a desire to understand rationally, logically, to see things as they are and not as we would like them to be. No god who is not both personal and impersonal can altogether satisfy human nature, compounded as it is of heart and head. The presence of these contradictory features in the conception of God accounts for confusions and compromises, some tragic and some ridiculous, which afflict civilized humanity.[29]

To this he adds a little further:

> The intellectual gymnastics to which the Church Fathers were prompted by this perplexing situation are a monument to man's resourcefulness, and, in particular, to his ability to believe the unbelievable in order to live content. The achievements of

29. Ibid., 52–53.

these men equal probably any other self-deception achieved by humanity.[30]

It may be said that the position of Leuba is extreme. Are there not other psychologists of religion who are favorable to the Christian faith? We reply that Leuba's position is extreme only in its manner of statement. Some other psychologists of religion are more courteous in their rejection of Christianity than is Leuba. That is really the only difference. We may as well face this situation. The psychology of religion literature says in effect that Christianity reduces experience to absurdity. The only way in which to meet this charge is to show that the opposite is true. When Leuba speaks of believing the unbelievable we point out that he, together with others, has denied the very law of non-contradiction.[31] He and his confreres have virtually given up every effort to give an intellectual interpretation to the phenomena of experience. They simply think of religion as a function with which man helps to adjust himself to an ultimately irrational environment. Let us look briefly at the religion of the psychologist of religion.

RELIGION AS THE JOYFUL SUBMISSION TO THE INEVITABLE

Some years ago a series of Outline Bible Study Courses proceeded from the University of Chicago. Professor Kingsbury, a psychologist, tells us in it what the good life is. He says that the good life is the "*well-integrated* life."[32] Personality itself appears upon the universe somehow. It must integrate itself somehow. It must seek the unification of its motives. "Unification of motives is not something we start with and then lose, as did grandfather Adam in the Garden of Eden. Oneness is an achievement, worked out, if at all, only in the struggle and effort of living in a difficult world."[33] Thus the task of personality begins to take shape. Personality is here somehow in a universe which is here somehow. The personality and the universe

30. Ibid., 57.
31. This is the case because all religions, even if they contradict one another, are deemed to be "legitimate."
32. Forrest A. Kingsbury in *What Religion Does for Personality*, by Shailer Mathews, Forrest A. Kingsbury, Charles T. Holman, et al. (Chicago: American Institute of Sacred Literature, 1932), 70.
33. Ibid., 77.

are somehow evil as well as good. In this chance conglomeration human personality is somehow going to achieve integration.

If we fear that this integration is not likely to be effected, we turn to the philosopher Wieman.[34] He assures us that there will somehow be something stable in the accidental universe. At least he tells us that if the universe were only accident and chance, integration would not take place. "Change without something that retains its identity throughout the change is meaningless. All purpose, all meaning, all progress, all hope, requires that something changeless persist throughout the sequence of transition."[35]

To this we can but reply that it spells the condemnation of the whole effort put forth by the psychology of religion. That whole effort is confessedly based upon an ultimate philosophy of flux. But we must believe the unbelievable and see what happens. If we become disheartened and think that on such a basis the whole of life and religion is a delusion, Wieman assures us that it is not.

Let us call to mind that the aspect of the universe called God is a pervasive aspect constantly and intimately operative in our lives and in the world round about us. In so far as we yield ourselves to it, indescribable possibilities for good hover over us and open before us. But in so far as we yield ourselves to the destructive aspects of the universe great evils hang over us and open before us. At regular seasons of worship let us cultivate this sense of divine presence, with the attendant possibilities for good and evil.

But we must not stop with this sense of divine presence and vivid apprehension of the attendant possibilities. Each of us must recognize, and through regular seasons of meditation clarify, the definite part which he is fitted to play in bringing the divine aspect of the universe into dominance, with all the consequent good, and in reducing the evil aspects with their consequent disasters.[36]

34. Henry N. Wieman (1884–1975), a philosopher and theologian, spent most of his teaching career at the University of Chicago. He was one of the most ardent defenders of theocentric naturalism in the twentieth century.

35. Henry N. Wieman in *What Religion Does for Personality*, by Mathews et al., 92–93.

36. Henry N. Wieman in *Experiments in Personal Religion*, by Edward Scribner Ames, William C. Bower, Georgia L. Chamberlin, et al. (Chicago: American Institute of Sacred Literature, 1928), 78–79.

Finally in order to enlist our energies in making the divine aspect of the universe dominant Wieman identifies it with popular notions of the kingdom of God:

> This genuine possibility for maximum good inherent in the universe may be called the cause of Christ, the will of God, the Kingdom of Heaven, the utmost welfare of mankind, etc., but its specific nature and the best way to promote it is something about which only the fanatic is sure; and he is probably most mistaken of all.[37]

Thus religion becomes something entirely subjective. It is an attitude to brute facts for which we have no metaphysical or epistemological justification. If the universe is nothing but a mass of brute facts then we have no right to assume that we can integrate our personalities. Religion on this basis becomes nothing but acceptance of the inevitable. Wieman himself virtually admits this when he says:

> One is free of demoralizing fear just as soon as he is ready to accept the facts precisely as they are. . . . There is record of a man who found he was going blind. As long as he clung to his failing eyesight he was fearful and depressed. But when at last he saw there was no hope, resigned himself to inevitable fact, and set to work to cultivate his sense of touch in order to become an expert flour-tester, his fear departed. . . .
>
> Now this state of complete self-committal, this total self-surrender to reality, with consequent command over all the resources of personality, is possible when one fills his mind with the thought that underneath all other facts is the basic fact upon which all else depends. This basic fact can be called the structure of the universe or it can be called God. Whenever we commit ourselves in love to God, accepting him with affection and all things else for his sake, we are free from fear. This state of mind requires cultivation.[38]

---

37. Ibid., 95.
38. Ibid., 138.

Thus religion becomes the joyful submission to the inevitable. But perhaps it will be said that the inevitable is not as inevitable as it used to be. Has not recent scientific research shown us that determinism must be replaced by indeterminism? Does not this give human personality an opportunity that it did not formerly have, to integrate itself? We do not think so. As pointed out before, human personality is no better off with a chance universe than with a determined universe. The psychology of religion literature, together with modern science in general, assumes a philosophy of chance. Upon such a basis no predication is possible and religion itself becomes unintelligible.[39] Christianity alone does not destroy reason, and therefore it alone does not destroy religion.

39. When Van Til says that "no predication is possible" apart from Christianity, he means that there is no meaningful way to affirm predication unless Christianity is true. In this context, if all religions are in some way justified, then there can be no truth, since religions contradict each other. Thus, religion itself becomes unintelligible; no meaning can be ascribed to it since it is divorced from the world and embedded only in subjective experience.

SOME RECENT SCIENTISTS

I n this Appendix we shall concern ourselves with some more recent developments in the philosophy of science and its methodology.

For all the differences between the various schools of recent philosophy and science that have made their appearance since Kant's three *Critiques*[1] were published, there are three notions that all of them have in common.

1. There is first the assumption that the would-be autonomous man, not God, is the ultimate starting point and final reference point of all human predication. If anyone suggests that man is what he is as a created image-bearer of God and ought, therefore, from the outset of his investigation of his environment subject his interpretation to the revelation of the triune God of Scripture, he is ruled out of court.

2. Secondly there is the notion of the world of fact as a purely contingent one. If anyone suggests that the world of space and time is what it is, and that therefore the facts that constitute it are what they are because of a prior interpretation of them by the triune God of Scripture, he is ruled out of court.

---

1. Van Til is referring to Kant's *Critique of Pure Reason*, his *Critique or Practical Reason* and his *Critique of Judgment*.

3. In the third place there is the assumption that any principle of unity that is to be used must be one of pure form.[2] Anyone who suggests that the plan of God as revealed in Scripture be taken as the principle of coherence for the scientist is ruled out of court.

Recent scientists continue to carry on the motif of Renaissance man. Renaissance man thought he had come of age. He needed no help from God, least of all from the God of Christianity.[3]

The Renaissance man enters upon the future with the expectation of carving out the kingdom of man without reference to the Christ who offers to save him. Such men as Copernicus, Kepler and Galileo insisted on having what they called a free mind (*animus liber*). The Renaissance man does not want the "theologian" to interpret him and his universe in terms of the narrative of Scripture. Wilhelm Windelband says:

> *Natural science* acquired its decisive influence upon the development of modern philosophy by first gaining its own independence with the aid of a conscious use of the scientific method, and then from this position being able to determine the general movement of thought as regards both form and content.[4]

FRANCIS BACON[5]

In complete independence of every form of authority and revelation, Francis Bacon, the typical Renaissance man, sets out to dwell "purely and constantly among the facts of nature."[6] If he makes any mistakes, he argues, he has given to others the means of correcting him. Speaking of his general methodology he says: "And by these means I suppose that I have established for ever a

2. For example, in Kant's *Critique of Pure Reason*, the noumena, which is unknowable, is necessary for the phenomena. But the noumenal God is "pure form," so there can be no content given to him because no experience of him can be had.

3. Fritz Heinemann, *Neue Wege der Philosophie* (New Paths of Philosophy) (Leipzig: Quelle & Meyer, 1929), 27.

4. W. Windelband, *A History of Philosophy*, trans. James H. Tufts (New York: Macmillan, 1901), 378.

5. Francis Bacon (1561–1626) is usually thought of as a transitional figure from the Renaissance to modern thought. He was a pioneer in empirical science and natural philosophy.

6. Francis Bacon, *The Great Instauration*, in Edwin A. Burtt, *The English Philosophers from Bacon to Mill* (New York: The Modern Library, 1939), 11.

true and lawful marriage between the empirical and the rational faculty, the unkind and ill-starred divorce and separation of which has thrown into confusion all the affairs of the human family."[7]

Bacon has set aside "the mischievous authority of systems, which are founded either on common notions, or on a few experiments, or on superstition."[8] Having renounced all classes of idols Bacon promises to lead us into what he himself calls "the kingdom of man."[9] The prophecy of Daniel will now be fulfilled to the effect that in the latter days "knowledge shall be increased."[10] God the Father, God the Son, and God the Holy Ghost, says Bacon "will vouchsafe through my hands to endow the human family with new mercies."[11]

We shall find that Bacon's style of combining science and philosophy with religion is fairly typical of modern times, even of recent times. Modern science and philosophy operate in complete independence of the creator-redeemer God of Scripture. Man and his spatio-temporal environment are assumed *not* to be what Scripture says they are. Man is assumed to be not a creature of God. He is *not* a sinner in the sight of God. How could he possibly be said to be in need of forgiveness for what he does as a scientist and as a philosopher? Is he not as a scientist and as a philosopher himself the great benefactor of mankind?

Of course, even Renaissance man knows that he is surrounded by ultimate mystery. What may come forth from that realm of ultimate mystery, who can know? To build the kingdom of man, the future must be wholly open. The possibilities offered by the future must be infinite. There must be no predetermination of the future by a God whose plans for that future do not, at least to an extent, coincide with those of man. Surely we shall continue to worship God the Father, God the Son, and God the Holy Ghost, but we do this because we know that this triune God will, with his infinite powers, seek to establish the work of our hands.

Recent scientists carry on their work in the spirit of Renaissance and, more particularly, in the spirit of Kant.

---

7. Ibid., 12.

8. Francis Bacon, *The New Organon; or, True Directions concerning the Interpretation of Nature*, in Burtt, *The English Philosophers from Bacon to Mill*, 45.

9. Ibid., 48.

10. Ibid., 66.

11. Bacon, "The Great Instauration," 12.

Kant has enabled us to see that by the idea of true inwardness of the human self we may overcome the hopeless reduction of fact to logic or of the hopeless reduction of logic to fact. We now see that the notions of pure contingency and of pure system are correlative and therefore necessary to one another. In the on-going process of human experience man needs both, the ideal of absolute openness of the universe and the ideal of the absolute comprehension of experience. But he cannot have both unless he takes them as correlative to one another.

With this we are prepared to appreciate the significance of post-Kantian thinking. Generally speaking, the various schools of science and philosophy during the nineteenth and twentieth centuries have wanted to build on Kant in order then to go beyond him. Again generally speaking, there are those schools of thinking which stress the need of *system* and there are other schools of thought which stress the need of contingent factuality. But, and this is important, it is always a matter of emphasis. It is not, as it was before Kant, a matter of exclusion.

Historically, those who have stressed the need of system prevailed during a good portion of the nineteenth century, and those who stress the need of contingent factuality prevailed in the twentieth century. When, therefore, Gilbert Ryle edits a book with the title *Revolution in Philosophy*, he refers to the common spirit of reaction on the part of such men as G. E. Moore, Bertrand Russell, the Vienna Circle, Wittgenstein, and others, against a position such as that of the great Idealists, F. H. Bradley and Bernard Bosanquet.[12]

Writing on Bradley in the book mentioned, R. A. Wollheim says that, according to Bradley, "To consider anything, we must consider everything."[13] According to Bradley, says Wollheim, "we can never talk about isolated events. And, worse still, he said there were no such things."[14] Bradley's view is monistic. For him, "Reality is an indivisible whole."[15] However much we may try to find an isolated event, we can never succeed in doing so. I may say: This

---

12. In other words, the "system" of idealism, with its emphasis on the whole of reality, is being replaced, in the twentieth century, by an emphasis on contingent facts.

13. R. A. Wollheim, "F. H. Bradley," in *The Revolution in Philosophy*, ed. Gilbert Ryle (London: Macmillan, 1957), 20.

14. Ibid., 16.

15. Ibid., 13.

bird is brown. I may then distinguish the particular brownness of this particular brown bird from the particular brownness of other brown birds. But however many descriptions I may add to my first statement, "there is always the chance that there is some other bird that they also fit: and so this one here and now, is not singled out. The generality of language is our undoing."[16] Even when we say that this particular brown bird "here" and "now" is different from all other birds "here" and "now" we have not reached absolute uniqueness. "If we try to specify the time and the position from which we are actually speaking, we are back in the world of descriptions."[17] "The moral that Bradley draws from this is that our only way of securing uniqueness is to specify the relations of our object with all other objects in the world, past, present, and future, actual and imagined: and to do this is, of course, to introduce the whole of Reality."[18]

What the men who write in Ryle's book, together with others, are trying to do is to save the reality of space-time fact from being swallowed up by Bradley's Absolute. Therefore they hark back to the empiricism of Locke, Berkeley and Hume. But they admit to having learned something useful from Idealism. Such men as Thomas Hill Greene, F. H. Bradley and Bernard Bosanquet proved convincingly that the traditional empiricist tradition was mistaken when it thought it could build up experience out of independent building blocks composed of sensations. The idealists were right when they argued that the *judgment* rather than the *concept* is the unit of human interpretation. No one can ever find an absolutely individual fact or have an absolutely individual concept. If thought is not to stand unalterably over against reality then we must assume that *this* bird and the *brownness* of this bird are identical. On this point the recent movement in science wants to follow Kant rather than Hume.[19] D. F. Pears says: "What Russell did was to absorb this part of the idealist tradition, and put it at the service of empiricism.

---

16. Ibid., 16–17.
17. Ibid., 17.
18. Ibid.
19. Kant was insistent, over against Hume, that knowledge was dependent on judgments, not on ideas. Kant's *Critique of Pure Reason* was written to answer the question, "Are synthetic a priori judgments possible?" Hume answered no to this question; Kant argues for an affirmative answer.

For the new philosophy is really an empiricism based on judgments or propositions, instead of being based on ideas."[20]

When recent philosophers and scientists such as G. E. Moore, Bertrand Russell, A. N. Whitehead and others are out to *save* science from the *absolutism* of the idealists, they do so within the limits of a basically Kantian approach.

The new scientists and philosophers are, without exception, opposed to what they call *metaphysics*. Well, the idealists were also opposed to metaphysics. Friedrich Hegel is often called a rationalist. Did he not hold to the idea that the real is the rational and the rational is the real? True, but while saying this, he did not want to revert to a pre-Kantian metaphysic. In fact he abhorred what he called, the "old metaphysic," the metaphysic which thought that the presence of the activity of an absolute God could be identified in the space-time world. Hegel and his British idealist followers were indeed committed to the need of holding to the idea of God as the Absolute. But for them, this notion of God as absolute was not a constitutive, but a *limiting*, concept. To distinguish their notion and function of logic in human experience from that of the Greeks, they accordingly spoke of the view of the Greeks as being that of an abstract universal and of their own as that of a concrete universal. If the Greeks tended to deny the reality of time and space, the modern idealist definitely included space and time into the life of the Absolute. It is for this reason that the Absolute of modern idealism is itself eternally growing by means of the absorption of the temporal into itself.[21]

It is only when these points are taken into consideration that we may be saved from much misunderstanding with respect to modern philosophy and science. When recent scientists and philosophers differ among themselves, these differences are differences among brothers who, as members of the same family, oppose Idealism.

Again, when recent scientists or philosophers and idealists like Bradley differ from one another, we remember that by means of their common concept of contingency they oppose the Greeks.

---

20. D. F. Pears, "Logical Atomism: Russell and Wittenstein," in *The Revolution in Philosophy*, ed. Ryle, 42.

21. As Van Til constantly argued, the Absolute of idealism requires, in order to be absolute, the relative of the space-time world. Thus, it is not really absolute at all.

Again, when recent scientists or philosophers together with modern idealists oppose the Greeks, we remember that by means of their common concept of human autonomy they oppose the historic Christian position.

What all of these schools have in common is a stress on the necessity of escaping the notion of an abstract, timeless Universal. They are all opposing what they speak of as the interpretation of human experience in terms of static concepts, i.e., abstract universals. They all oppose medieval and earlier modern views of reality in so far as these were influenced by the timeless Absolute of the Greeks.

But then, what frequently happens is that the Greek notion of God and his relation to the world is virtually identified with what is called the God of the historic Christian confessions. This point will engage us again as we deal with theology. For the moment we mention it only for the purpose of clarifying the issues engaging recent scientists and philosophers.

These scientists and philosophers, speaking in general, oppose modern idealism in the interest of the significance of human temporal-spatial experience. But modern idealism opposed ancient philosophy for the same reason. And ancient philosophy itself becomes intelligible only if it is seen as an expression of those who, as descendents and followers of Adam, with him insist on the idea that man can understand himself and his experience of his environment only if he thinks of himself as deciding on the nature of reality without reference to what God says about it. When therefore the British philosopher Alexander writes a book, *Space, Time and Deity*; when the French philosopher Bergson writes a book, *Creative Evolution*; when the German philosopher Heidegger writes a book, *Being and Time*; when the Russian philosopher Nicolas Berdjaev writes a book, *The Beginning and the End*; and the American philosopher John Dewey writes a book, *The Quest for Certainty*, they all express the recent spirit of opposition to modern idealist absolutism, and back of that to Greek absolutism, and back of that to the only absolute who is not a virtual projection of self-sufficient man, namely, the God of historic Christianity. When these various writers are out, as Kant was, to *save science*, they are seeking to save it from the destructive principles of historic Protestant thought from which their predecessors had not been altogether able to liberate themselves.[22] It is this God and only this God who controls in advance all that the space-time continuum produces and thus at one stroke kills the very idea of open factuality which the scientist needs as bread and butter. It is this God and only this God who insists that man's principle of coherence as it rests on the activity of the mind of man rests, back of this, upon the activity of the mind of God.

The modern scientist and philosopher has no other tools with which to save science than that of human autonomy, of pure contingent factuality, and of abstract self-existent rationality. The Greeks operated with these principles, Renaissance man operated with these principles, Kant and Bradley operated with these principles. In each case science was not saved and the Christian religion was arbitrarily excluded as not even possibly needed by science and philosophy, in fact as destructive of science. In each case the problematic was how to get a network of purely conceptual and absolutely comprehensive relations into significant contact with an endless number of unrelated facts. How then does recent science and philosophy seek to save science?

1. Bertrand Russell[23]

Speaking negatively, recent scientists and philosophers are in full agreement with one another on the fact that wherever any left-over of metaphysics may be found, it must be eradicated. Both the gathering of facts and their ordering into laws can be and therefore must be accomplished without so much as a glance in the direction of the creator-redeemer God of the Bible. Empiricists of the pre-Kantian school were, these men feel, not clear on this point. They were unable to show the complete independent ability

22. Kant's famous dictum, that he determined to define knowledge (science) in order to make room for faith, grants to the domain of science an autonomy that is explicit, and it sets scientific knowledge in antithetic relation to religion.

23. Bertrand Russell (1872–1970), together with G. E. Moore and Ludwig Wittgenstein (see below), is considered to be the founder of analytic philosophy. Analytic philosophers, with all of their differences, were unified in their rejection of Absolute idealism and its focus on the analysis of meaning by way of propositions. Initially an idealist, Russell rejected his idealist views in favor of what he called "logical atomism." A complex doctrine, logical atomism seeks to focus not on an "Absolute" to make sense of contingent things (as in idealism), but on the contingent things themselves. The world, Russell argued, was made up of many distinct entities, which themselves can be analyzed without recourse to their relations to other things or to the human mind.

of man to interpret reality for himself. Such men as Locke did not see that man has within his own make-up the power of uniting the facts of experience into unity. But now, since Kant, we have a "new kind of empiricism." Russell calls it "logical atomism."[24]

Russell even speaks of logic as "the Essence of Philosophy."[25] Pears quotes Russell as saying that philosophers should "give an account of the world of science and daily life." Pears says for Russell: "If only we can succeed in understanding the way we talk and think about the ordinary world, we shall not be led to reject it in favour of another world behind it."[26] We must not say, as Bradley did, that all analysis falsifies. Analysis does not refer to anything hidden behind the world of science. But, as Pears points out, the logical atomism of Russell and, as he adds, of Wittgenstein is, after all, a "metaphysical theory."[27] Russell uses his logical analysis in order to obtain what Bacon in his day sought to obtain, namely, the reduction of "empirical concepts . . . to a few simple elements." Russell is looking for "indivisible logical particles."[28]

But, Pears asks, "What sense can be attached to the notion of logical indivisibility"?[29] At this point, he adds, the theory of logical atomism "becomes metaphysical." It is when the theory of logical atomism "is extended to particular things that it ceases to be plausible."[30] Suppose I make the statement: "This fountain-pen is black." You know what I mean by this statement "from the context in which I make the statement." Bradley tries to obtain the "uniqueness of reference" that he needs for the purpose of making such a statement by adding "more and more general descriptions of the thing." Russell "thought that he could achieve uniqueness of reference by moving in the direction of greater and greater simplicity until he reached particulars."[31]

Russell's argument is that the experiences of daily life can be explained only if we assume that there are "absolutely simple particulars" somehow present in them. As an empiricist Russell rejects

24. Pears, "Logical Atomism," 42–43.
25. Ibid., 45.
26. Ibid.
27. Ibid., 46.
28. Ibid., 50.
29. Ibid.
30. Ibid., 50–51.
31. Ibid., 52–53.

Bradley's Absolute. The introduction of the notion of an Absolute is, to Russell's mind, to explain the known world of daily experience by an unknown world foisted upon it by a false logical theory. But Russell himself introduces *another* world, a world foisted upon experience by sheer logical theory. The effort on the part of Russell to refute Bradley's idealism indicates the fact that they operate on a common basis. The "new empiricism" cannot speak of itself except in terms of the old idealism.

Russell reduces the facts of experience to indivisible logical atoms. He needs these in order to manipulate existence by thinking. Then how can he bring these "indivisible logical atoms" into relation with one another except by absorption into one all comprehensive logical thought which no thinker has ever thought or can ever think?

Of course Russell wants to maintain his realism. But he cannot do this unless he is inconsistent. Pears says: "If a philosopher begins by saying that things are, from a logical point of view, like Chinese boxes, then he really must carry this theory through to the end: he should not lose his nerve and say that inside the last box there must be something which, unlike the boxes, is solid and indivisible, something which cannot be described but only named, an individual substance."[32] Thus Russell the realist, says Pears, produced a theory "which is, in the deepest sense, Platonic."[33]

From the Christian point of view, we may add that not only do all those who claim to have no metaphysic in reality have one, but that they have an anti-Christian one, whether or not it be platonic. To pretend to be able to give any essentially true interpretation of the world of space and time without reference to the work of the Creator-Redeemer God of the Bible is like going on a privately owned estate and claiming that one can explain the shrubbery without reference to the question of ownership.

2. G. E. Moore[34]

The next position we consider briefly is that of G. E. Moore. In 1917 Moore wrote an article with the title, "The Conception

---

32. Ibid., 53–54.
33. Ibid., 55.
34. G. E. Moore (1873–1958), together with Bertrand Russell and Ludwig Wittgenstein, was one of the pioneers in the development of analytic philosophy.

of Reality."[35] This article was directed against the idea "that Time is not real." The interest back of this sort of contention is, says G. A. Paul, that a world beyond the temporal world would give a foundation for ethics, i.e., "some warrant for rules about how we are to behave towards one another." "Moore would not have it."[36]

Moore was not a positivist. "But he *was* an 'analyst'."[37] So he picks out one question in order to see what is involved in it. His question is, "What is good?" This, Moore says, "is *the most fundamental* question in all Ethics."[38] How then does he define the good? His answer is that the good cannot be defined.[39] Moore "had no programme." " 'Even if I prove my point', he wrote, 'I shall have proved nothing about the Universe in general.' "[40]

What Moore actually demonstrated is that he, like Socrates, has no need of God and of Christ in his investigation of the nature of the good. Pretending to say nothing about the Universe in general he is, nonetheless, in effect, making a universal negative judgment about it. If Moore's philosophy were true, the Christian story cannot be true.

3. Logical Positivism (The Vienna Circle)

For a brief description of *Logical Positivism*[41] as it originated in the so-called *Vienna Circle*, we listen to A. J. Ayer.[42]

It is remarkable, says Ayer, in speaking of the *Vienna Circle*, "how many of their most radical doctrines are already to be found in Hume."[43, 44] "The positivist flavour of their thought," Ayer continues,

---

35. G. A. Paul, "G. E. Moore," in *The Revolution in Philosophy*, ed. Ryle, 57.
36. Ibid.
37. Ibid., 58.
38. Ibid., 59.
39. Ibid., 60.
40. Ibid., 59–60.
41. Logical positivism was a diverse movement in the twentieth century, difficult to characterize precisely and doctrinally. It seemed to be unified around a rejection of idealism and an emphasis on the empirical as the primary, if not the only, ground for knowledge and for meaningful predication.
42. A. J. Ayer (1910–1989) set forth what was considered to be the main tenets of logical positivism, or logical empiricism. He was the main proponent of such a view in the English-speaking world.
43. A. J. Ayer, "The Vienna Circle," in *The Revolution in Philosophy*, ed. Ryle, 73.
44. Much of the antimetaphysical bias and the focus on propositions began in earnest with Hume's radical empiricism. Hume argued that there are only three kinds of propositions—analytic propositions, in which the subject is contained in the predicate; synthetic propositions, which depend on experience for their meaning; and nonsensical propositions,

"comes out most strongly in their hostility to metaphysics."[45] Any "attempt to describe Reality as a whole, or to find the purpose of the Universe, or to reach beyond the everyday world to some supra-sensible spiritual order" was thought of as metaphysics.[46] They condemned metaphysics "not as being unduly speculative, or even as being false, but as being literally nonsensical. They reached this conclusion by the application of a criterion of meaning which is known as the verification principle."[47] "Roughly stated," says Ayer, this principle "lays it down that the meaning of a statement is determined by the way in which it can be verified, where its being verified consists in its being tested by empirical observation."[48] Judged by the verification principle, statements of metaphysics as above described "are ruled out as factually meaningless." Statements of metaphysics, that is, "are not capable of stating facts." Wittgenstein expressed this contention succinctly in the last sentence of his *Tractatus* by saying: "Whereof one cannot speak, thereof one must be silent."[49] Neurath,[50] one of the members of the circle, wants to go further than this. He wants to make sure not only that we cannot *speak* of metaphysical entities, but that there *are* no such entities. "When it comes to metaphysics, said Neurath, 'one must indeed be silent, but not *about* anything'. Or as the Cambridge philosopher, F. P. Ramsey, an enthusiastic but critical follower of Wittgenstein, put it: 'What we can't say we can't say, and we can't whistle it either'." Ayer himself adds: "A great deal of bad philosophy comes from people thinking that they can somehow whistle what they cannot say."[51]

On what, someone may ask, does the verification principle itself rest? Could one verify the verification principle? Of course not, says Ayer. "It was put forward as a definition, not as an empirical statement of fact. But it is not an arbitrary definition. It purports to lay down the conditions which actually govern our acceptance, or indeed our understanding, of common sense and scientific

which are neither analytic nor synthetic. If we can have no experience of something, we cannot meaningfully talk about it. Thus the death of metaphysics in philosophy begins.

45. Ayer, "The Vienna Circle," 74.
46. Ibid.
47. Ibid.
48. Ibid.
49. Ibid., 75.
50. Otto Neurath (1882–1945), as a member of the Vienna Circle, focused his attention almost exclusively on the philosophy of science and its implications for empirical thought.
51. Ayer, "The Vienna Circle," 75.

statements, the statements which we take as describing the world 'in which we live and move and have our being'."[52]

If a metaphysician replies "that there may be other worlds besides the world of science and common sense, and that he makes it his business to explore them," then we reply that "the onus is on him to show by what criterion his statements are to be tested: until he does this we do not know how to take them."[53]

What we insist on, argues Ayer, is that the statements made by the metaphysician must not be entered as scientific hypotheses. If they enter their statements as something other than scientific hypotheses, "then we want some information about the conditions under which this different race is run."[54]

We have done with metaphysics. Now to the task of interpreting science and daily life by observation of facts and by testing any statement of observation by the verification principle.

It is obvious that in scientific interpretation of facts we must connect our individual observations by means of logic and mathematics. Now if logic and mathematics are themselves empirical generalizations, as was held, e.g., by John Stuart Mill, then how do we account for their necessity? Without necessity we have no firm ground under our own position. How then shall we deny metaphysics?

Well, the Vienna Circle allowed that logic and mathematics are necessary "but only because they were true by definition. They were said to be tautologies, in Wittgenstein's somewhat special use of this term."[55] "Logic and mathematics have, on this theory, the important function of making it clear to what our use of symbols commits us. . . . A priori statements are not themselves descriptive of anything, but their use enables us to pass securely from one descriptive statement to another. Wittgenstein, like Eddington, applies to our conceptual system the simile of a fisherman's net. Logic and mathematics are concerned only with the structure of the net, and therefore only with the form of the fish. Their truths are certain because we do not admit the possibility of their being falsified."[56]

52. Ibid.
53. Ibid., 75–76.
54. Ibid., 76.
55. Ibid.
56. Ibid., 76–77.

The Vienna Circle has now accomplished the exclusion of all metaphysics and has shown us the foundation on which it stands when it accomplishes this exclusion. If the theologian wants to continue to make statements about a world beyond the world of science, he may be permitted to do so on condition that he regards his statements as emotive rather than informational. As for the philosopher, since he too must cease to be metaphysical, we assign to him the task of "a sort of intellectual policeman, seeing that nobody trespasses into metaphysics."[57] "It is science that gives us our knowledge of the world; there is not, there cannot be, a philosophical brand of knowledge which would compete with science in this field."[58] This was, says Ayer, essentially Wittgenstein's view in the *Tractatus*.

The Vienna Circle wanted to give the philosopher a second, a positive form of employment. The task of the philosopher would be to refine scientific statements by analysis.[59] "The result of philosophizing is not to establish a set of philosophical propositions, but to make other propositions clear."[60]

At this point Ayer asserts that the Vienna Circle had not solved the basic epistemological problem. What is really meant when we say that a statement is verifiable? Does it mean merely that statements about facts are internally coherent with one another? Does it not also mean that statements must be verifiable in relation to facts? Then, if I make statements about my experience of facts, how can I convey the meaning of my experience to you? For my experience is private to me, and your experience is private to you; how then, if we each have to interpret every statement of fact as referring to our own experience, do we ever succeed in communicating with each other?

Morris Schlick's[61] "solution of this difficulty was to say that while the content of our experiences is indeed incommunicable, their structure is not. What I call 'red' may look quite different to me from the way what you call 'red' looks to you; we can never tell;

57. Ibid., 78–79.
58. Ibid., 78.
59. Ibid., 79.
60. Ibid.
61. Moritz Schlick (1882–1936) was thought by many to be the leader of the Vienna Circle since, when he came to Vienna in 1922, he formed a discussion group with the mathematician Hans Hahn and Otto Neurath, which came to be called the "Schlick Zirkel."

it is doubtful even if the question whether they are or are not the same has any meaning. But we can at least discover that we apply the word on the same occasions; so that whatever may be the difference in the content of our private worlds, their structure is the same."[62] This answer of Schlick's, says Ayer, does not withstand analysis. Here are "a number of people immured within the several fortresses of their own experience, and then considering what they can convey to one another." It is obvious that if they are so immured as Schlick says they are, "there would be nothing they could convey, not even structure."[63]

In connection with this problem a difference of opinion developed within the members of the Vienna Circle. They disputed between themselves about what they called "protocol statements." Protocol statements are "the basic reports of direct observations, by reference to which the truth of all other empirical statements was supposed to be tested."[64] But must not these protocol statements themselves "be inter-subjectively verifiable?"[65] And to be inter-subjectively verifiable "was taken to imply that they must refer to physical events; for it was assumed without argument that physical events were accessible to all alike."[66] The language of physics, Neurath argued, "is a universal language; universal in the sense that every empirical statement can be expressed in it."[67] This, says Ayer, "is the old doctrine of materialism, in a modern guise."[68] It may also be called physicalism.

In opposition to Neurath, others of the Circle thought protocol statements need not be inter-subjectively verifiable. "They alone were verified directly: all other empirical statements were verified indirectly through them."[69]

The physicalists "took away from protocol statements their special character as records of experience: and they then went on to deny their function. It makes no sense, they said, to speak of comparing statements with facts. Statements can be compared only with one

62. Ayer, "The Vienna Circle," 80–81.
63. Ibid., 81.
64. Ibid.
65. Ibid., 81–82.
66. Ibid., 82.
67. Ibid.
68. Ibid.
69. Ibid.

another. Accordingly, they were led to adopt a coherence theory of truth: they maintained that the criterion by which it is to be decided whether a statement is true is not its correspondence with fact but its consistency with other statements."[70]

Then, if someone objected by saying that "many incompatible systems of statements may each be internally consistent: and since they are mutually incompatible they cannot all be true," then Carnap is ready with his reply. "Carnap's answer to this was that we were to regard as true that system which was accepted by the scientists of our culture circle."[71] Finally, if each of several competing systems claimed that it alone is accepted by the scientists of our culture, then Carnap is ready again with his reply. "What Carnap meant was that the true system was that which they *in fact* accepted."[72] Ayer's comment on this final answer of Carnap's is: "But if a reference to fact is to be allowed in this case, why not in others also? Experience might even show that contemporary scientists sometimes made mistakes."[73]

"On any view of philosophy," says Ayer near the end of his discussion of the Vienna Circle, "this inner-outer problem is extremely difficult, and I shall not attempt to give a solution of it here."[74]

EVALUATION

Ayer can point to plenty of evidence to prove that the problem of inner-outer has proved not only difficult but impossible of solution by referring to such efforts as we have discussed.

Bacon and his followers wanted to study the facts of nature "as they are" without any pre-interpretation. Their exclusion of the creative-redemptive activity of the Triune God of Scripture in the world was, in principle, as absolute as any member of the Vienna Circle might wish. But in excluding the self-identifying Christ of Scripture from their enterprise they encumbered themselves with a problematic that is inherently artificial and insoluble. Separating man from God they also separated man from man and man from

70. Ibid., 82–83.
71. Ibid., 83.
72. Ibid.
73. Ibid.
74. Ibid., 84.

"nature." They made for themselves a false ideal of knowledge. Man must know all reality exhaustively or he knows nothing at all. Then if man would know everything, he would know everything about nothing. All diversity would be reduced to blank identity.

Modern scientists inherited this false ideal of knowledge from the Greeks. Parmenides saw the vision of reality as one, to which nothing had ever been or could ever be added. Kant followed his modern predecessors; the idealists followed Kant; the "logical atomists" and the "logical positivists" in turn follow the idealists. The "revolution in philosophy" which we have traced so far is a revolution within the Kantian revolution, within the Renaissance revolution, within the Greek revolution, within the revolution of Adam.[75]

To escape the nemesis of success by showing that nature must be what mathematics based on the notion of human autonomy says it must be, modern scientists and philosophers, like Heraclitus before them, must assume that all reality is flux. The idea that all reality is flux is as necessary to modern science and philosophy as is the idea that all reality is changeless. These two ideas, that *all* reality is changeless and that all reality is flux, underlie the various schools of modern science and philosophy as well as the various schools of ancient philosophy.

There is, therefore, one false problematic that underlies all these schools, as there is one basic ethical hostility that comes to expression in them. Men are victimized intellectually by their ethical opposition to the self-identifying Christ of Scripture.

If Christian believers would evaluate various schools of modern science or philosophy, they would be well advised if they took note of this basic similarity between them. Taking note of this similarity may keep them from thinking that one school of man-centered science or philosophy is less sympathetic to Christianity than another.

It is often thought that because of its anti-metaphysical bias, modern positivism is more hostile to Christianity than were the idealist, the spiritualist and the theist philosophies of the modern and the ancient past. To think so is to deceive one's self. Modern

75. As Van Til summarizes the history of philosophy here, his main point is that virtually all philosophical movements and positions have begun their work by excluding the Christian God. Such an exclusion will inevitably lead to irrationalism, no matter what the particular philosophy is.

anti-metaphysical speculation is simply more openly and perhaps more honestly, more outspokenly "immanentistic" in its view. The great service that such movements as logical atomism and logical positivism may render is to show that the more consistently the principle of human autonomy works itself out, the more clearly it appears that once man leaves the father's home, he cannot stop till he is at the swine-trough. The verification principle of modern positivism can verify nothing. It has separated absolutely between a formal rationality that is like a turnpike in the sky and a bottomless swamp of factual ooze on which the turnpike must somehow rest. Goethe's dictum *spricht die Seele so spricht ach schon die Seele nicht mehr* appears anew and more clearly than ever before to be a true description of any form of interpretation of human experience that is not based on the self-identifying Christ of Scripture.

The "Vienna Circle," says Ayer, "did not accomplish all that they once hoped. Many of the philosophical problems which they tried to settle still remain unsolved."[76] We may add that they will always remain unsolved so long as men seek to solve them in terms of (a) human autonomy, of (b) brute factual reality, and of (c) self-subsistent and self-sufficient logic. There will, on this basis, always be an absolute dichotomy between contingent factuality and purely formal logic.[77]

Yet it is upon the basis of an interpretation of the world of everyday experience in terms of these principles that many recent scientists and philosophers boldly assert that "metaphysics" is a meaningless phrase. We readily grant the truth of this point if by metaphysics is meant the speculations of Greek and of modern philosophy from Descartes to Dewey. But the reason why the metaphysics of these men is "meaningless" is because it is built upon the same anti-Christian assumptions as those on which recent "anti-metaphysical" speculation is built. Recent anti-metaphysical schools of philosophy and science are just as metaphysical as was what is actually called metaphysics of the past. And, more importantly, the various forms of anti-metaphysical positivism constitute, in effect, a type of metaphysics that *excludes* Christianity. It not merely *ignores* the God and Christ of Scripture but, in effect, *denies*

---

76. Ayer, "The Vienna Circle," 86.
77. The dichotomy is expressed in that the contingent facts change and the formal laws do not. How then can the two ever meaningfully meet?

him. It is as though men picked the fruits and vegetables of a garden, ignoring the signs of the owner that are obvious everywhere.

Recent positivisms still deal, in effect, with "the ponderous enigmas of metaphysicians." There is the same sort of "system construction" which leads to purely *a priori* logic which, by definition, says nothing and, by definition, never will be able to say anything about facts. There is the same sort of fact which forever recedes as one seeks to say something about it.

In terms of recent scientific and philosophic theory no fact can ever be identified in its uniqueness. As soon as it is identified it is no longer unique. Again in terms of recent scientific and philosophic theory, no fact can be intelligently related to any other fact. There is no intelligible principle of verification by which scientific hypotheses may be tested in terms of experience.

When Ayer, as a young man, wrote his book, *Language, Truth and Logic,* he was quite certain that he had discovered a principle of verification by which a solid body of scientific knowledge could be built up. A number of years later he was less sure of himself. He no longer claims that a proposition can be "conclusively established in experience." He now says that a proposition is said to be verifiable "in the weak sense, if it is possible for experience to render it probable."[78] He now knows that the truth of a scientific proposition can never be established. It "never could be; for however strong the evidence in its favour, there would never be a point at which it was impossible for further experience to go against it."[79] How else can science discover what is new unless the universe be completely open at every point? Ayer had, apparently, in his zeal to exclude all metaphysics, for a moment forgotten this. But Ayer hastens on to tell us that the universe is not so open, but that there are some "basic propositions" which can be verified conclusively. These basic propositions can be "verified conclusively" because "they refer solely to the content of a single experience."[80] Such basic propositions may therefore be said to be "incorrigible." It is "impossible to be mistaken about them except in a verbal sense."[81] In short, it is a case of "nothing venture, nothing lose." Ayer adds: "It is, however,

78. Alfred Jules Ayer, *Language, Truth and Logic* (New York: Dover Publications, 1952), 9.
79. Ibid., 9–10.
80. Ibid., 10.
81. Ibid.

equally a case of 'nothing venture, nothing win,' since the mere recording of one's present experience does not serve to convey any information either to any other person or indeed to oneself; for in knowing a basic proposition to be true one obtains no further knowledge than what is already afforded by the occurrence of the relevant experience."[82]

Obviously Ayer is in great straits. He is frank and honest enough to say so. He needs an absolutely open universe in which the future might prove everything that has been said in the past to be wrong, except for the fact that there are "basic propositions" which could never be shown to be wrong. That is, they could never be shown to be wrong because they could never be shown to have any communicable meaning to anyone. Of course a "dictionary" might be written by means of which statements can be shown to be verifiable. But then "the statements which constitute the dictionary" must be regarded as "analytic."[83] By means of this dictionary we could keep the metaphysicians from invading the realm of science.[84] But then the dictionary itself can, on Ayer's view, at best be composed of an infinite number of descriptions of "basic propositions" which, as Ayer insists, not even he who makes them knows what they mean.

Thus Ayer's dictionary records the usage of words conventionally agreed upon by a group of scientists and philosophers, even though none of these scientists or philosophers has been able to give himself or others an intelligible account as to the reason for his usage of words. There is a common assumption on the part of the contributors to this dictionary that though the "basic propositions" on which every possible use of the dictionary depends are utterly meaningless to those who make them, yet, together, they prove that the presence of the activity of God and of Christ in their own consciousness and in the facts must be denied as meaningless.

To Ayer's imaginary dictionary we may write an imaginary introduction to the effect:

(a) None of the contributors knows what the basic propositions they report mean to themselves. They have no intelligible notion of themselves; when they seek to identify themselves to themselves, they must do so by concepts which generalize and therewith destroy

82. Ibid.
83. Ibid., 13.
84. Ibid., 14.

their uniqueness. What all of the contributors do know is that every man is in the same position of not being able to identify himself and of communicating with himself or with others.

(b) It follows that the historic Protestant claim with respect to Jesus Christ as the self-identifying one, who has from all eternity been in full self-conscious communication with the Father and the Son[85] and who offers himself as the Savior of all those who have entangled themselves in mental and spiritual confusion, *cannot* be true. If it were true, then man would not be the one who makes "basic propositions" and he would not hide himself in a position where he could say "nothing venture, nothing lose" or "nothing venture, nothing win," for in that case his very attempt to make "basic statements" constitutes an insult to the self-identifying Christ. No one can steal tomatoes in God's garden while in his deepest heart knowing that it is God's garden (*gnontes ton theon*)[86] and expect to escape the wrath of God by claiming that he does not know what he is doing.

The name of the self-identifying Christ must therefore be pressed anew upon the men of science and of philosophy in our day in order that they might be saved. If Roman Catholic and Arminian thinkers fail to do this they therewith do not press the breadth and depth of the liberating power of the gospel upon men. Christ came to save the whole man. Christ came to save science and philosophy. Kant was not able to save it by his Copernican revolution; the recent scientists have not been able to save it by their revolution. Each new scientific-philosophic revolution, short of the revolution that springs from the work of Christ and his Spirit, leads the non-Christian scientist and philosopher more deeply into his hopeless program of interpreting reality in terms of a self which can never identify itself.[87]

There is evidence to show that at least some modern scientists and philosophers realize that they have not come in sight of solving their problems. In concluding his survey of the Vienna Circle, Ayer says, "It will be seen that the Vienna Circle did not accomplish all

---

85. Van Til likely meant "Spirit" here.
86. This is the initial phrase in Romans 1:21: "knowing God."
87. Van Til's analysis of the history of philosophy here is, in some sense, confirmed by that history itself, in that philosophers are perpetually denying previous views and seeking to answer the same questions differently. Thus various "schools" of philosophy are born.

that they once hoped. Many of the philosophical problems which they tried to settle still remain unsolved."[88] Ayer might better have said that they have solved no problem. No problem *can* be solved if the problem of the relation between concept and fact is not solved. So long as an infinite number of wholly independent "things" must be related to one another by an infinite number of wholly independent "minds" by their being reduced to a oneness that absorbs all things and all minds, so long there is no solution for any problem.

LUDWIG WITTGENSTEIN[89]

We take Ludwig Wittgenstein as a final witness to the fact that the most brilliant of scientists are unable to offer a foundation for human speech so long as they reject Christianity.

In his early period, the period of the *Tractatus Logico Symbolicus*, Wittgenstein was a disciple of Russell. With Russell, Wittgenstein was in violent rebellion against Bradley's idealism. In their introduction to Volume 2 of *Philosophy in the Twentieth Century*, William Barrett and Henry D. Aiken give an account of Wittgenstein's philosophical development. I make grateful use of their survey.

The *Tractatus* gives us "the most radical restatement of some of Russell's most influential theories."[90]

> Wittgenstein developed in that work the clearest formulation of the Russellian notion that the world, as it would be described by a perfectly lucid and logically immaculate language of science, is composed of elementary "logical atoms" which constitute the irreducible and simple elements of what there is. "The world," he said in the gnomic sentences which comprise the *Tractatus* "is everything that is the case." But the world also "divides into

88. Ayer, "The Vienna Circle," 86.
89. Ludwig Wittgenstein (1889–1951) was one of the most influential and brilliant philosophers of the twentieth century. As Van Til notes, there is an earlier and a later (and some would even say a "middle") phase to Wittgenstein's thought. His early phase, contained in his *Tractatus*, was later rejected by him, under the influence of some in the Vienna Circle, who themselves had been influenced by him. His *Philosophical Investigations*, which he authorized to be published posthumously, characterizes his later phase.
90. William Barrett and Henry D. Aiken, eds., *Philosophy in the Twentieth Century: An Anthology*, 4 vols. (New York: Random House, 1962), 2:487.

facts," any one of which can "either be the case or not be the case, and everything else remains the same." (Shades of both Russell and Moore.) "What is the case, the fact, is the existence of atomic facts," and "An atomic fact is a combination of objects (entities, things)," and "The configuration of objects forms an atomic fact." Any "object" which can enter into a "configuration," and which is not itself a configuration, must be an unanalyzable and simple "entity." The basis of any true and perspicuous science must be statements which describe atomic facts, that is, configurations of things that are themselves absolutely simple. Such statements, moreover, are themselves logical "pictures" of atomic facts, and from an analysis of their essential forms, one can gain, as it were, a logical photograph of the elementary atomic structure of the real world. In short, an analysis of the basic forms of a proper scientific language, automatically provides a kind of mirror of the fundamental structure of reality itself. Of course, no general science, as it stands, is concerned with the description or picturing of particular atomic facts. But at this time it was still Wittgenstein's belief that all general scientific truths are nothing but logical compounds of true atomic propositions, that is, again, propositions which picture basic atomic facts.[91]

To attain the ideal of science, Wittgenstein needs a "perfectly logical language." Only such a perfectly logical language could decide which ordinary language statements are and which are not statements of atomic facts. A perfectly logical language would:

establish a clear boundary line between sense and nonsense by a clear and explicit statement both of the conditions for the uniqueness, simplicity, and reference of all referential terms in the language and of the logical conditions of their combination and recombination in sentences. In short, an ideal language would resemble a calculus whose logic or syntax is absolutely explicit and whose basic terms are quite clear, simple, and unambiguous.[92]

91. Ibid.
92. Ibid., 488.

If this description is at all fair, as I believe it is—but the readers of the *Tractatus* may judge for themselves—then we have in Wittgenstein a well nigh perfect exhibition of the nature of the impasse of recent scientific thought discussed earlier. For Wittgenstein, the scientific ideal is that of exhaustive logical analysis of reality by man. Then, if this exhaustive analysis were successful, if the perfectly logical language were available, all newness would be lost. If the perfect language were available we would be unable to relate it to ordinary language. But the perfect language is not available. We must, therefore, get along with ordinary language. And, we started looking for a perfect language because of the ambiguities of ordinary language.

Accordingly, Barrett and Aiken conclude: "There remained in any case many problems which, for a critical and honest reader, the *Tractatus* had left unsolved."[93]

We add again that not many but all problems are left unsolved and admit of no solution so long as men insist that to know anything man must have exhaustive conceptual knowledge of everything.

Not sensing this basic difficulty, Barrett and Aiken conclude that "even if formal logic itself provides nothing more than the transformation rules for getting logically from one statement to another, the analytical philosophy of language and of logic enables us to *show* what the metaphysical traits of 'being' really are."[94]

But what does it mean to *show* us what the metaphysical traits of "being" really are, when, admittedly, nothing can be said about these traits? And are we not supposed to be done with metaphysical traits and with a "being" of which no one can say anything? It were better if Wittgenstein had included science as well as metaphysics when he said, "*Wovon man nicht kann sprechen, daruber soll man schweigen.*"[95] Modern science has imposed silence upon God but in doing so, it was compelled to impose silence on itself. Modern science boldly asks for a criterion of meaning when one speaks to him of Christ. He assumes that he himself has a criterion, a principle of verification and of falsification, by which he can establish for himself a self-supporting island floating on a shoreless sea. But when he is asked to show his criterion as it functions in experience, every fact

---

93. Ibid., 489.
94. Ibid.
95. I.e., "Whereof one cannot speak, thereof one shall be silent."

is indeterminate, lost in darkness; no one can identify a single fact, and all logic is like a sun that is always behind the clouds.

The net result of our story is that it is now more obvious than ever that the traditional Thomist-Butler apologetics cannot be of service to the modern scientist, to the modern philosopher or to the modern theologian as in their ethical hostility to the self-attesting Christ of Scripture they cannot even strangle themselves in the tangle of their views because they cannot even identify themselves. Modern science, modern philosophy and modern theology have shown anew the truth of the words of Paul: "Hath not God made foolish the wisdom of the world, for after the world by wisdom knew not God it pleased God by the foolishness of preaching to save them that believe."[96] Only Reformed apologetics seeks to be true to Paul when it contends that only on the presupposition of the truth of what God has revealed to man in Christ through the Scriptures can there be any intelligible predication.

96. 1 Cor. 1:20–21.

Cornelius Van Til (1895–1987) was born in Grootegast, the Netherlands, and emigrated with his family to America in 1905. He attended Calvin College and Calvin Seminary before completing his studies at Princeton Theological Seminary and Princeton University with the Th.M. and Ph.D. degrees.

Drawn to the pastorate, Van Til spent one year in the ministry before taking a leave of absence to teach apologetics at Princeton Seminary. When the seminary reorganized, he was persuaded to join the faculty of the newly founded Westminster Theological Seminary. He remained there as professor of apologetics until his retirement in 1975.

Van Til wrote more than twenty books, in addition to more than thirty syllabi. Among his best-known titles are *The Defense of the Faith, Christian Apologetics, An Introduction to Systematic Theology,* and *Christianity and Barthianism.*

K. Scott Oliphint (M.A.R., Th.M., Ph.D., Westminster Theological Seminary) is professor of apologetics and systematic theology at Westminster Seminary, Philadelphia. He is the author of *Reasons for Faith* and *The Battle Belongs to the Lord,* and is coeditor of *Revelation and Reason: New Essays in Reformed Apologetics.*